Imagined Museums

Imagined Museums

Art and Modernity in Postcolonial Morocco

Katarzyna Pieprzak

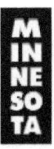 University of Minnesota Press
Minneapolis • London

The University of Minnesota Press gratefully acknowledges the financial assistance provided for the publication of this book from Williams College.

A version of chapter 2 was published in *Journal of North African Studies* (Spring 2003). An earlier version of chapter 3 was published in *Yearbook of Comparative and General Literature* (Fall 2001). Two sections of chapter 5 were published in *MESA Bulletin* (Summer 2008) and *Studies in Twentieth and Twenty-First Century Literatures* (Winter 2009). This previously published material is reprinted here, with alterations, by kind permission of the journals.

Poetry from "Made in Morocco," by Izhar, was first published in *Lamalif* 12 (May 1967): 18; reprinted with permission from *Lamalif*. Poetry from "Chebaâ" and "Table ronde," by Abdellatif Laâbi, was first published in Abdellatif Laâbi, *Petit musée portaif* (Al Manar, 2001); reprinted with permission from Al Manar.

Published by the University of Minnesota Press
111 Third Avenue South, Suite 290
Minneapolis, MN 55401-2520
http://www.upress.umn.edu

Library of Congress Cataloging-in-Publication Data

Pieprzak, Katarzyna.
  Imagined museums : art and modernity in postcolonial Morocco / Katarzyna Pieprzak.
    p. cm.
  Includes bibliographical references and index.
  ISBN 978-0-8166-6518-1 (hc : alk. paper) — ISBN 978-0-8166-6519-8 (pb : alk. paper)
  1. Art museums—Morocco. 2. Art and state—Morocco. 3. Postcolonialism and the arts—Morocco. I. Title.
  N3810.M8P54 2010
  069.0964—dc22

                                                                2009031573

Printed in the United States of America on acid-free paper

The University of Minnesota is an equal-opportunity educator and employer.

20 19 18 17 16 15 14 13 12 11 10   10 9 8 7 6 5 4 3 2 1

Contents

Note on Translation and Transliteration

Unless otherwise noted, all translations from French and Arabic are mine. In Morocco, many Arabic words have standard transliterations, often derived from the French, and I used these whenever possible. Likewise, I used the standard and accepted spelling of Moroccan names. All other transliterations follow the style of the *International Journal of Middle East Studies*.

Acknowledgments

The list of people who contributed directly and indirectly to this book is long, and I cannot begin to do justice here to the intellectual and emotional support that I received throughout this project.

First, I thank my friends and colleagues in Morocco. The Chami family in Fez opened my eyes to cultural politics in the country, and Najib Chami patiently humored me through many of my museum visits around Morocco. Ali Amahan, Hassan Najmi, Saïd Ennahid, Abderrahman Nazih, Amina Touzani, Sylvia Belhassan, Hassan Darsi, and Abdellah Karroum have all been generous with their time and knowledge, providing invaluable insights on Moroccan art and its politics. Aicha Hariri welcomed me to her home in Rabat, and her good humor, cooking, and wise counsel sustained me in my research.

I thank my colleagues and friends in Middle East studies and museum studies in the United States, especially Susan Slyomovics, Barbara Kirshenblatt-Gimblett, Stacy Holden, Susan Miller, Holly Edwards, Mary Vogl, Felicia McCarren, Shaun Lopez, and Laila Lalami, for their support, incisive comments, and willingness to read or listen to parts of this project and push it further. The summer I spent in Istanbul as a Getty Fellow under the mentorship of Irene Bierman and Jere Bacharach was crucial to the development of this book, and I thank them for the inspiring seminar and the opportunity to meet and work with wonderful scholars.

This book started many years ago as a doctoral dissertation at the University of Michigan under the careful supervision of Frieda Ekotto, Simon Gikandi, Matthew Connelly, Anton Shammas, and Richard Candida Smith. I thank them for their comments and continued support. My friends and colleagues at Williams College have, in turn, been eager readers and wise counselors. I thank the entire Romance Languages department, as well as Magnus Bernhardsson, Armando Vargas, and Kenda Mutongi, for their critical engagement with this work. Theo Davis, Mérida Rua, and Jennifer French have graced me with continued friendship and intellectual support over the years.

I thank the anonymous readers of the manuscript for their constructive and challenging criticism and for their redeeming praise. The University of Minnesota Press staff has expertly guided this book through its many forms, and my utmost thanks goes to Richard Morrison, who was so generous in both his interest and his faith in the book.

Hassan Darsi and Abdellah Karroum deserve special thanks not only for their willingness to engage with my project but also for the beautiful images they contributed to this book. Writer and editor Samuel Shimon went far out of his way in an attempt to secure permission for the use of Mohamed Melehi's photographs, and I thank him sincerely.

Not unlike a public museum, a public library is a precious resource. This book was written into various manifestations at numerous libraries, and I acknowledge the staff at the Oriental Division of New York City Public Library, the Performing Arts Research Library at the New York Public Library, the Clark Institute Library, the Bibliothèque Générale du Maroc (now the Bibliothèque Nationale du Royaume du Maroc), and the library at La Source in Rabat. These institutions gave me space to read, think, and write; their librarians and staff offered the advice, aid, and daily banter that helped me to continue working.

I have been extremely lucky to have such supportive and understanding friends and family. They have heard me talk about this book for too many years. Thank you, Nirmala, Jean, Kris, Kyle, Camilla, Shana, and Magali, for your friendship. My family, especially my parents and my late grandmother, have given me unconditional love and never lost faith in me. Finally, to Matthew, my husband and best friend, thank you for always being my first and most engaging reader, both in my work and in my life.

Introduction

Entering the Museum

As we walked the crowded streets of the Fez medina toward the Batha Museum, high school student Najib Chami turned to me and asked, "Why should I go to a museum when I live in one?" Apart from a general contempt for tourism as something for foreigners, Najib's question revealed his awareness of his own limited possibilities. A teenager stifled by his family, trapped in his ancient city, he wished to leave and transcend his past. The Fez medina, full of medieval mosques and *madrasas,* with intricate arts and crafts reproduced and sold in its stalls throughout the centuries, was a living museum, and to Najib, it held no place for dreams of a future outside its walls. Moroccan writer Abdelfattah Kilito describes the medina as "ancient history, stagnant water. . . . Protected by its walls, the medina is a closed territory. Once you turn your back on the outside world—looking back won't help; it's disappeared, lost."[1] Najib bemoaned his entrapment in this living museum. Visiting yet another space dedicated to the preservation of the Moroccan past would not facilitate his escape into the present, into a modernity that lay elsewhere, in the outside world.

It did not help Najib that much like his suffocating medina, the Batha Museum is yet another depressing site for the young and rebellious mind. Rather than inspiring a cathartic or uplifting transformation in the visitor, the overall feeling created by the museum's collection is one of lack, loss, and disappointment. Upon entering the gates of the former palace on the edge of the medina, the visitor is faced with a mosaic courtyard and a disheveled garden that feels empty and abandoned. The collection itself is very small and does not inspire anyone to think about a glorious Moroccan past. Najib tried to imagine living there as a prince, but his reference point for richness and artistic treasure stemmed from glimpses of opulent shops and hotels in the medina and the *ville nouvelle,* from stories and histories he had learned from his relatives, but not from the museum collection itself. Faced with an imagined modernity elsewhere and a poor representation of a supposedly glorious past, the young Moroccan was not granted access to either but forced to imagine their existence through lack. He remained stuck in a melancholic other world, which, to use the words of Stefania Pandolfo, is "populated only by the ghostly presences of absent interlocutors."[2]

While attempting to stress the beauty of what *is* present in their museums, the Moroccan Tourist Board unwittingly performs the same condition of absence and lack by narrating the museums through a ghostly and incomplete past. The official publication on Moroccan museums distributed by the board in association with the Ministry of Culture is a glossy and attractive pamphlet. On the cover, a photograph of a Roman-era mosaic presents a partly clothed woman reclining suggestively as another partially represented figure wafts soft winds toward her. This visual image of ancient luxury is a fitting choice for the textual introduction. On opening the booklet, the reader is greeted with a photograph of old keys and the following text:

> Inhabited since prehistoric times, with a culture that goes back thirty centuries, at the crossroads of Roman, Berber and Arab civilizations, Morocco is rich in museums overflowing with treasures. These magical places are entirely devoted to admiration. The touch of a master transforms the humblest objects into masterpieces. Carpets, pottery, garments or arms, here everything is a work of art. . . . A visit to the museums of Morocco is not merely a means of understanding more about a different culture, nor merely an introduction to part of humanity's heritage; it is in fact an opportunity to experience a total enchantment of the spirit and the senses.[3]

The keys juxtaposed with the text invite the reader to open the magical doors of Moroccan patrimony and explore the architectures that house national treasures from centuries past. Sumptuous photographs of museum courtyards and building interiors reflect the architectural preoccupation of the text. The Museum of Moroccan Arts in Tangiers is described as an "imposing silhouette" that "dominates the Tangier Kasbah," "a worthy setting for works of art from all over Morocco."[4] The ethnographic museum in Chefchaouen is introduced as "a haven of peace in a magnificent Andalusian garden," the Oudaya Museum in Rabat as "an opulent lodge," the Dar Si Said Museum in Marrakesh

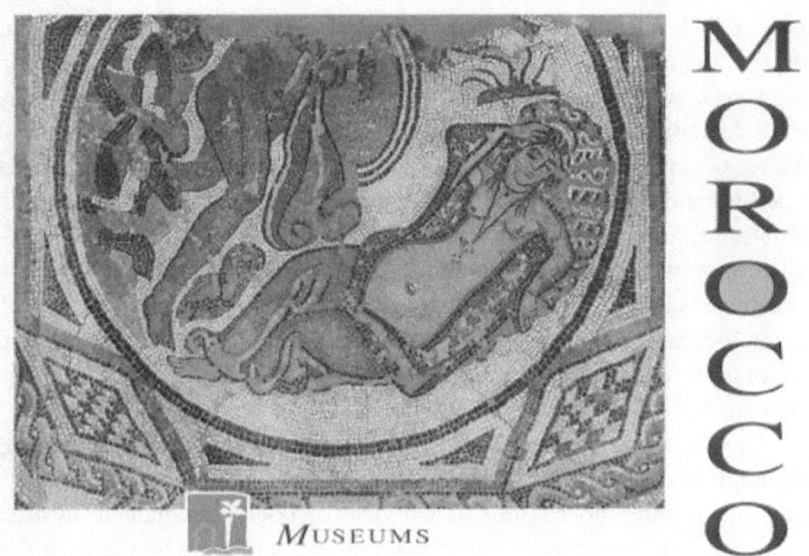

Cover of the publication on Moroccan museums. From Moroccan Tourist Board,
Morocco: Museums.

as "a sumptuous palace housing the very quintessence of Moroccan art."[5] The
pamphlet proclaims of these architectures of beauty and pleasure, "Moroccan
museums are very often monuments in their own right. Even empty, they would
be well worth a visit."[6] This last statement is especially significant because in
reality, these magical places *are* empty—*quite* empty.

If we look at Moroccan national museums today, we find buildings with
few objects and even fewer visitors, empty palaces grafted onto a vibrant and
crowded Moroccan landscape. It is true that these buildings are often architectural wonders, that they are monuments in their own right, but monuments
to what? What event do they mark? What do they ask us (local and international visitors) to remember? In speaking of Moroccan museums, the former
museum director of Morocco, Ali Amahan, told me, "I am not interested in
national museums of the Third World. Memory that is useless is useless to
preserve."[7] According to Amahan, Third World museums are symbolic pres-
tigious architectures that promote the national image abroad and have nothing to do with Third World reality. He argues that in a docile acceptance
of their colonial past, Moroccan museums function as inherited state regalia,
maintaining outdated narratives of Moroccan culture and failing to give the

Moroccan public any sense of possession of or access to their patrimony. Sakina Rharib, former director of the Marrakesh Museum, goes even further, stating that the only function of the museum in Morocco is to be a depository for objects, "ni plus, ni moins" (no more, no less).[8] But what sort of storehouse is it, asks cultural critic and anthropologist Amina Touzani, when a small collection of only two hundred thousand pieces is distributed among fifteen museums and the annual collection rate is only 5 percent, with the majority of objects coming from archaeological digs? Rumors abound that the king takes whatever he wants to his palaces and that corrupt officials have sold objects to wealthy private collectors. Touzani exclaims that Moroccan museums are truly at the "degree zero of museology: museums are visually depressing, take no notice of the public and do not fulfill any roles traditionally associated with a museum."[9]

Unvisited by a disinterested local public and summarily walked through by disappointed tourists, national collections of ethnography and art lie quietly out of date, often housed in colonial villas or poorly maintained historical buildings. The disjunction between what these places could be and what they are is heartbreaking to those who believe in the museum's potential to transform and engage the individual, to preserve art objects, to educate, to house collective memory, and to bring people together. Lynn Szwaja and Tomás Ybarra-Frausto argue for the relevance of museums around the world, underscoring "the transformative potential of these institutions in the public sphere, institutions that resonate with memory, history, pain, beauty, and resilience."[10] Yet with extremely small curatorial staffs, a lack of funding, and outdated permanent collections, national museums in Morocco can do very little for any public. So if all one sees is the failure of the museum, should it still exist? Why is it still there? How can we read this anemic shadow of an institution? And what is its relevance in both Morocco and the world of museums in general?

When I started studying museums in Morocco in 1998, I quickly encountered repeated narratives of failure. The history of such discourse stretches from the 1960s to the present and permeates almost all discussions of art institutions. It claims, quite simply, that despite fifteen state-run museums and a small number of private museums and foundations, on a fundamental level there are no museums in Morocco. When I first encountered this negation, it seemed merely as though an adjective was missing. Was it that there were no "successful" museums in Morocco? Or perhaps no "art" museums? Or was it perhaps just a question of definition? And who was to set the terms? As someone who teaches primarily literature—the work of imagination and the creation of narratives in which "truth" is relative and not necessarily at stake—I found my attention shifting from reading the exhibits of existing museums as entries into the Moroccan cultural politics of representation to reading the stories of those who claimed that there was no museum and pronounced its failure as entries into the Moroccan cultural politics of the imagination.

Despite the criticism leveled at existing institutions, no one went so far as to claim that museums should be abandoned or that art and artifacts do not need to be collected or displayed. What these narrators wanted was a better public museum—a museum that did not function as an outdated technology, a private storehouse, or a second-rate colonial import from Europe. Museums in Europe and the United States underwent fundamental changes during the second half of the twentieth century, shifting their identities from Enlightenment nation-building collections to better reflect and serve diverse publics. What Moroccan museum critics want today is this same transformation in their outdated national museums and private art collections so that the museum as an institution can actively participate in the public landscape, becoming a better place to account for the past and the present and to collectively and individually imagine a relationship to the future.

How should we approach the national museum and its failure? The field of postcolonial museum studies has grown since Benedict Anderson wrote about colonial museums and the imagination of empire and nation-states and Arjun Appadurai and Carol Breckenridge encouraged scholars to think about postcolonial museums by examining display practice in India in "Museums Are Good to Think." Today we can count a number of excellent studies of museums of the Middle East and Africa led by scholars such as Irene Maffi, Heghnar Watenpaugh, Anne Gaugue, and Wendy Shaw that look at postcolonial state formation through the lens of national museum projects, examine the manipulation of imperial history and national identity through exhibit display and curation, and treat the museum as an institution of state negotiation in the production of heritage and its related narratives of nationalism and empire.[11] For the most part, these studies read existing museums as relatively stable, even if contested, material carriers of state narratives and/or limit their analytical scope to the nation-building era. I think the time has come to answer Appadurai and Breckenridge's call to think about the museum in a different way, and the key is to destabilize the museum itself as a grammar of nationalism, analyze its limits, and examine how other museums have emerged in its failure. What happens when national institutions decompose? What other narratives of art and cultural memory are presented outside the national museum's often crumbling walls? How are alternative museums constructed, and what is their relationship to dominant national and global discourses of art and culture?

In ten years of conversations with Moroccan friends, artists, writers, and curators, any discussion of museums has always begun with declarative statements of negation and short narratives of failure. Productive discussions appeared to necessitate an initial recognition and erasure of what was considered a bleak reality; for a generative discourse to take shape, degeneration and ruin had to be acknowledged and even emphasized. These discursive habits reflect the actual process occurring in the museum world in Morocco, where new museums emerge and disappear in response to the deteriorating condition or absence of state museums. In approaching the museum in its many incarnations in Morocco, I have chosen to focus on these intertwining processes of decomposition and creation rather than exhaustively documenting sites, chronologies, or histories. The disintegration, decomposition, and decay of public spaces of art and memory have invited generative, creative, and tactical interventions that resist the complete unraveling of the museum as an institution in Morocco.

This book is thus divided into two parts that trace these interrelated strands of movement: the first, "Monumental Sites of Discourse: National Museums, Corporate Collections, and Cabinets of Curiosity," addresses three types of museums that exist as physical institutions and reads the imagination that they house and their relationships to collective or inclusive practices of art and memory. As national museums have decayed, corporate and private spaces have opened with ambivalent relationships to the general public and with contradictory rhetoric and practice when it comes to providing public access to patrimony and narratives of creation and memory in Morocco. I have named these institutions monumental in the sense that they have erected discourses that seek to monumentalize certain scripts of history and identity. In so doing, these institutions reveal their anxiety to mark both space and time, to control collective memory and limit the intervention and participation of inappropriate actors. The second part of the book, "Tactical Architectures of Art: Discursive, Ephemeral, and Nomadic Museums," focuses on discursive, ephemeral, and nomadic museologies and how they intervene in the process of monumental exclusion in material museums. Using tactics that destabilize monumental categories, these museological practices seek to imagine different visibilities, different narratives, and different ways to display art and memory. In some respects, these museological practices reflect the work of what Michael Fehr has named "counter-museums": "spaces that present the fiction we require to find our bearings in the world, *as fiction,* and as rooms that comprehend the viewer as a historical subject and emancipate him vis-à-vis history." In other words, museums can become "second-order systems, within which visitors can become observers of the rise and decay of orders."[12] Although Fehr achieves this through his radical curation of the Karl Ernst Osthaus-Museum, I would argue that the juxtaposition of multiple museums in Morocco and their intersecting and often jarring narratives of culture and history reveals the rise and decay of orders such as modernity, the nation, and globalization in Morocco.

The structural division of the book is a porous one and aims to reveal a contentious imaginary in which we can read claims, statements, and negotiations about identity, value, history, and culture in Morocco. Here we can read the negotiations over the sovereignty of art as an autonomous sphere against the tension in institutional identity in corporate galleries. We can read struggles over controlling patrimony between progressive artists, the state, and private collectors. We can read articulations of the role and relevance of self-described modernist art in a socioeconomic landscape that is struggling to address the material concerns of its inhabitants. And ultimately, in this imaginary we can trace a struggle over cultural capital and status, over meanings of modernity and claims to be modern. Corinne Kratz and Ivan Karp tell us:

> Reproduced, adapted, and transformed globally, museums are not just a place or institution but have become a portable social technology, a set of museological processes through which such statements and claims [about identity, history, place, and value] are represented, embodied, and debated. Whether they define their scope as national, regional, or community based, museum spaces can become global theaters of real consequence.[13]

In this book I propose that Moroccan museums in their multiple incarnations and intersections are theaters of real consequence.

The Museum, Modernity, and Modernization

Although this book is primarily interested in telling the intertwined stories of various museums in Morocco, there is another set of deeply related narratives that it wishes to reveal: the stories of modernity, modernization, and modern culture in Morocco. If, as Timothy Mitchell argues, modernity is a practice of representation that stages the contested line between the modern and the non-modern and endlessly organizes the world to represent the reality effect it creates, nowhere do we see this dynamic in play more clearly than in the museum, which as an institution is all about the staging and representation of time, subjectivity, history, and progress.[14] The museum as both a physical and a conceptual site provides us the analytical means to enter into the hall of mirrors that defines the subject and his possessions, his lacks, and his desires. In preserving the past, the museum promises to clear the way for the future; in narrating history, it defines the present. Donald Preziosi has described this mediating performance in the museum as an embodiment of the dynamic of modernity: "Museums are our modernity's paradigmatic artifice, modernity's art par excellence, and the active, mediating, and enabling instrument of all we have learned to desire we might become . . . [of] what it is we imagine we see when we see museums imagining us." For Preziosi, the museum incarnates Mitchell's contested line between the modern and the nonmodern as an "edge between the material residues and relics of the past and the adjacent empty space that the future is imagined to be, demanding to be filled."[15] The museum thus participates in staging the practice of being and becoming. Tony Bennett theorizes this in another way by arguing that "museums are best understood as distinctive cultural machineries that, through tensions that they generate within the self, have operated as a means for balancing the tensions of modernity. They generate and regulate both how, and how far, we are detached from the past and pointed toward the future."[16] In these understandings of the museum, modernity is defined as both a condition and a practice of representation of the world. The museum is a structure that mediates the instabilities caused by modernity's condition and provides a site of embodiment for its practice as a form of representation. The museum serves as modernity's art and artifice.

Although scholars of the museum world often theorize the subject of modernity and the museum in this fashion, I would like to shift the terms and argue that rather than modernity's art and artifice, the museum discloses the artifice and art of modernity as a functioning "native category." In different ways, Frederick Cooper and Paul Rabinow have argued for the use of the term *modernity* as a "native category" as opposed to an analytical one. Cooper writes:

> Scholars should not try for a slightly better definition so that they can talk about modernity more clearly. They should instead listen to what is being said in the world. If modernity is what they hear, they should ask how it is being used and why; otherwise shoehorning a political discourse into modern, antimodern, or postmodern discourses, or into "their" modernity or "ours," is more distorting than revealing.[17]

Rabinow puts it in slightly different terms when he writes, "The debates about modernity are endless: since it has no essence, and refers to so many diverse things, it seems futile—or simply part of the modernizing process—to worry extensively about abstract definitions. It would seem more heuristic and more ethnographic, to explore how the term has been understood and used by its self-proclaimed practitioners."[18]

By reading the museum's exhibits and narrative imagination, we can see how modernity is a concrete set of claims defined and debated by those who invest in it as a category, its "self-proclaimed practitioners." The history of the museum in Morocco intersects with discourses and claim-making of modernity in numerous ways: as a colonial architecture that participates in contradictory constructions of modernity, as a symbolic architecture of the responsible nation-state in postcolonial modernization processes, and as an abandoned national structure and privatized space in light of neoliberal economic policy. The museum is thus not just a stage for modernity as a representational process but a stage on which and through which different actors (colonial, global, and local) stake claims and construct narratives of status and legitimacy. Whether the museum is colonial, national, corporate, or private, it functions as a site of claim-making about status in local and global society by creating and engaging narratives of what it means to be modern. And so we can use the museum to carefully listen to how people and institutions petition for inclusion in "universal" narratives that exclude them while articulating claims of modernity that in turn exclude others. Furthermore, as certain museums decay, they present us with sites in which to read the decay of various claims to and definitions of modernity.

The goal of this book is thus to explore various manifestations of Moroccan museums over the past century not only to see what they can tell us about the workings of troubled national architectures but also to see how different groups use the institution to make claims about cultural modernity and their relationship to modernity at large. How do museums produce "useful" memory for modernization efforts? How is modern art used to enhance status and construct modern identity by the state, corporations, and banks? How are claims to modernity as a set of rights and material privileges articulated through the museum at various stages of its history? How does a cultural elite that sees itself producing aesthetically modern works negotiate the socioeconomic disjuncture between their modernist ambitions and the lived reality of modernization and lack in Morocco? How do Moroccan artists negotiate their peripheral marginalization in art-historical movements that claim universality?

If we listen closely to what is said about modernity in Morocco, we can see how the creation of multiple museums and multiple scripts that define what it means to be modern seeks to deal with an imagined singular Western modernity that has evaded the majority of Moroccans and is located elsewhere. In writing of inaccessible modernity, James Ferguson tells us that although anthropologists and cultural critics are eager to stress plural African modernities in order to valorize practices that have long been ignored or discriminated against, local African discourses stress lack and absence:

> Modernity has thus been a way of talking about global inequality and about material needs and how they might be met. In particular, it has indexed specific aspirations to such primary "modern" goods as improved housing, health care, and education. . . . Where anthropologists proclaim Africa always already modern, local discourses on modernity more often insist on seeing a continuing lack . . . a lack that is understood not of cultural inferiority but of a political-economic inequality.[19]

As development discourses and neoliberal economic policies fail to bring promised political and economic equality on the world stage and universal access to education, housing, health care, nutrition, justice, and the ability to speak freely, a sense of despair at the static status and worsening of life conditions grows across the African continent, including in Morocco. Whether during the period after the country achieved independence from France in 1956, when the referent for what it meant to be modern primarily came from a certain vision of France, or in the early twenty-first century, when artist collectives engage with the concept of a universal modernity in a critical or ironic fashion, modernity as a material end state is still defined through a lack that cannot be replaced or satisfied by local alternative modernities or hybrid bricolage. The reference to Morocco as a society "en mutation" (in transformation) has been repeated obsessively by Moroccans since 1956. What if this transformation and the unstable condition of "being pulled willy-nilly towards Europe" are actually static?[20] Ferguson argues that today there is "a different understanding of modernity in which, no longer promised as a *telos,* it has come to be simply a status—a standard of living to which some have rights by birth and from which others are simply, but unequivocally, excluded."[21] Moroccan historian Abdallah Laroui echoes this position when he writes that modernity in the Arab world is bound to a history of domination and exclusion, a position that rings even more true in the political climate of U.S. aggression in the Middle East: "Arab lives are determined elsewhere, where the balance of power lies in the industrialized West; this is how 'today's humanity is really partitioned.'"[22]

This book is not invested in "provincializing Europe," critiquing Eurocentric thinking, or rethinking European institutions by examining how they became modern through their interactions with colonial and non-Western societies, though these are important projects.[23] It is more interested in noting how Moroccan museum institutions, intellectuals, and artists have addressed their positions on the periphery of a proclaimed and often imagined modernity emanating from the West and how they have navigated their identities over a period of historical instability since it achieved independence. Their negotiations are not about regulating a cultural inferiority complex but rather about the use of art to access the right to participate equally on local and world stages. The first three chapters thus address how the museum as an institution has been manipulated, transformed, and used by three sets of actors concerned with modernity and the processes of modernization and globalization in Morocco: the state, corporations and banks, and private individuals. These actors have used the museum as a symbolic beacon of modernity and a protected haven for culture against an often contradictory and antagonistic landscape of growing unemployment, bread riots, civic unrest, torture, imprisonment, and the rise of Islamism. In chapter 1 I examine how after independence the Moroccan state used inherited colonial museums and their discourses on the deterioration and safeguarding of Moroccan culture as national museums to symbolize the state's commitment to processes of modernization. By examining the creation of categories of memory—the "useless" and the "useful"—I aim to show how art is collected and displayed in service to a naturalized national history and broadcast in an international context to testify to modernization efforts. In chapter 2 I examine Moroccan corporate art museums. As neoliberal economic policies replaced state modernization discourse in the 1980s, financial institutions started investing in art, arguably as a spur to national development but ultimately to help themselves by creating global identities for their institutions and clients. Finally, in the last chapter of Part I, chapter 3, I look at a private art museum established in the late 1990s that has seemingly opted out of modernization and discourses of development and takes the neoliberal privatization of culture to an extreme by creating a cabinet of curiosities that functions as a cave to protect Moroccan arts from the outside world and its unsuitable publics. The historical trajectory of the establishment of these art institutions points to a growing exclusion of the Moroccan public from art and patrimony at the same time as the social divide between the wealthy and the poor is widening in Morocco. From the national museums of the 1960s and 1970s to corporate modern art museums of the 1980s, housed within corporate headquarters, to the cave of the 1990s, which through a logic of nostalgia has become a gated community, visible museums in Morocco have become progressively less visible to the Moroccan public at large. This dynamic is disturbing at best. It ultimately confirms the complaints of Moroccan museum critics that there are no museums in Morocco and that ordinary Moroccans are kept at a distance from art and cultural patrimony.

From the Monumental to the Tactical

When material museums fail their publics, we must dig deeper and uncover their imaginary and invisible counterparts. If existing museums lack objects, collective memory, and public participation and appear more concerned with visible status than with visible art, what other unseen museums might we turn to in order to speak about history, memory, art, and value? Faced with the void of a public museum, Moroccan artists and intellectuals established discursive and ephemeral museums that respond to the politics of modernity in Morocco and attempt to bring the public to patrimony and art. If we think past the museum as solely a physical architecture or a material collection to the museum as an imagined, discursive, or portable technology through which one can muse on art, society, and memory, then through museums past, present, and absent in Morocco, we can visit an unexplored but extremely important imaginary.

In their 2004 project *Kinshasa, the Imaginary City,* Filip De Boeck, Marie-Françoise Plissart, and Koen Van Synghel showed that in a context of material decomposition and lack, the invisible is as important as the visible, if not more so. By filming and photographing invisible, imagined, unstable, and ephemeral urban infrastructures, they started with material absence in order to reveal the city and its practices as a mental space and performance at war with visible and official constructions:

> The urban landscape of Kinshasa, its activities, its praxis and its spaces particularly charged with signification (the parcel of land, the bar, the church, the street) should be read not only as geographical urban realities that are visible and palpable, but also and foremost as a *mundus imaginalis,* a local and mental landscape, a topography and historiography of the Congolese imaginary that is no less real than its physical counterpart.[24]

In this project they were interested not only in making visible an unstable urban fabric but also in showing that the deceptive promises of modernity had created an "arsenal of physical and symbolic violence."[25] Their focus on spaces of lack and the creative bricolage that filled them was not a celebration of alternative modernities but an examination of landscapes of material degradation in order to address political and economic inequality. Likewise, the goal of this book is not to celebrate the ability of Moroccans to imagine modern art institutions in their absence but rather to understand the topography of the imagination as it grapples with this absence.

Ferguson's articulations of decomposing modernity or a nostalgia for the modern—that modernity has already come and left Africa—are extremely useful and provocative in the context of Moroccan imaginary museums. Although

in the aftermath of independence modernization discourse promised to construct state architectures committed to modern culture, as time passed and the
promise of a modern public art museum failed to be realized, artists and intellectuals grappled with a growing nostalgia for the modern institution that almost
was. In chapter 4 I look at the creation of what I term a "discursive museum"
that attempts to write itself into existence in the face of an unraveling "modernity that almost was" in the national museums. Working to suspend, reposition,
dissect, and re-present dominant narratives on art and modernity in both the
Moroccan context and the international art world, the discursive museum created textual rooms to confront the place of Moroccan modern art vis-à-vis the
politics of representation in Islamic art, the popularity of naïve or unschooled
painting, the pressures of nationalist art, and the tensions between universalism and cultural specificity. From the mid-1960s to the mid-1970s, the discursive museum housed the most dynamic cultural discourse in postcolonial
Morocco; artists and intellectuals were animated by the desire to create new
art and a new society that would reflect the exuberance and hope felt in the
aftermath of independence. The museum was built through the work of three
cultural journals of the time: *Souffles* (1966–1972), founded by poet Abdellatif
Laâbi; *Lamalif* (1968–1988), founded by Mohamed Loghlam and journalist
Zakya Daoud (a.k.a. Jacqueline Loghlam); and *Integral* (1971–1978), founded
by painter Mohamed Melehi. When the 1970s brought with them military
coups, university strikes, state paranoia, and a repressive atmosphere that ultimately put Abdellatif Laâbi in prison and declared Zakya Daoud an enemy of
the people, the journals either closed down or were forced to limit their discussions of art as a tool of societal critique. Moumen Diouri describes the
Morocco of this period as a society held ransom to violence and repression as
it moved forward at "two speeds."[26]

Despite the crackdown on expression, the discursive museum consolidated
its place and served as an important museological space of reflection, memory,
and Moroccan art that would increase the cultural elite's agency in controlling,
developing, protecting, and disseminating modern Moroccan culture. This
pedagogic dynamic appears most clearly in the local press, where public transcripts on art were formed to encourage the neobourgeois Moroccan to replace
his or her idea of facile entertainment for cultural betterment and to link the
acquisition of wealth to the acknowledgment of art as a source of cultural capital. As artists worked to dispel the image of naïveté that had been assigned
them by international art markets and discourse, they also desired to educate
the Moroccan public and bring them out of their position as undiscerning
consumers of modernity, or "naïve spectators."[27] However, their strategies of

containment in disciplining taste in art ironically re-created many of the exclusionary dynamics and barriers of the museums they sought to redefine. The discursive museum did not knock down its exterior walls.

Where the discursive museum worked to extricate artists from discourses that marginalized them, ephemeral outdoor museums take art to the streets and work to bring the marginalized public to art. In chapter 5 I trace the history of bringing modernist and contemporary art to the streets through five projects, some more ephemeral than others: the populist art manifestations during the late 1960s by the Casablanca School, the work of Mohammed Benaïssa and Mohamed Melehi in creating the yearly Asilah art festival, the urban projects of the contemporary Casablanca art collective La Source du Lion, the curatorial practice of L'appartement 22, and the creation of a community museum in Aït Iktel. These sites and projects bring museum practice—display, collection, preservation, and education—to the streets and redefine the place of a museum within the urban fabric as something other than a single static temple of culture. Temporary or malleable in nature, the ephemeral museums allow heterogeneous publics to engage with visual art and become sites that have the potential to function as "contact zones" or "conversable civic space."[28] Going beyond reductive and exclusionary architectures of the nation in their acceptance of a plural and pluralistic staging of culture, they encourage people to reflect on more intimate and immediate relationships such as those between the spectator, art, and the city itself. The wall-less nature of these spaces of cultural representation invites a transformation in the identity of art institutions as hierarchical architectures of knowledge to that of a more democratic and dynamic form of cultural exchange and process. This type of museum has the potential to invite nonhierarchal organization of knowledge and to cross the cultural divide between popular and elite. Rather than engaging categories of nation, memory, and identity from the top down, these spaces work from the ground up, drawing on the individual and his memory as starting points. Likewise, rather than replicating state-produced narratives of the nation, these spaces work to redefine those categories from a constellation of positions and sites: the city, the family, the rural, and the nomadic.

Global Art Museums and Border Crossings

Recently Mubarak Muhairi, director general of the Abu Dhabi tourism authority, declared: "We believe the best vehicle for crossing borders is art. And this region is in need of such artistic initiatives."[29] The United Arab Emirates is one of the latest arrivals to the booming museum construction site that has blossomed in the Gulf States. The I. M. Pei–designed Qatar Museum in Doha opened December 1, 2008; Dubai is building a "Culture Village"; and Sharjah is fashioning itself as the cultural capital of the region with its art museum. Abu Dhabi's museum efforts seek to surpass these developments by constructing a Frank Gehry–designed Guggenheim Abu Dhabi, a Jean Nouvel–designed Louvre franchise, and a Zaha Hadid performing arts center on Saadiyat Island. The art development project also envisions a national museum, an art college, and pavilions to house international biennales. The Canadian consulting firm that is guiding the project, Lord Cultural Resources, advertises that its mission is "Creating Cultural Capital."[30] Art museums in the Gulf will serve as cultural capital in a "high-end" international economy of prestige and exclusivity. But who will they really serve in the region? How will they fulfill their missions as public museums? What memory will they create? Who will have access to these collections? As Salwa Mikdadi has written, although museum officials appear committed to art education and outreach, "there have been no studies done, such as focus groups or community meetings, to understand how the art museum can serve the native community or how the audiences' response to art will be heard."[31]

In 1968, the Lebanese poet "adonis" (Ali Ahmad Said) exclaimed: "Today we are submitted to the disastrous consequences of our attitude from the last fifty years. This attitude consisted in attaching ourselves to superficial events and neglecting our interior beings. Arab life knows how to copy, and at a speed that would cause vertigo, the multiple appearances of European and American civilization. But the man remains unchanged."[32] For adonis, Arab modernity existed as a simulation of the Western world, as a mask from reality. What might he think of the Guggenheim Abu Dhabi? Although global megamuseums like the Guggenheim, and now the Louvre, sell their logos around the world and support tourist industries interested in attracting older and wealthier tourists, the museum's message of societal transformation through art rings false in its exclusion of local communities and their material and cultural needs.

In the Conclusion to this book I examine two small and mobile Moroccan counterparts to the monumentally scaled universal museums that supposedly cross global borders through art. These are the portable and the nomadic museums. While the Moroccan Ministry of Culture attempts to compete with international trends in art museum development and digs deeply into the ground to pour the foundations of the long-awaited National Museum of Contemporary Art in Rabat, Abdellatif Laâbi has created a portable literary museum that through poetry and art speaks of exile, abandonment, and the painful history of postcolonial Morocco. Likewise, through their proclaimed nomadism, the Expedition Projects of Abdellah Karroum and the articulations of identity by the video-art collective Videokaravaan unravel the notion of the state and its symbolic use of the arts in favor of museum projects that are inherently stateless, defined primarily as traveling *through* countries rather than originating or returning to them, situated in the points of unbelonging. These museums have created architectures for the collection, preservation, and display of art not through imitations of monumental global or national architectures imported from the West but rather through institutions that have meaning to Moroccan artists and the public on a local level. In operating from the margins, they can maintain a critical engagement with dominant discourses.

Methodology from the Margins and Other Directions for This Study

I am not an art historian but a scholar trained in comparative literature and Middle East studies. This book's interdisciplinary methodology reads art institutions and their symbolic spaces as verbal and visual texts that engage theories of representation, memory, and identity. By deploying the research strategies of several disciplines (anthropology, museum studies, literature, and art history), this study attempts to open a path that is empirically informed but theoretically engaged. Comparative literature at its best dislocates assumed centers of dominant discourse and does not conform to "authoritative" disciplinary modes of scholarship. Rather than analyze Moroccan culture solely through established Western academic theoretical or philosophical lenses, I strive to place Moroccan cultural debates and critical perspectives in conversation with each other and with academic work in Middle East studies, African studies, and art history. It is this negotiation between international theoretical discourses and what is actually practiced on the ground that led one scholar to call my approach a form of "radical localism" that privileges voices from practitioners of art and literature in North Africa and does not subsume their position into dominant academic discourse.

My methodology embraces and interrogates sources that range from the archival to the seemingly trivial, sources that I believe raise important questions about cultural politics. I conducted archival work in Morocco at the Bibliothèque Générale Nationale in 2000 and again in 2004, focusing on the postcolonial French and Arabic press as well as memoirs and letters of colonial administrators. In order to access a wider group of voices from the French Protectorate and postindependence ministerial archives, I have also relied on the thorough research and often ingenious retrieval of history by scholars such as Hamid Irbouh, Stacy Holden, Amina Touzani, and Muriel Girard.[33] However, rather than rely solely on archival materials (what is placed in the archive anyway, and how?), I have also chosen sources that would not perhaps be in the archives and that by their very nature vis-à-vis dominant discourse will be unsystematic; these include travel narratives, visitor comments, and blogs. These are not "authoritative sources" for the history of museums, and they are useful precisely because they fall on the edges of disciplinary acceptability and hence raise critical issues for specialists and nonspecialists alike regarding the nature of the museum. Although complex discussions on the organization of a museum may be in the archives, what has interested me here are the interpretations of display by visitors and the general public. How does a museum engage the imagination of those who think, speak, or write about art in Morocco?

Every book has its limits, and I would like to reveal mine by noting some approaches that I have taken here, along with some very worthy directions that I have not. Perhaps most obviously, my chosen subject is the larger discourse around the art museum, which in most cases precludes a detailed analysis of the objects of collections and of individual artworks. For those readers who would like a deeper analysis of art objects, the history of art, and the rich field of visual culture in Morocco, I would suggest several excellent studies to consult: Cynthia Becker's book on Amazigh arts, Edmond Amran El Maleh's work on painting, Abdelkebir Khatibi's book on contemporary Arab art, and Susan Ossman's treatment of visual culture.[34] Although this book addresses many museums in Morocco, it is not an exhaustive biography of the museum institution in Morocco. Museums have come and gone over the past fifty years, and I am sure that as you read this, many more will have emerged and disappeared. The majority of my research over the past ten years has focused on northern urban centers such as Rabat, Casablanca, and Fez. Tourism in the Moroccan south and the recent spread of small private, family-run museums in rural areas deserve critical attention that I have not been able to offer here.

Throughout this work I examine museums of art and ethnography and navigate in discourses that assign the term "artisanal" to certain objects and "art" to others. It is my hope that the book reveals the politics behind such designations, especially in chapters on the national and discursive museums. Ultimately, you will note that the focus of this book is on primarily academic, modernist, and contemporary visual art and how their practitioners have intervened in discourses of modernity staged by various museums. This is not a value judgment on my part. There are many other important directions that should be taken and types of artistic production that should be analyzed more closely. These directions include a more anthropological approach to how and what individuals collect and display as art, as Susan Ossman has done through her groundbreaking study *Picturing Casablanca: Portraits of Power in a Modern*

City and as Jessica Winegar's admirable work on Egyptian art communities and collecting, *Creative Reckonings,* attests. Recently, in response to the collecting practices of the Moroccan king, there has been a surge in collection of neorealist art among the Moroccan bourgeoisie with the establishment of three auction houses in Casablanca. How do different communities collect art in Morocco and in diaspora, and how do these practices define what art is? Also, how does diasporic collection reveal definitions of Moroccan artistic patrimony? What do families who live between Europe and Morocco take with them to display in their homes when they leave these countries? These are all questions that fascinate me, but unfortunately they fall beyond the scope of this book.

Finally, the majority of art discourse that I cite here is in French. Academic art discourse in Morocco has been primarily conducted in French over the past five decades, revealing many things: that modernist or academic visual art is a language that was learned in art schools in Europe, that the use of French reflects a desire to be heard and to participate in a Western-controlled international art sphere and market, and that audiences for both the museum and its artwork tend to be imagined as Francophone. Apart from occasional newspaper coverage of gallery exhibits in Arabic-language dailies, reviews and articles in art journals were published predominantly in French. Likewise, in the museums, French has dominated. For example, although today there are many object labels in both French and Arabic, the object histories in the national Oudaya Museum in Rabat are solely in French.

Although French has been the dominant language of academic arts in Morocco, artists have also creatively rerouted it from the language of the dominant power structure to a language used to circumvent exclusion. French continues to serve as a lingua franca that unites Moroccan artists not only to Europe but also to Francophone Africa. And recently curatorial practices by a new generation of artists reveal a polyglot intervention into French-dominated discourse, easing the elite identity of the language in a Moroccan context. For example, through Radio L'appartement 22 Abdellah Karroum broadcasts interviews with artists in Moroccan Arabic, conducts cutting-edge multilingual contemporary art projects in the French and Amazigh languages, and is devoted to curating multilingual discourse as an art medium. Although I do not examine this new dynamic in great depth here, it is an important development worth pursuing: how is discourse on art changing with linguistic shifts? If, as Abdellah Karroum proposes, discourse is itself a new medium in art, how does this polyglot medium fundamentally shift directions in art, its collection, and its display?

When young Najib asked me in the streets of the Fez medina why he should visit a museum, I should have risen in defense of the institution. I could have told him about the many revolutionary and transformative things museums can do. I could have told him that the museum world in Morocco was much richer than the Batha Museum, the Fez medina, and the Louvre itself. That although material conditions of the institution in Morocco are perhaps lamentable, the counter-museums that Moroccans have created over the past fifty years to negotiate the absence of a public space for visual art are truly remarkable. That the museum was not just for tourists but a collective space of memory for all Moroccans. But I did not. Instead, all I saw were his feelings of entrapment and exclusion and his image of a museum as a prison. I hope that now that I understand Moroccan museums more clearly, in their visible and less visible forms and in their decomposing and generative forms, this book can open their doors and through their exploration show the potential of Moroccan art and its architectures of intervention as a radical transformative social force and reveal the museum as a central site for the negotiation and staging of the future.

PART I

Monumental Sites of Discourse

*National Museums, Corporate
Collections, and Cabinets of Curiosity*

One

Degeneration and Decay in the National Museum: Useful and Useless Memory in Modern Morocco

Moroccan museums do not exist. Moroccan museums are failed institutions. These two statements are the most common responses that Moroccan artists, curators, and academics initially give when asked to talk about museums in Morocco. The museums that they refer to are the national museums, and their critique of the institution is ultimately a critique of state support for arts infra- structures. National museums do not respond to local needs; there is no devel- oped arts education in primary and high schools, there are no art departments in Moroccan universities, there is no national inventory of sites of patrimony, and ministerial politics reward political friendships over merit and quality. As cultural anthropologist Amina Touzani declares, "If one visits them today, one can ask oneself in what measure these bric-a-brac and aging bazaars can be qualified as museums, given the way in which they were created and the qual- ity of objects that they house."[1]

Although such complaints are frequent in discussions of Moroccan art today, they are not new. They initially emerged in the immediate postindepen- dence period and were the first signs of dissatisfaction with triumphant dis- courses of postindependence nationalism. They reveal discontent that colonial infrastructures remained in place after independence and that, although the nation-state used Moroccan arts and inherited museums symbolically as signs of the nation's commitment to culture and modernity, there was little actual invest- ment in their development. Rather, museums created by the French Protectorate

Fine Arts Administration as sites for the collection of authentic cultural prototypes turned into stagnant depositories and did nothing to reflect the postindependence energy and excitement to reassert and redefine what it meant
to be Moroccan. Disappointment in the museum was more broadly tied to a
nostalgia for the promise of the modern and its cherished institutions. Would
Moroccans be granted access to more than a rhetorical veneer of modernity,
or would state rhetoric continue to disguise dire socioeconomic and cultural
realities? In the 1970s, the stagnation in the national institution led Moroccan
museum officials to start rethinking the function of the museum as something
more than just a depot. However, their theoretical goals were never realized due
to a lack of funding, trained personnel, public interest, and political will. By
the end of the century, the museum had degenerated even further into an empty
symbol used primarily in international prestige politics.

In order to address the half-century of lack, disappointment, and disaffection stored in the archives of public discourse on the museum in Morocco, it
is important to understand how the museum as an institution first appeared
in Morocco and to read the stories, the memory, and the imagination it housed
and suppressed. The concept of decay guides my reading of museum history,
for such a concept invites an examination of processes of disintegration at work
in dominant discourses such as those regarding authenticity, tradition, and
modernity. Reading for the decay of a site can reveal the pitfalls in the totalizing grammars that have constructed it. In this respect, the work of Walter
Benjamin on the decay of bourgeois institutions can be helpful.[2] As he wrote,
"In the convulsions of the commodity economy, we begin to recognize the
monuments of the bourgeoisie as ruins even before they have crumbled."[3] By
reading the convulsions of the museum in a colonial and postcolonial economy, we might begin to recognize monuments of its foundation as ruins before
they crumbled. By examining the naturalized grammars of progress and modernization at the core of these institutions, we can better understand the
dynamic of degeneration that marks their history. And so in this chapter I offer
an overview of the museum's origins and history in Morocco from 1912 to the
turn of the twenty-first century using memoirs, travel narratives, and interviews
that speak to how the museum was used, seen, and imagined before it failed,
decomposed, and became an absent institution.

Though the museum certainly affected the lives of nonelite Moroccans
through its "re-education of artisans" during the Protectorate period (1912–1956);
its employment of administrators, guards, and workmen after independence;
and its central role in tourism during both periods, I argue throughout this
chapter that the museum in Morocco was never founded as a public institution

with the interest, collective practice of memory, or civic education of a general Moroccan public in mind. Rather it functioned as a conservatory for artisanal practices valorized by colonial administrators and a depository for objects collected through a Protectorate discourse on dying local culture and modernizing reform. Up to the present day, the national museums have struggled with this identity, ultimately failing to make themselves relevant to any public save in their symbolic use in the most abstract modernization politics. What nation do these national architectures represent?

Colonial Museums, the Degeneration of Moroccan Culture, and the Creation of Useful Memory

The fundamental mission behind the establishment of museums during the Protectorate period was to collect samples of artwork in order to restore artisanal practice in Morocco. And this mission was articulated through various narratives of local failure from the very beginning: Moroccan culture was asleep, degenerating, and/or on the brink of destruction. The Protectorate museums would protect and revive Moroccan popular arts and make them useful in the development of the Moroccan economy. In 1911, one year before the official establishment of the French Protectorate, Maurice Tranchant de Lunel, the man who would become the first director of the Protectorate Fine Arts Administration, spoke of Moroccan art in the following terms: "The princess from Perrault's tale wasn't dead, she was merely sleeping."[4] In 1917, Raymond Koechlin, president of the Friends of the Louvre, echoed Tranchant de Lunel's rhetoric when he wrote: "Let us not exaggerate, in truth Moroccan art is not dead, but it was sleeping. Without a doubt it was going to die when we intervened and taking it under our protection, we have awoken it."[5] At the discursive core of the museum project in Protectorate Morocco was a desire to create an institution that through collection and "re-education" would save slumbering local arts from a certain death. Rhetorically, Moroccan art became the feminized object of a self-mythologizing, princely French mission.

The primary intellectual concern of the Protectorate Fine Arts Administration, as reflected in official literature of the time, was to save what it considered a local architectural and craft culture in decay, a valuable material culture left exposed to great insecurities due to the emergence of new technologies. Alongside actions to save historical sites such as *madrasas,* there were equal efforts to restore local industries in weaving, ceramics, and woodwork. When art historian Prosper Ricard replaced Tranchant de Lunel as the head of the Protectorate Fine Arts Administration in 1912, it was his involvement with artisanal production that guided the policies of the administration. In 1915, he opened the first Moroccan museum, the Batha Museum in Fez, in the nine-teenth-century Dar Batha Palace, originally constructed by Moulay Hassan, the last powerful Sultan before the establishment of the Protectorate. Ricard adhered to Tranchant de Lunel's mission statement to restore monuments and sites using "pure" or historically accurate methods and created a museum that would function as a repository of Moroccan art for restoration purposes. In Ricard's own words, the goal of the Batha Museum was to collect "the most interesting specimens of both urban and Bedouin artistic production that could serve as models for the work of restoration presently undertaken."[6] Likewise Ricard founded the École des Arts Indigènes (School of Indigenous Arts) in the Oudaya Museum complex established the same year. The school was com-mitted to the restoration of artisanal techniques in order to "bring Moroccan techniques of illumination, of sculpture and painting of wood, of bronze en-graving, of wool and silk dying for carpets or embroideries, back to life."[7] Con-ducting interviews with artists, Ricard compiled volumes of works on textiles and carpets, including technical charts for patterns, many of which had been threatened with oblivion. He was obsessive in his categorization of art, seek-ing the most unadulterated models for the museums and classifying complex and hybrid production by teasing out the various strands that defined it and eliminating obvious European influences. As Muriel Girard notes, "Artisanal production, dynamic and plural, was constantly categorized by Ricard: Berber, urban, neo-, pseudo and 'fake' when produced by Europeans. These catego-rizations condition discourse on tradition and the policies that are taken."[8] A rhetoric of purity legitimized the objects as fitting blueprints for the restora-tive process, and a comparison of superiority made with Algerian art was a rhe-torical norm.[9]

This classification and documentation of art also revealed an anxiety re-garding the taste of local artisans, an anxiety that ultimately reflected issues of power and control and asserted who should exercise the authority to define what was authentic Moroccan art. In one case, when speaking of the work of carpet weavers and their desire for brighter palettes, M. Fleury, the director of public instruction in fine arts and antiquities, remarked that Ricard's directives served as a "guard rail against the fantasies of the natives on which he imposed a theme that maintained the symphony of colors within reasonable limits . . . and preserved it from mistakes in taste, the gravity of which we Europeans sus-pect in advance."[10] The Batha Museum functioned as a conservation laboratory where Moroccan arts could serve as prototypes for the re-education of artisans, and it limited local experimentation for more "authentic" traditional prac-tices valorized by French academics. In 1917, Tranchant de Lunel exclaimed that through the establishment of museums, conservatories, and artisanal schools, "we are ensuring that industrial Moroccan art never takes on that impersonal character, hideous to those people of good taste, that we find in modern fabrication in general."[11] Moroccan arts would be brought into the industrial era with the aid of the Protectorate; however, their premodern characteristics would be protected. Tranchant de Lunel articulated a critique of modernity through nostalgia for a "purer" past, a time before the modern industrial age in which personally and individually produced objects had created uniform standards of "good taste."[12] Pierre Bourdieu has argued that good taste is legitimized as universal and disinterested by the ruling class.[13] In the Moroccan colonial context, imposing good taste was the purview not only of a local ruling class but of a French ruling culture that brought with it a French history of class relations regarding art and modern fabrication and an academic understanding of local class relations. Quoting the goals of royalist Protectorate Resident Governor Maréchal Lyautey, Tranchant de Lunel was adamant that the means of production in the local arts industry would not change: "In all, the program of the Fine Arts [Administration] is perfectly clear. It can be summarized in these words: Touch everything without changing anything."[14] For the administration, preservation meant stepping back in time and re-educating Moroccan artisans with academically defined "pure Moroccan taste."

Rhetoric on good taste and authenticity in Moroccan culture served as the discursive foundation for the museum in Morocco. In their quest for authenticity, the administrators established a canon of prototypes for authentic cultural practice that reigned in contemporary creativity. Furthermore, concerns for authenticity underlying the production of carpets and the creation of models and pattern sheets ironically also supplanted local memory and practice. As Girard notes, "This return to 'tradition' was detrimental to the habitual modes of apprenticeship based on the memorization of gestures, because from now on weavers would receive models from which to work."[15] Reading a model replaced months of memorization; in the words of Ricard, "a young weaver who would have taken months to learn certain motifs through memorization can now execute them instantly by simply reading."[16] Preserving tradition increased industry, the circulation of appropriate commodities and the usefulness of Moroccan workers themselves.

In his work on colonial art education, Hamid Irbouh writes about the archetypal canon of arts created through the museums. According to Irbouh, the prototypes were carefully chosen not only to serve as guarantors of authenticity for the work of restoration and heritage but, perhaps more *usefully*, to bolster a new section of the economy, the craft industry: "Prototypes from these museums served as authentic sources on which new Moroccan craft productions emerged." Irbouh links the museum project to a colonial ideology that attempted to re-educate and refashion Moroccan society through the establishment of new work forces: "French authorities established the vocational schools for the Moroccan poor and created what Michel Foucault has called 'disciplinary careers' in which various educational and pedagogical methods set in motion a process of work regulation and ethics."[17] Holden takes this reading a step further and ties it to specific urban economic politics, arguing that "French administrators themselves enunciated an intention to preserve the medina so as to maintain employment opportunities for Moroccan craftsmen and other workers, an economic policy intended to prevent political unrest among the urban masses."[18] Creating "Le Maroc utile" (useful Morocco) became a slogan in Protectorate Morocco that extended to all sectors of society, even to art. Indeed, the museum and its artisan ateliers worked to create both useful art and useful people.

The museum also functioned as a cornerstone for another nascent industry: a new culture industry that marketed and sold Moroccan heritage to eager tourists wanting an authentic Moroccan experience. In addition to his academic writings, Prosper Ricard wrote for the *Guide bleu,* claiming that it was the Fine Arts Administration's "duty to help the tourist understand Morocco well."[19] However, as Muriel Girard notes, faithful to his concern for the real and authentic, Ricard differentiated between the cultivated and "fake" tourist, condemning the fake tourist as one who cannot distinguish the beauty of the authentic and instead "often rushes towards cheap rubbish with a perfect thoughtlessness and sometimes an unqualifiable ignorance, encouraging the fabrication of junk in the worst of taste."[20] For Ricard, the true tourist was one who recognized the differences in quality in Moroccan culture, and his guidebooks served to give this tourist the textual tools to understand the collections in the museums.

Inside the Museum and the Canon of "Good Taste"

Let us finally step inside the physical museums themselves and read their displays. According to Ricard's descriptions, there were seven divisions to the Batha Museum. The first section, archaeology, was comprised of a room and two galleries that included an eclectic mix of paneled doors and sculpted wood, ancient varnished faience mosaics, and marble tombstones with inscriptions and chiseled plaster work that were called "examples of the most pure traditions of hispano-mauresque art." The second section launched the visitor into contemporary artisanal production with two rooms full of objects that could be purchased in the Fez or Meknes marketplace, including enameled pottery, women's embroidered belts, silk and gold embroidery in both ancient and contemporary styles, leather and bronze work, jewelry, painted and sculpted woodwork, and leather-covered chests.[21] The museum would serve as a stamp of authenticity for objects that intrigued visitors wished to buy in the marketplace. And by 1921 (the edition date of the guidebook), Moroccan arts had become both intriguing and profitable in the French marketplace. As early as 1917, a number of articles appeared in French art journals documenting an explosion of Moroccan art on the French scene through a series of exhibits in Paris at the Pavillon de Marsan and the Musée des Arts Décoratifs. In visiting this room in the Protectorate museum, it was hoped that the tourist or commercial trader, already familiar with its contents from exhibits in France, would be inspired to purchase similar items while in Fez. European representations of Moroccan culture thus engaged in a movement in which the location of their authority to describe what was authentic or valuable shifted back and forth between the metropole and the colony.

The third section of the museum housed a display of Berber arts, primarily carpets and textiles.[22] Although Ricard mentioned the different regions from which objects were taken, he rather summarily described Berber art as having one style: an ornamentation that is rectolinear. If value judgment is missing from Ricard's comments, one can still detect the ethnic politics exercised by the French administration in regard to Berbers and Arabs in the exhibit's construction. Most significant is the museum's separation of Berber art from Arab art as culturally and historically distinct bodies of work. This delineation between Arab and Berber arts fell in line with Protectorate policies of race and ethnic relations in Morocco in which differences between the two groups were emphasized on all levels. For the most part, in official discourse the Berber group was represented as the aboriginal and "pure" inhabitants of the land, even distant cousins of Europeans, while the Arab group was presented as itinerants in a land of ancient traditions.[23] The rhetoric of valorization extended to cultural production. As Pierre Champion wrote in his 1927 book, *Le Maroc et ses villes d'art*, the Berber pottery displayed in the Batha Museum was similar in style to a valorized European form: ancient pre-Hellenic, Minoan pottery. In exclaiming that "the analogy [between Berber and European forms] is striking and has nothing to do with Fez ceramics," he separated and distanced Arab arts as less significant than those of Berber communities.[24] In 1965, Abdellatif Laâbi summarized this "berbérophilie":

> Colonial studies on the Berber world were conducted through a perspective that
> disturbed all objectivity and ended up, for the most part, by concluding that the
> Arab grip on the land was a failure: restrained Arabization, superficial Islamization

seen through the survival of pagan beliefs and practices, antagonistic social and economic practices. . . . Berberphilia was not a sincere attempt to revalorize or save a culture, a language or civilization from oblivion before a national or universal patrimony, but rather a political option in the service of pacification, and later full colonization.[25]

Laâbi, suspicious of French valorizations of Berber civilization, linked cultural policy to a greater political effort to pacify Berber communities and bring them into the Protectorate.

Although conservation and commercial promotion of artisanal production were at the heart of the museum, other sections of the museum created more overt political narratives and included weapons and pieces of artillery from Morocco and Italy, as well as eccentric historical objects or ethnographic scenes that narrated and legitimized the end of Moroccan history and the arrival of French modernity. The Section des Souvenirs Imperiaux (Room of Imperial Memories) exhibited "the sofa upon which Moulay Hafid received in 1912 the first French governor of Morocco, a painted carrying chair, a cage in which Moulay Hafid imprisoned the rogue Ben Hamara."[26] All three objects highlighted in this section had an imprint of power; more specifically, they were physical objects that represented exchanges of political power. What was meant by classifying them as objects of imperial memory? Why were they in an "art" museum? And how were they "useful"?

By associating French imperialism with imperial Morocco under Moulay Hafid, the museum presented the Protectorate as a natural continuation of the many imperial dynasties in Moroccan history. The exchange of power from sultan to governor as commemorated by the 1912 sofa marked the entry of a new empire, the French Empire, onto the scene. By clearly showing that Moroccan imperial activity was a thing of the past, effectively ended by the presence of the sofa, the museum exhibit underscored that the future of Morocco lay with France and the modern world. Objects of Moroccan imperial power would be relegated to the category of "memory," that is, to the past. Yet although the sofa and the carrying chair had their historical memory preserved, at the same time it was undercut as these seats of power became artistic objects to be admired for their craftsmanship. French empire was real, political, and powerful, while Moroccan empire became something aesthetic, something of the past. This "useful" work of memory in the museum exhibit reinforced a colonial discourse of French imperial might.

In order to further understand how the museum created these political narratives through art, it is necessary to understand not only what was displayed but how and the effect that exhibits could have on visitors. The 1917 article by Tranchant de Lunel in *Les arts* provided a photograph of the interior of the Batha Museum that most probably represented the section of artisanal production. As we can see, the walls were covered with plates and rugs, and the floor was littered with bronze trays, wooden boxes, and more rugs. There were no labels that specified the origin or provenance of the objects, explained their regional specificity, or gave the dates of their production. Objects were not isolated on their individual aesthetic merit, and they were not displayed entirely in situ either. Though located in a nineteenth-century palace, the room did not resemble a domestic Moroccan interior. Although one might argue that the absence of labeling and the display technique were appropriate to ethnographic museums of the period and that the guidebook would have provided the visitor with the necessary contextual information, the lack of scientific organization in the room speaks to contemporaneous practices in the display of non-Western cultures in museums and at world's fairs in the late nineteenth century and even the early twentieth century, where the exotic was displayed as outside teleologies of Western history, or en masse, in a jumble that delighted

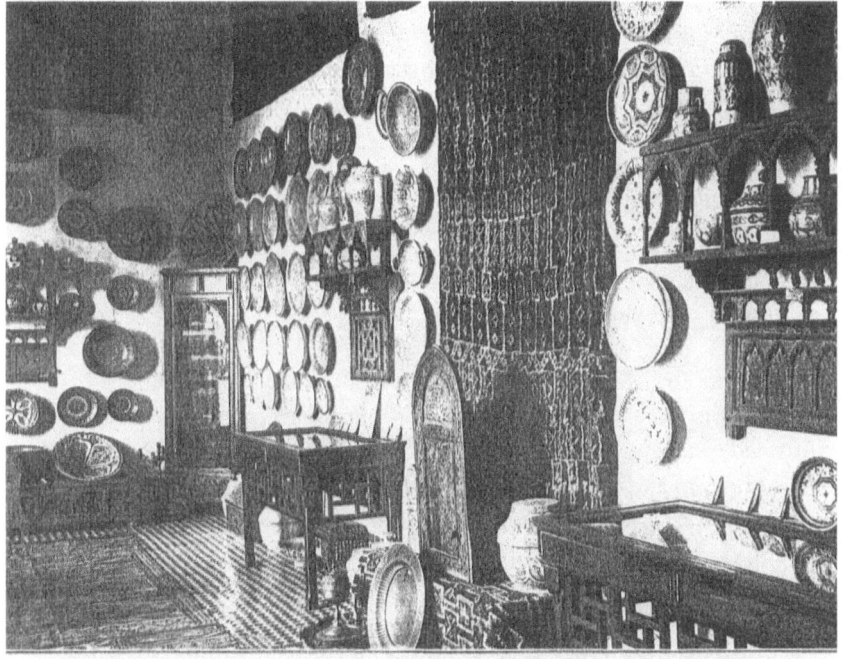

MUSÉE DE FEZ

Interior of the Batha Museum in Fez, 1917. From Tranchant de Lunel, "Le Maroc artistique," 28.

the senses. For example, in the 1905 exhibit of Algerian art in Marseilles, the curator Georges Marçais, a fellow scholar of Prosper Ricard, created spaces that were filled to capacity with precious objects. The exhibition was more concerned with showing the spoils of French domination in Algeria than with placing them into an ordered narrative or aesthetic frame. As Nabila Oulebsir describes the process of collecting art objects in colonial Algeria, collection was inseparable from military excursions; art was literally war bounty.[27]

In her essay "'A Jumble of Foreignness': The Sublime Musayums of Nineteenth-Century Fairs and Expositions," Meg Armstrong writes about the dynamics of spectatorship in exhibits of non-Western cultures at late nineteenth-century fairs and expositions. She argues that the interpretation of exhibits by visitors did not emerge solely from the exhibits themselves but that the referent for understanding the exotic was a widespread visual culture of exoticism: "Illusions of voyage, exotic objects displayed at exhibitions, world fairs, in curiosity cabinets, department stores, or operatic sets encouraged the dreaming or hallucination of the exotic other and exotic place."[28] The writings of a British traveler in Morocco provide a glimpse into how seemingly unordered displays in the Moroccan museums amplified the dreaming of and hallucinations about the exotic other. In visiting the Batha Museum in the late 1940s, the English poet and editor Wrey Gardiner was immediately attracted to the Room of Imperial Memories. It captured his attention and certainly his imagination:

> There are modern palaces in which you can see the tiled Moorish world which never varies very much whether it is 9th or 19th century, such as the Dar Batha, now a museum of arts and crafts. An interesting exhibit is the iron cage in which the pretender to the throne of Sultan Moulay Hafid, Ben Hamara, was exposed to the populace before being thrown to the lions. This occurred not five hundred years ago, but in 1909.[29]

Predictably, the "Moorish" world appeared unchanged over time for this museum visitor. Wrey Gardiner was not a connoisseur, nor was he necessarily a cultivated tourist by Ricard's definition, but as a white European he had access to the museum and the discursive power to frame the exhibit and generate his own narrative.[30] In the absence of a chronological narrative to guide him through the art pieces, he was left with his own perception that the aesthetics of the objects remained constant and existed in a certain timelessness. This same timelessness and lack of history in art could also be transferred onto the objects from historical events that appeared in the Room of Imperial Memories, and that is exactly what Gardiner did, concluding that the Moroccan judicial system also remained outside of modern time, as "barbaric" as it had been five hundred years earlier. In Gardiner's reading of the Batha Museum's exhibit organization, Morocco was narrated as a country on the doorstep of modernity, outside the European family house of progress, enlightenment, reason, and justice.

In the Oudaya Museum in Rabat, Gardiner took even more time to reflect on the barbaric nature of the "Moor." Although he mentioned the ceramics on display in passing, his attention was captured by the physical architecture of the museum, an old fort complex:

> It was cool inside, and examples of the pottery of every town in Morocco poured a cool dream-like quality back into my tired over-heated mind. The rich blue of the pottery of Safi was particularly beautiful. There was, as usual, the room once occupied by the Sultan's Favourite. It was always the most beautiful of all and somehow its dark corners, coloured by rich carpet hangings on the walls, or blue tiled alcoves, managed to evoke the ghost of some richly clad girl with the dark haunting eyes looking from under blackened lashes. And where were the other forgotten wives gnashing their teeth in the ill-lit chambers of outer darkness and neglect? In Moorish palaces you pass up a few steps here, and down a few more there, and always around the corner is something new and barbarically splendid. Here it was, walls covered with chains and instruments of torture that had been used on the Christian prisoners who had the misfortune to be captured by the pirates, or who had just been washed up on this coast which was not called Barbary for nothing.[31]

Gardiner was more preoccupied with seeing the barbaric splendor of the "Moorish" palace than the display of ceramics before him. Aesthetic objects such as plates, tiles, and rugs triggered images of Orientalist harems with forgotten wives "gnashing their teeth in the ill-lit chambers of outer darkness and neglect." For Gardiner, a juxtaposition of chains and instruments of torture with delicate pottery effectively served to remind him that behind the beauty of Moroccan civilization there was, "as usual," an Islamic barbarism that needed to be disciplined.[32]

Armstrong writes of European fairgoers in the late nineteenth century and their construction of exotic and political orders, and she explains that "the agency of the fair-goer arises in his activities as a rag-picker, a bricoleur of foreign objects (or "events") on his visual plane that will contribute to his own museum of exotica and to which he will give an aesthetic order."[33] Fifty years after the world's fairs that Armstrong describes, we see Gardiner using the same practice of bricolage to order the Islamic world in the museum. Rather than seeing a National Museum of Moroccan Arts organized by region with rooms of carpets and textiles from Rabat and Salé, pottery and furniture from Fez, jewelry from Sous and Meknes, Gardiner focused on random objects to engage his imagination and ultimately reproduced stereotypical and racist knowledge of the time. Gardiner perceived Moroccan culture as barbarically exotic, and, like a safari, the museum provided the safety and controlled environment that allowed the visitor to be pleasurably frightened and appalled by the creatures on display, whether lions or native Moroccans.

In *Exhibiting Cultures,* Ivan Karp, among others, has argued that the exhibition is a "field in which the intentions of the object's producer, the exhibitor's arrangement and display of the objects, and the assumptions the museumgoer brings to the exhibit all come into play."[34] At this point, I hope that I have given the reader a glimpse into how Moroccan museums and their directors created various narratives that valorized "traditional" culture as a commodity in the modern Protectorate economy and insisted that these premodern arts be kept as pure as possible, protecting the object but sacrificing the history of the practice and gestures of its creation. Likewise, the narrative of Wrey Gardiner reveals how pervasive preconceptions and assumptions about Moroccan culture and history were read onto exhibits and effectively placed Moroccan culture outside of history and modern time.

By 1950 the number of museums in Morocco had multiplied more than threefold, for with the establishment of the Batha and Oudaya museums in 1915, other peripheral exhibition venues were opened throughout the Protectorate. At first, these venues were linked to the *estampillage* (stamping) of carpets and described in tour books as places to see fine carpets before they were shipped off for sale. However, by 1920 a regional museum was opened in Meknes in the Dar Jamai; in 1932 the newly restored palace of Si Said in Marrakesh was opened as a Fine Arts Administration museum; Rabat gained an archaeological museum; a small museum of French art in Casablanca came under construction in 1950; and on the Spanish side of Morocco, a museum and school of Moroccan arts opened in Tetouan in 1925. On the one hand, the Protectorate sought to preserve Moroccan visual culture from the ravages of the modern world, and on the other, it worked to modernize certain infrastructures in the kingdom in order to allow Moroccan arts to more easily participate in an imperial commodity economy.

The irony in the colonial museum project in Morocco is that in attempting to save what was seen as a decaying culture, the museums built a depository of dead objects. The desire to limit what was authentic to pure models of the past created a canon that for the most part excluded contemporary experimentation. Barbara Kirshenblatt-Gimblett writes that the ethnographic exhibit is always created out of ruins and fragments excised from living cultures: "Like the ruin, the ethnographic fragment is informed by a poetics of detachment."[35] Moroccan Protectorate museums detached and excised models of Moroccan culture from living contexts and in the end reified these models for economic purposes. Ultimately these prototypes attempted to discipline local artisanal memory and practice for a new type of productivity.

As an institution, the Enlightenment museum in Europe in the nineteenth and early twentieth centuries became the incarnation of a weal for temperance and education in the hope of creating an enlightened middle class.[36] Its desired audience was a public at large. Although Moroccan museums created useful culture and useful people, they were never founded to instill a sense of community or nation in the Moroccan public at large. Unlike French museums of the time, which were interested either in edifying the public with master narratives of the nation and the empire through art consumption or in educating the public about technological development and "the social problems of the contemporary world" through the model of the Conservatoire des Arts et Métiers or the Musée Social, the colonial museum in Morocco functioned more as a closed laboratory of conservation for the education of a specific group of people: primarily administrators, academics, and "re-educated" artisans.[37] The official Protectorate bulletin published for the 1930 Colonial Exposition exclaimed:

> In the spirit of its organizers, the museums of indigenous art that unite a selection as perfect and complete as possible of works of ancient art of the country and construct an inventory of historical documents, are the indispensable instrument of the projected renovation of the country, in that they should serve to educate diverse individuals: administrators, artisans, lovers of art and buyers of it.[38]

The museum was certainly not established to forge a new Moroccan middle class but rather created an artisanal working class in urban medinas.

While Resident Governor Lyautey invited reform and invested in the rhetoric of modernization, ultimately the improvement or creation of public facilities for Moroccans such as schools, hospitals, and other institutions was limited. As Paul Rabinow has argued, "The most teetering flaw was the static conception of space allotted to the Moroccans. Despite all the rhetoric of modernization, no provisions for growth or change were made."[39] In her archival work on preservation policy in the Fez medina from 1912–1932, Stacy Holden supports Rabinow's reading and reveals that "the French deliberately chose to reinforce the physical infrastructure of a pre-modern economy, perpetuating a system of urban labor based on handcrafts, not industrialization."[40] Located in historic buildings in the medinas, colonial museums suffered from this static conception of space and time. The colonial museum did not participate in the creation or improvement of public space for the performance and remembrance of Moroccan culture through visual arts, nor did it make provisions for imagining a future of growth and change. Built on a totalizing discourse of authenticity based on exclusive "traditional" models, the museum's very definition and application of that authenticity would eventually result in its own ruin.

Moroccan National Museums and Developing a Veneer of Modernity

In many post-colonial countries today, national museums serve primarily as political symbols in nationalist movements and modernization processes to prove to an international community that the state is fulfilling the responsibilities of a modern nation-state. They testify to the state's commitment to culture and along the way, through culture, create narratives that naturalize and legitimize national history, placing the modern nation-state at the teleological end of the country's history. To a certain extent, it does not matter that many of these institutions are in a state of disrepair. It is the concept rather than the execution that is most important in the global game of status and signification. This is particularly the case in Morocco. During the Protectorate, museums embodied Protectorate policies to both save and define traditional visual culture while modernizing and industrializing other sections of life. After Morocco gained independence in 1956, the museums did not lose their function as monuments to modernization but were entered into a discourse of Third World development by the Moroccan state. By keeping these architectures in place, the Moroccan state used them as symbols of modernity playing directly into world prestige politics. Protectorate museums of premodernity thus made the transition to national monuments to the modern, and a new usefulness for the memory they housed was defined through the symbolic discourse of modernity.

The national museum as an institution is all about claiming modernity. In theorizing its European Enlightenment identity, Tony Bennett writes that the museum functioned as a modern "technology" of culture.[41] The concept of the museum itself was imbued with an ideology of progress: the museum was to represent the democratization of knowledge and the incarnation of an entity called the nation. The objects in its halls defined not only the state's wealth but the character of a nation itself. And the ordering of those objects in turn narrated the history of the nation and its citizens, placing art and culture in a teleology of progress based in technological and scientific gain. As Bennett argues, the effectiveness of these "narrative machineries" was contingent on their abilities to mobilize the visitor into a performance of their logic:

> The superimposition of the "back-telling" structure of evolutionary narratives on to the spatial arrangements of the museum, allowed the museum—in its canonical form—to move the visitor forward through an artefactual environment in which the objects displayed and the order of their relations to one another allowed them to serve as props for a performance in which a progressive, civilizing relationship to the self might be formed and worked upon.[42]

The nineteenth-century museum in its organization allowed the visitor to "perform" evolutionary civilizational advancement by walking down the path to progress in one afternoon. The national museum allowed its visitor to walk through the history of the nation, with the modern nation-state as its logical conclusion. Objects and art aided the performance and naturalization of the relationship between the nation and the self.

In Morocco, the rhetorical translation from colonial to national occurred quite rapidly. By the early 1960s, what had formerly been colonial apparatuses and European institutions had become Moroccan national museums. Examples of this terminological transfer in the public sphere can be read in the state-run tourist magazine *Morocco Tourism,* in which museums were literally expunged of their colonial pasts. In the autumn 1968 issue Mohamed Serghini, director of the Fine Arts and Folklore School in Tetouan, wrote an article about "the national role" of the school. Serghini underscored the importance of what he labeled a specifically national institution and avoided the mention of its colonial foundations. Yet the aims of the national museum that he narrated remained essentially unchanged from those of the colonial one: "Its main aim is to train perfectly qualified craftsmen to restore historic monuments, maintain or resuscitate them in their authentic original forms and thus contribute towards the preservation of the national heritage."[43] In the summer 1968 edition of the magazine, an article on the Antiquities Museum in Rabat performed a similar erasure by not acknowledging the role of French archaeologists in the establishment of said institution:

> In a quiet little Rabat street not far from the Royal Palace is a small building set in a garden built in 1930 according to the plan of a Roman house. It contains the Antiquities Museum where a good selection of artifacts bearing witness to the presence of man in Morocco has been assembled. . . . Surveys undertaken in the 19th century and systematic excavations in the 20th have brought to light traces of many civilizations that have succeeded each other.[44]

The date of the museum's establishment as well as the dates of the excavations should be sufficient as signifiers to alert the reader that the period of archaeological work fell directly under French colonialism, but there is no explicit acknowledgment that the archaeologists or museum directors were French.

Furthermore, the mention of the royal palace situates the museum even more firmly in the sovereign domain, presenting the institution and its collection as part of a purely Moroccan patrimony.

Although rhetorically the museums had become nationalized, little had changed physically within their walls during the first decade of Morocco's independence. As mentioned earlier, this was due in part to a lack of funding and trained personnel and was a problem common to many decolonizing African states. Anne Gaugue tells us, "In the large majority of newly independent states, the museum was conceived as a tool for the diffusion of the idea of the nation. However, this representation of the nation to be built was most often assigned to Europeans, often to the same people from the colonial era."[45] Such was the case in Morocco, where French museum directors and administrators stayed on in Moroccan museums throughout the period following independence maintaining a national architecture that housed a primarily colonial imagination. As Adou Koffi notes in the case of postcolonial national museums in West Africa:

> In Côte d'Ivoire, and perhaps elsewhere in Africa too, the tradition of museums that goes back to the colonial period cannot easily be continued because of the fact that the collections were often acquired without the participation of nationals and the sole criteria that governed their selection were aesthetic delight and ethnographic curiosity. Precious information was over-looked, making much of the collection unusable. Furthermore, the newly independent states that have resolved to continue the museum tradition, far from overcoming the shortcomings of the institution, have chiefly been concerned to make it a prop of national prestige.[46]

In the Moroccan context, the Room of Imperial Memories and the juxtaposition of chains and pottery in the Oudaya Museum serve as examples of problematic narratives that were based on aesthetic delight and political discourse, and they were eventually removed. This process was slow, but according to the 1971 dissertation of Abdelhak Sekkat, by the late 1960s several colonial museums had been appropriately "modernized." In his short list, Sekkat mentioned the Oudaya Museum in Rabat: "It has been modernized during the past few years. It is worthy of modern museology through its conception and through its presentation of the collections."[47] Rather than a storehouse of premodern culture, the national museum was to present "objective" and modern representations of Moroccan culture.[48]

The museum as a modern institution was to work in the grammar of the modernizing process as a key symbol of development. In 1966, on the tenth anniversary of independence, the Moroccan government published *Le Maroc:*

Aperçu historique and introduced the expression *symboliser le Maroc moderne* (symbolizing modern Morocco). Although it specifically referred to Mohamed V's change in title from "sultan" to "king" (a political substitution that discursively sought to bring Morocco out of an exoticized Middle East of despotic sultans into the modern Western sphere of constitutional monarchies and democracies), the term was indicative of a dynamic of symbolization that was taking place on all levels of state and in all areas of life.

The same year, the government published *10 ans d'independence, 1956–1966,* to illustrate Moroccan progress in development with articles and photographs depicting modern economic infrastructures and projects: ports, railroads, programs in professional training, urban planning, electricity plants, and the national civilian airline, Royal Air Maroc. As James Ferguson writes, symbols of modern status in postcolonial African nations often included "suits made in London and a national airline."[49] And as though it were a literal interpretation of W. W. Rostow's runway to development, the national airline became a symbol of modernity throughout Africa, introduced to the world by sexy and sophisticated airline stewardesses wearing the latest international airline fashions.[50] As early as 1961, the Ministry of the Economy declared that "an analysis of the potential of Moroccan economic development over the course of the next decade shows that she has attained, according to Rostow, the stage of '*décollage.*'"[51] At least in rhetoric, both the economy and the stewardesses were ready to go.

In addition to testifying to successful industrial modernization in Morocco, this symbolism attempted to disguise the dire socioeconomic realities of the period. Morocco of the 1960s was a country beset with social, economic, and political turmoil. In search of a better life and employment, peasants migrated from the countryside at unprecedented rates. Bidonvilles, sprawling shantytowns without running water or any waste management, sprung up around Casablanca. This public sought the benefits of a modernizing country but found very few. On the political stage, repression was at a high point, and governments were dissolved one after another. With the ascension of Hassan II to power, stories of torture in the Dar al-Mokri and Derb al-Sharif and the construction of an underground prison in the High Atlas mountains, Tazmamart, spread quickly by word of mouth. The monarchy was anything but constitutional. Although opposition parties managed to exist, their leaders were constantly making the trip to and from prison. A few, like the leader of the opposition party UNFP (Union Nationale des Forces Populaires), Mehdi Ben Barka, led their lives in exile in France and Algeria, but they could not completely escape the state's grasp either. In 1965, Mehdi Ben Barka was kidnapped in Paris, presumably by Moroccan intelligence officers, and was tortured and killed. The affair became one of international significance, with France momentarily suspending her political ties with Morocco. In Casablanca, on March 23 of the same year, students went to the streets to protest an edict prohibiting adolescents over eighteen from attending high school; at least a thousand were killed by the army. Two military coups were staged to overthrow the monarch, in 1971 and 1972, both failing and resulting in either the execution or the life imprisonment of all involved. In December of 1972, university students and professors went on strike to protest the government. The strike lasted until the spring of 1973, when it was finally suppressed by government forces.[52]

With the social, political, and economic reality in Morocco so distant from the goals and values of its proclaimed modernity, the state resorted to symbols and symbolic gestures in order to attest to its allegiance to modernization. Symbolizing, representing, and testifying to Western industrial modernity and modernization for the purposes of acquiring international prestige extended into all areas of official discourse, including the arts. Howard Becker has written, "Many states regard art as more or less a good thing—at the very least, as a sign of cultural development and national sophistication, along with modern highways and a national airline."[53] And this is where the museum reappears. The ability of the institution to imagine the past and the future served the interests of a state that did not want to dwell on the present.

In "Art Museums and the Ritual of Citizenship," Carol Duncan argues that the art museum is used as a symbol of prestige by Third World "despots" who wish to make symbolic overtures to the West attesting to their espousal of democratic tenets. She writes:

> The West then, has long known that public art museums are important, even necessary, fixtures of a well-furnished state. This knowledge has recently spread to other parts of the world. Lately, both traditional monarchs in so-called underdeveloped nations and Third World military despots have become enthralled with them. Western-style art museums are now deployed as a means of signaling to the West that one is a reliable political ally, imbued with proper respect for and adherence to Western symbols and values. By providing a veneer of Western liberalism that entails few political risks and relatively small expense, art museums in the Third World can reassure the West that one is a safe bet for economic or military aid.[54]

Duncan's statement is notable in its political reading. The use of the museum as a symbol of allegiance to an international modern community points to a historic and continuing relationship between culture and development in the Third World and reveals how narratives of modernity in artistic production are embraced for development gains.

A contemporary example of this relationship between art and economic development can be seen in United States Trade Representative Robert Zoellick's June 12, 2004, opinion piece for the *New York Times,* in which he praised the renewal of free trade agreements between the United States and Morocco. Zoellick did not begin his piece, titled "When Trade Leads to Tolerance," with a description of democratization efforts in Morocco or a discussion of economic reform in the kingdom. Rather he opened his remarks with a comment on art:

> In Tangiers' Museum of Antiquities stands one of the most famous mosaics in Morocco, "The Voyage of Venus." It can best be appreciated by stepping back and taking in the full picture, so that each brightly colored tile blends into the others. As the United States signs a new free trade agreement with Morocco next week, we need to recognize the full mosaic of interests at stake. The larger picture is one of a new and deeper economic and political partnership with Morocco, a bright light of reform and moderation in the Islamic world.[55]

Zoellick's introduction reaffirms that Moroccan museums and the cultural patrimony they preserve are cultural signposts on the road to international modernity: a nation that invests in preserving art and history is responsible and committed to modern state infrastructures. The Tangiers Museum of Antiquities, situated at the Moroccan geographic point closest to Europe, and the Roman mosaic "The Voyage of Venus" serve as apt symbols of Morocco's rapprochement with the West, allowing Zoellick, among many others, to muse on the "bright light of reform and moderation in the Islamic World." Senegalese President Abdou Diouf noted this relationship between culture and economics in his opening remarks at the 1998 Biennale for Contemporary Art in Dakar: "No economy can be considered healthy if its culture is unhealthy."[56] In order to attract economic investment, the state must exhibit its modernity through culture. The museum in Morocco allows the state to generate aesthetic images of Morocco as a means to stake claims to shared history and modernity and to attract investor capital by "marketing heritage."[57]

If the national museum has long been regarded as a fixture of the modern state in the West, in a Third World context it should be read as part and parcel of the negotiation for modern state identity and status. As a modern architecture from the colonial period, it is a physical marker of and testament to the various projects of modernization that it inhabits. To further this claim of allegiance, in the late 1960s the Moroccan state added several museums to those established during the colonial period. A Postal Museum and a Museum of Mining were both placed in the capital city testifying to the process of modernization in Morocco through exhibits detailing Moroccan technological advances in science and engineering. Museums were thus not only repositories of ancient and historic culture—buildings that held the cultural identity of the nation—but also architectures that narrated how socioeconomic modernity was underway in Morocco.

To fully understand how museums functioned as monuments to modernization and symbols of modernity in the 1960s and 1970s, it is important to examine them in the context of Western tourism in Morocco. If they were indeed symbols of modernity for the West, they must be understood through the image of Morocco that the state produced and packaged for the West. National museums in Morocco were not intended for a local public as much as they were for the rest of the world.[58] In the 1960s, Morocco chaired the African Council on Tourism, and in March 1967 the magazine *Morocco Tourism* went into publication. French, English, and German editions invited and encouraged Europeans to enjoy Morocco with pictures of bikini-clad models water-skiing, sunbathing, and dancing in nightclubs. Published by the National Office of Moroccan Tourism, the quarterly magazine was sponsored in part through advertising, and its pages were replete with images promoting cigarettes, wine, cruises, and luxury hotels. Articles covered such events as golf tournaments, horse shows, and car rallies. The image of Morocco projected was one of modern wealth. In the summer of 1969, Morocco hosted the Miss Europe pageant, and the rhetoric of the article written about it reflected the general image of the country for which the National Office was striving: "The 21st International Festival of Beauty and Elegance was held this year in Morocco in the luxurious setting of the Rabat Hilton."[59] Morocco was to be seen as a land of beauty, elegance, and luxury replete with modern amenities such as international hotel chains.[60] One advertisement that recurred in the magazine over several years was for Sacha's Boutique on the Casablanca corniche and included the following message embracing the spirit of modern capitalism: "There is a nice spot on the seaside where good food can be had and where at the same time you can go shopping for all the fashionable frivolities and novelties cunningly displayed to entice you."[61] Fashion and frivolity were signs of modern prosperity, and the epitome of this image can be found in the cover article of the fall 1970 issue, "Mr. Playboy in Morocco": "Morocco has just had the visit of an exceptional personality—Hugh Hefner, the boss of 'Playboy' and himself a playboy."[62] The short article continued to praise Hefner and the way he himself landed his Bunny Jet on Moroccan soil.

Although one cannot deny that presenting an international jet-set Morocco was one of the Tourism Office's primary goals, the office was not interested only in that. Realizing the hundred-year fascination of Europe with whitewashed Kasbahs and colorful mosaic floors, the office sold Moroccan culture and the arts as a heritage industry as much as it could. Thus, in each issue there were articles about traditional wedding dresses, wood carving, carpet weaving, *moussems* (festivals) in the south, and the architectural quaintness of Riffi villages. In the same spirit and through the same dichotomization present in Protectorate-era guidebooks, the Tourism Office advertised timeless culture alongside modern convenience. In each issue we can read images of Morocco and Moroccan culture defined by categories such as modern and traditional, contemporary and ancient. The Tourist Office successfully navigated between these often contradictory and problematic binaries, producing from each the most aesthetically pleasing image of Moroccan life. Thus one can find on the cover of the summer 1968 issue a portrait of a beautiful young Moroccan woman wearing a richly embroidered caftan covered with gold jewelry. Her hair is loosely covered, by both cloth and shadow, and she is gazing off toward the left side of the frame in a meditative pose. The image evokes Orientalist paintings of Arab women depicted as sensual, mysterious, and melancholic and comfortably plays into long-established Western stereotypes of Arab women. The following issue, however, bears a cover showing a young man and woman sailing off the Moroccan coast. He is at the helm, while she, wearing a bikini, turns and waves. Although the cover presents the portrait of a wealthy modern couple, inside the magazine one of the feature articles concerns traditional wood painting and jewelry at the Fine Arts and Folklore School of Tetouan. Tourists were enticed to visit Morocco through the image of its ability to straddle two worlds. The selling point was beauty, and the Morocco being sold was one that combined the ancient and exotic charm of another world with the modern convenience of Europe and the United States.

The museum factored into this tourist economy as a guarantor of authenticity. As Ning Wang shows in his study *Tourism and Modernity*, the desire for authenticity and its fulfillment is a complex but integral dynamic in tourism. Authentic experience is vital to "ethnic, historical or cultural tourism, all of which involve some kind of presentation or representation of the Other or of the past." The museum in Morocco created authenticity on two levels: first of all, the objects it housed were certified by professional art historians to be original and authentic, and secondly, the museum collection served to legitimize culture outside its walls, such as local crafts available for purchase by the tourist in the marketplace. As Wang writes: "Authentic experiences in tourism and the authenticity of toured objects are constitutive of one another."[63] In a metonymical relationship, the legitimacy represented by the museum legitimates the entire Moroccan experience for the tourist.

Barbara Kirshenblatt-Gimblett writes that heritage "is created through metacultural operations that extend museological values and methods (collection, documentation, preservation, presentation, evaluation, and interpretation) to living persons, their knowledge, practices, artifacts, social worlds, and life spaces."[64] Between the traditional arts and the modern tourist economy the Tourist Office publication *Morocco Tourism* inserted yet another symbol of modern Morocco and its heritage: contemporary Moroccan painting. Although all "Oriental" cultures might be seen by the foreign readership as imbued with exotic and ancient traditions, the magazine rationalized that the best way to show Moroccan heritage and attest to Morocco's allegiance to the modern world was partially through the display of living modern culture itself. In almost every issue there appeared a short piece on a Moroccan painter in which the artist explained his commitment to a larger international community of art and to local Moroccan traditions. In the winter 1968 issue, an article on the Tetouan Folklore Museum was juxtaposed with an article on the Moroccan painter Benkemoun. In the latter, art critic and intellectual Edouard Roditi exclaimed that "Morocco has had a voice in the international art world for only ten years or so" but that Benkemoun was one of its leading proponents.[65] After a brief analysis of Benkemoun's style of painting, Roditi listed the numerous international galleries that had exhibited his work, including several in Paris, New York, Washington, D.C., and Los Angeles. Reinterpreting traditional art, artists like Benkemoun were to provide a "new" Moroccan art. The importance of the visually modern was crucial to the image of a nation engaged in the modern world, body and soul. Moroccan culture needed to be exotic enough to attract Europe's money but also modern enough to attract Western trust and join an international community of "equals" on all levels.

In a 1960 catalogue published by the Ministry of National Education titled *Jeune peinture marocaine,* the Moroccan state made the following rather vague promise: "We hope that in a relatively near future we will take on the organization of a museum consecrated to the work of our modern artists."[66] But no concrete plans were made. The desire for a modern art museum resulted in a litany of complaints and demands from Moroccan artists and intellectuals alike throughout the 1960s and 1970s, starting with a seminal meeting of painters in the Moroccan press in August 1965. While the state used the art museum as a prop of prestige, as a symbol of modernity, Moroccan artists used the call for a "Modern Art Museum" as a trope for their demands for a fair and true modernity and a fair and real cultural policy. They wanted a museum of modern culture instead of mere monuments to modernity. And this brings us to the critical practice of decomposing the museum and narrating its absence.

From Useful to Useless Memory and Culture: Decomposing the Museum

The postcolonial Moroccan state used culture to shield the tourist from the socioeconomic realities of Moroccan life. *Morocco Tourism* seamlessly combined the traditional with the modern in its presentation of the contemporary, and, like successful official narratives, it silenced voices of dissent. Although it mobilized art and museums as symbols of Moroccan modernization and authenticity, many artists resented being used to create a veneer of modernity. In 1967, the same year that *Morocco Tourism* went into print, the Moroccan cultural journal *Lamalif* published the following poem. The author's name was substituted with an alias, Izhar,[67] and the title was given in English: "Made in Morocco." The text follows in both the French original and my own English translation:

La musique andalouse	Andalusian music
Pour oreiller	For a pillow
Le matelas de chomage pour les autres	A mattress of unemployment for others
Des méchouis	Mechouis[68]
Pour maintenir le métabolisme	To maintain the metabolism
Après la pastilla	After the pastilla[69]
Avant le thé à la fleur d'oranger	Before the orange-flower tea
L'indice du coût de la vie	Indicators of the cost of life
Qui diminue de zéro virgule zéro, zéro . . .	That diminish from zero point zero zero . . .
Pour les autres.	For others.
La danse du ventre	Belly dances
Pour l'émancipation de la femme	For women's emancipation
Les "Fatma" pour enrichir le Revenu national	Fatmas[70] to enrich the national revenue
Les khamas pour travailler	Khamas[71] to work
Et le kif	And kif[72]
Pour oublier	To forget
Les bidonvilles . . .	The slums . . .
Des Mosquées	Mosques
Pour valoriser le métre carré	To give value to the squared meter
Exorciser la sécheresse,	To exorcise the drought
Pour maintenir la stabilité	To maintain an apolitical
Apolitique (Ah. Politique)	stability (Ah. Political)
Des crédits pour poser la première pierre	Loans to place the first stone
Des soldats pour en jeter un autre	Soldiers to throw another
Des Fantasias	Fantasias[73]
Des Marabouts	Marabouts[74]

Pour maintenir le génie national	To uphold the national spirit
Et puis des complexes	And then the complexes
qui font le physique de l'emploi	That make sport out of work
Des discours truffés d'indéfectibles attachements	Discussions stuffed with indestructible alliances
Des femmes en "you-you"	Women ululating "you-yous"[75]
Pour voter	To vote
Des libertés qui oppriment.	Liberties that oppress.
Des oppresseurs sensés	Sensible oppressors
Des turbans aux assemblées fantoches	Turban-wearers in phantom assemblies
Des partis de gauche	Parties of the left
A leur droite . . .	To their right . . .
Des laveurs de morts	Washers of the dead
Content de leur sort	Happy with their fortune
Des ministres aigris	Ministers embittered
Par des rentes non indexées	By nonindexed salaries
Des cimetières pour Fassis	Cemeteries for Fessis
D'autres pour martyrs	Others for martyrs
Fosses communes pour scolaires.	Communal graves for teachers
Bref, un Maroc utile	In brief, a useful Morocco
Dont il est inutile de parler.[76]	Of which it is useless to speak.

Using valorized images of Moroccan culture and modernity to show the depths of societal despair, the poet painted a composite of Moroccan society. From the opening lines Izhar presented two Moroccos intertwined: that of culture, patrimony, and folklore with another of bitter economic and social reality. He asked: Can culture mask the pain of unemployment and poverty? Can Andalusian music, according to some Moroccans the apogee of the musical arts, serve as a pillow for the destitute? Can belly dancers incite the emancipation of the Arab woman? Can prostitutes enrich the national revenue? Through these questions, with their implied answers "no," the poet examined how cultural, social, and economic categories valorized by both Moroccans and the West, by both traditionalists and modernizers, were used to disguise the reality of what was at stake in Moroccan society. He pointed out the absurdity of how these categories were supposed to change life in Morocco and asked, How are those who are working for change rewarded? While there are cemeteries for the rich, educators who work to better society lie in communal graves.

Through the juxtaposition of images of beauty and wealth with those of economic and political repression, Izhar showed the ironies of modern Morocco. The aesthetic does not remedy reality, but neither do "modern" architectures of the state such as housing credits and elections. In the closing lines the poet stepped out from the images he had evoked to provide an explicit commentary. The reader is immediately struck by the bitterness of the word "Bref"—In brief—as though none of it matters, as though even after a long list of injuries, it is all minor. The adjective "utile"—that which can give use, that can be used—coupled with "inutile" suggests the despair of the situation: it is useless to even talk about the useful. As I previously mentioned, "Le Maroc utile" was a Protectorate expression that signified economically exploitable sectors of Moroccan life. The poet presented images of traditional and modern culture that were often exploited for the good of the state but that in the end proved to be useless for the people. After a wealth of images, after the richness of culture, the poverty of reality.

Izhar's poem was published in *Lamalif,* a Moroccan cultural journal that was committed to culture "because one cannot live without culture, because culture is contestation, questioning and thus renovation because it is the deepest expression of a people, its problems, its aspirations, its own reality."[77] *Lamalif,* which spells out "no" in Arabic, was one of several journals that served as vehicles for artists and intellectuals dissatisfied with the mere veneer of modernity created by the state for tourism and promotion of the national image abroad. Zakya Daoud explained the journal's title and origins as "the staging of a position, a *No* openly plastered on everything that does not respond to the needs of the population and resolve the difficulties facing the country. . . . This sophisticated *No* that beats like a flag in the wind is also an avowed duality, a *Yes* to another Morocco, open, tolerant, dynamic, modern and more just."[78] *Lamalif* was eager to become a site in which culture was more than an image for export. Another journal, *Pro-Culture,* founded in 1973, went even further in its critique of the Moroccan love affair with exclusionary modernity and capitalism, explaining in its mission statement: "Why the journal 'Pro-C'? To be the witness and promoter of our culture, of our experience and our adherence to humanity in the face of a castrating and de-humanizing civilization: a civilization that is emptying itself and shrinking like a *peau de chagrin.*"[79] The director of the journal, Omar El Malki, used the term *peau de chagrin,* the title of a Balzac novel in which a magical skin or talisman shrinks every time its owner makes a wish until both the skin and the owner disappear, to critique the Moroccan state's misuse and abuse of culture to attract foreign capital.[80] What did these intellectuals and artists want? They wanted the government to actively and meaningfully invest in creating a modern state and not just the image of one. They did not want any more "useless" memory. They did not want a missing museum or an empty symbolic structure.

Filled primarily with plates and rugs, Moroccan museums simply did not reflect the excitement to reclaim the nation after independence: a process that nationalist politicians such as 'Allal Al-Fassi advertized would respond to "all material and moral needs of the population, and permit the individual to recover his dignity and to profit from modern civilization in participating in its progress."[81] Artists and writers engaged in the visual arts argued for an increased presence of modern art in this nationalist projection of a postcolonial modernity, and where better to place this art than in a national museum, an institution that was supposed to house the cultural identity of a nation? Moroccan artists and writers campaigned for a new museum: one that would reflect the dynamism and promise of the postindependence era. In the spirit of effecting change, they aired their complaints in public through the national press.

The Absent Museum of Modern Art

The first discussion of the missing museum occurred on August 4, 1965, in the national newspaper *L'opinion* when the Moroccan painter André Elbaz wrote: "A country without a museum is a country in which the artist, the genius that he may be, finishes by finding himself alone in his room between four walls, obliged to invent a language."[82] Speaking for himself and Morocco's best-known painter, Ahmed Cherkaoui, Elbaz lamented the lack of state attention to and comprehension of what they considered vital to the well-being of a living modern Moroccan culture. Eight days later, the poet Abdellatif Bennis wrote in support of Elbaz, declaring that the museum project was crucial for the development of the country.[83] And the following day, a Moroccan painter named Mohammed Bellal joined the conversation, exclaiming:

> The Ministry of Tourism deploys all its efforts in the construction of tourist centers and seaside resorts. But what percentage of Moroccan nationals benefit from these structures? To follow the idea of Mr. Elbaz, could we begin, and this would be a first step, with the creation of a meeting place for those unknown artists and for that public that does not know them: a museum! A museum for artists, what a school! But also a museum where the public will educate themselves. This public that is too used to "easiness," to painting that is called "commercial" or to painters, that have no idea of how to draw, and baptize their canvases as "modern." The public is too used to painting that has nothing to do with real art.[84]

For Bellal, the art museum would be the first truly modern cultural architecture in Morocco, and the paintings that it would house would be "real art." It would authenticate the project of cultural modernity through its institutional presence, educating both the local public and artists. The next day, Ahmed Cherkaoui joined the conversation, listing all the different ways in which the state could encourage and promote Moroccan arts. He concluded that above all, the state must create a museum: "This would be in the interest of the entire country."[85]

When the two weeks of exchange on the future of Moroccan arts came to a close, there was no published response from the Moroccan government, and the call for a museum continued. A few months later, in an essay titled "Reflections on Art and the Artist," the writer "C. E. Y." exclaimed yet again that the state should create a national art museum: "It is as indispensable as a bank vault."[86] One year later, in 1967, writer Salim Jay published an editorial in *L'opinion* in which he argued:

> Our artistic treasures continue to be exiled in Europe (these days this rings equally true for actual people, painters and sculptors). The Moroccan youth of tomorrow, will they have to go on a pilgrimage to the Museum of African and Oceanic Arts in Paris in order to celebrate and discover the genius of their fathers? This is what must absolutely be stopped from happening by those responsible for the culture and arts of Morocco. They must make themselves promoters of national museums, the absence of which is a dangerous and significant aberration that we have denounced in these columns many times before.[87]

Jay argued that as long as there were no meaningful museums in Morocco, Moroccan arts in all their forms would continue to be viewed through a colonial paradigm in which they were extracted abroad to museums of ethnography as exotic objects. Likewise, Moroccan painting deserved to be recognized as modern abroad but, even more important, in the nation. After all, if the state believed in the modern, why was it constantly located elsewhere? In 1968, in a state of abjection, the Moroccan painter Amine Demnati supported Jay's claim by stating in an interview with the journal *Lamalif*:

> It has been ten years now that one speaks of creating a museum of fine arts. Nothing has been done. Elsewhere one sees things being born, galleries, museums, things are being created. But here, nothing. There is no museum, no gallery and one must exhibit in back rooms and basements. . . . And what did the state do for Cherkaoui, whose work has made everyone abroad speak of Morocco? Not even a museum.[88]

Following Cherkaoui's sudden death in 1967, the Paris Museum of Modern Art had exhibited a tribute to his work, as had the 5th Biennale des Jeunes and numerous other groups and galleries. In Morocco, a group of Moroccan painters had organized an exhibit at the Bab Rouah gallery in Rabat one year later.[89] Demnati's bitterness shows the depth of institutional abandonment felt by artists vis-à-vis the Moroccan state despite this recognition of Cherkaoui in the nation's capital. The existing museums were so far from the experience and use of artists and the Moroccan public that they might as well not exist at all.

Although artists critiqued the inactivity of the state, the truth of the matter was that the government experienced great internal instability during the

1960s and 1970s (from 1956 to 1966 alone, the Morocco government changed eleven times).[90] Reflective of this political dynamic, various incarnations of the Ministry of Culture, created to oversee projects in the loosely defined domain of "culture," suffered from a lack of cohesive policy and organization from their very inception. Based on archival work on the politics of the ministry from the time of Morocco's independence to the present, Amina Touzani's 2003 book *La culture et la politique culturelle au Maroc* narrates the history of a ministry that underwent frequent leadership turnover and organizational restructuring, suffered from a lack of funding, and functioned primarily through ministerial personalities and their ambitions. As she writes:

> In Morocco, culture as a domain is less clearly defined than other areas, and its conception and objectives depend enormously on the personality of the minister in charge. . . . What follows is a personalization of "cultural power" to the profit of the minister, who in a sovereign manner, and in function of budgetary means put at his disposition by the government, chooses the projects and puts them into production.[91]

For example, while the first minister charged with cultural affairs and education, 'Allal Al-Fassi (1968–1971), favored literary arts and the Arabization of institutions, Mohamed Benaïssa (1985–1992) was primarily invested in painting and visual arts. As testimony to the individual power of the minister, Touzani recounts that, before Benaïssa's proposed subdepartment of arts had even been decreed by law, he had already appointed his close collaborator, artist Mohamed Melehi, to the director's post.[92] Each minister defined the goals of his administration and set out a rhetorical commitment to action; however, the disjuncture between rhetoric and action was often immense. Throughout the ministry's history, its articulated goals were rarely realized: "In the cultural domain as elsewhere, it does not suffice to identify seductive objectives or to sign decrees. It is necessary to translate discourse into reality and arrive at a coherent plan. This task is inaccessible if one doesn't dispose of material or human means. Yet, the ministry of cultural affairs has suffered from a flagrant imbalance between its ambitions and its means."[93]

In the context of museums, this imbalance among ambitions, means, and political will is clearly illustrated by the former head of museums in Morocco, Ali Amahan, who recently presented a bleak history of inaction in Moroccan museums: "At the beginning of the 1970s the Ministry of Culture started to reorganize the museums and their collections . . . and we realized that we didn't really have any museums, only depots for objects. . . . We tried to put in place a policy of acquisition and even a revision of the concept of the museum. But unfortunately these projects have dragged on and never come to term."[94] What Amahan critiqued was not only the lack of monetary means but, more important, the stagnation of political will for change that would transform the depository model of the museum created during the Protectorate into a museum that engages and serves the general public with dynamic exhibits that educate and also encourage everyday Moroccans to reflect on different cultural practices present in the nation and beyond.

If we look at late twentieth-century Moroccan museums, we can see that though narratives and exhibits have changed, museums remain far from public use and interest. Displays of excess in the colonial museums have been replaced by an arguably more "scientific" and modern system of display. Rather than hanging freely on walls like bounty, ceramics have been placed in display cases, for the most part, taken out of an ethnographic system of display, decontextualized and aestheticized. Rather than re-creating "scenes" or presenting collections of bounty, labels with dates and documented origin of objects serve as markers of context and identity.[95] In the Batha Museum, all objects are clearly labeled in both French and Arabic, and recently track lighting has been installed to appropriately illuminate the objects.[96] The Room of Imperial Memories and the chains have both disappeared from their respective sites, replaced by exhibits that offer other narratives. In the contemporary Batha Museum, for example, there is a room called "La Vie Spirituelle" (Spiritual Life) that includes a 1350 *minbar,* pages of Qur'ans, and painted miniatures depicting religious life. The organizing principle is a logic of continuity in which illuminated scripts from the fifteenth and sixteenth centuries *(anciens reliures)* are placed next to twentieth-century ones and painted miniature scenes of religious life from the nineteenth century are placed next to contemporary miniatures of men and women reading from the Qur'an.

Here religious life serves as the principal frame for a history of progress and continuity. By showing that the spiritual core of Moroccan existence has remained constant through political, technological, and scientific changes in the kingdom, the narrative affirms the purity of a Moroccan identity based in religion that is able to maintain its integrity in the midst of historical upheaval. This exhibit argues that the "soul" of the Moroccan nation resides in an incorruptible spirituality. However, the idea that the spiritual backbone of the Moroccan people has remained untouched by history is not apolitical. As Combs-Schilling and John Waterbury, among others, have written, the king as the spiritual leader of Morocco bases his legitimacy on his ascendancy from the Prophet.[97] Theoretically, he is the protector of the faith, and thus it is important to maintain the image that he, through his rule, has protected the Moroccan people

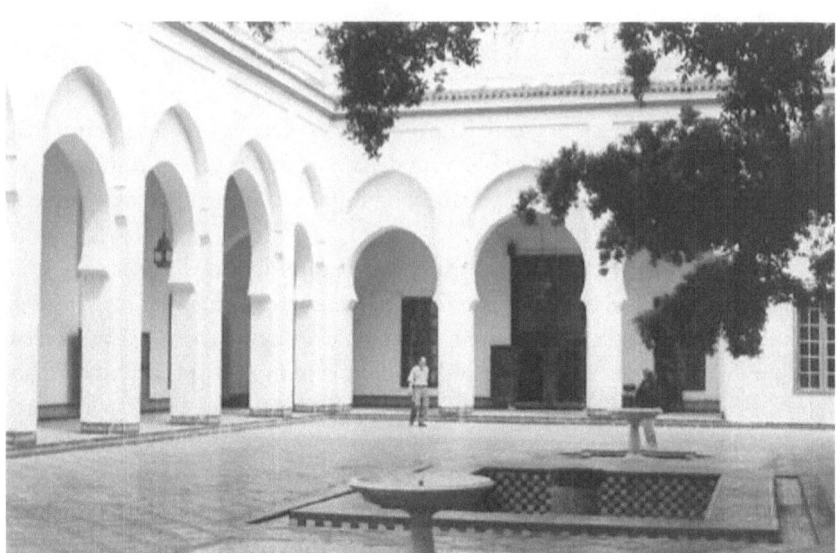

Interior courtyard of the Batha Museum, Fez. Photograph by the author, 2000.

from the ravages of the outside world, has secured and protected their spiritual life. In this room, French political formulations of "Imperial Memory" are thus replaced by another form of imperial and dynastic memory based in religion and religious life: Islam and the Alaouite dynasty have guided Morocco through history and will continue to do so into the future. This message is intended for the West as much as for a Moroccan public.

In the Oudaya Museum, the chains that evoked the barbary of Moroccan pirates are gone. As in the Batha Museum, objects have been placed securely behind glass and labeled in both Arabic and French. However, the fact that the only explanatory label of any length in the museum is printed solely in French testifies to the museum's Western and primarily Francophone audience. In Sekkat's 1971 description of the "modern" Oudaya Museum, he seemed less interested in actually describing the interior of the museum than in the museum's surroundings: "That which renders the museum even more agreeable is that it is situated in the Palace of the Oudayas near the picturesque neighborhood that bears the same name."[98] Rather than entering the museum, he spent his discursive time outside. Sekkat's description of the museum site echoes the advice of Protectorate-era guidebooks, in which a walk around the Oudayas was highly recommended.[99] And up to this day, the gardens and the Kasbah complex in which the museum and the neighborhood are located are a vibrant part of Rabat life, with more Moroccans than tourists sitting in the gardens and on the ocean-facing café terraces. The steps of the museum are a symbolic barrier between these two identities. While tourists enter the palace to examine the scientifically displayed modern exhibits of Moroccan patrimony, Moroccans typically remain outside. Children will climb the steps to look at the fish in the pond below, but they do not enter the doors to the museum. The symbolic space of the museum as something for tourists and foreigners is exactly the point and the problem of Moroccan museums that function as props of prestige.

In the December 2005 inaugural edition of the Moroccan art journal *La matrice des arts,* the editors declared that the situation of museums for modern and contemporary visual arts in Morocco is truly disgraceful. Although a small Museum of Contemporary Art has existed in Tangiers since 1996, no one except the Ministry of Culture seems to realize that it is there. Barely one year after its opening, journalist Karim Mariami published a piece on the International Day of Museums in the national newspaper *Libération,* deliberately ignoring the museum's creation and proclaiming the importance of creating an art museum in Morocco.[100] Mariami did not consider this museum legitimate, and if we read its politics, it is not difficult to understand his position.

Placed in the former British consulate villa, the museum houses approximately thirty paintings, lesser-known works from the most established and

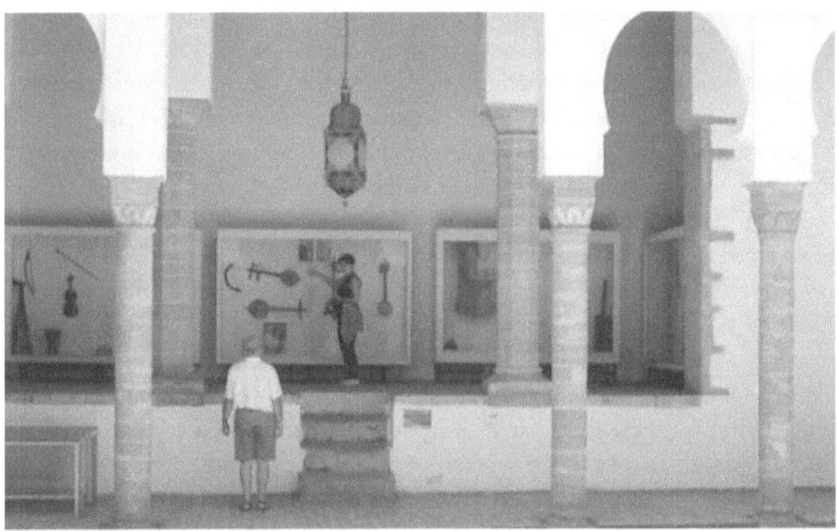

Interior of the Oudaya Museum, Rabat. Photograph by the author, 2000.

renowned Moroccan painters of the postindependence period, including Abdellah Hariri, Fouad Bellamine, Mohammed Kacimi, Mohammed Chebaâ, Mohamed Melehi, Hussein Tallal, and Chaïbia. There is seemingly no thematic organizational logic behind the exhibition, although paintings by unschooled painters such as Chaïbia and Fatima Hassan are placed together in a room of their own, nominally separated from the works of the academic painters.[101] The paintings that the museum houses are not the most representative of these artists' work; the entire collection stems from the 1980s, while the majority of the artists' celebrated works from the 1960s and 1970s are scattered around Europe and the United States, many located in the French Institut du Monde Arabe, arguably the largest collector of paintings from the Middle East and North Africa. As critic Salim Jay predicted in 1967, Moroccans have to travel to France to see masterpieces of Moroccan art.[102]

The former head of museums in Morocco, Ali Amahan, worked on the organization and creation of the Tangiers museum, and he has admitted that this small collection was really just a gesture from the state to the arts community. According the him, the collection is "insignificant" and the number of visitors negligible. When I asked him why the museum was opened in Tangiers and not in Casablanca or Rabat, the academic centers of Moroccan painting, without pausing he answered, "Because the space was great, and it was physically the closest to Europe."[103] The museum offered poor compensation for decades of state neglect and lack of investment in art. Yet even in this gesture to its artists, the state was more concerned with the museum as a sign to the West, the art for a Western audience.

It is thus not too surprising to find the guestbook of the Contemporary Art Museum of Tangiers filled with comments in French and English written by presumably foreign hands. A guestbook in a museum is a fascinating document of the imagination, for it invites the visitor to break the silence of the space and to respond verbally to a predominantly nonverbal experience and to an imagined community of curators, museum officials, and other visitors. As Susan Crane tells us, the guestbook can serve as an important register of "disaffection" in which the viewing public can inscribe their experience of the museum and express whether their expectations have been met.[104] When I first visited the museum in 1998, approximately 95 percent of the comments were written in languages other than Arabic, predominantly in French and English. Several comments penned in French were signed by people bearing Moroccan names. This act of Moroccans' writing about contemporary art experience in French is a worthy site of interpretation in which to read the politics of identity, class, and culture. For some, to write in a foreign language when visiting the museum may be only natural due to the perceived foreignness of both the institution and the art within its walls. For others, the choice to write in French is an act of distinction and self-identification with a bourgeois French-educated or diasporic group of Moroccans. By inserting comments in French next to other comments in French by Francophone tourists, yet others perform a rapprochement with a Western community of apparently shared values regarding art and culture. For a guestbook is not only a book in which people write; it is also a book in which people read. Perhaps this group of comments by Moroccans was written precisely to be read by foreign guests not to affirm the writers' status among other bourgeois or educated elite but rather to communicate with other worlds.

Although the majority of the comments expressed admiration, many expressed disappointment at the size of the collection, and one questioned whether the pieces could be considered "Art" at all. This comment was written in French with the signature blurred to illegibility, and it was difficult to find any trace of the identity, however superficial, of the writer of this last disaffected response, but the comment itself introduced the most vital questions: What standards for art and for an art museum was the visitor using in his or her judgment? To what was the Moroccan art inside the Tangiers museum being compared? And how could this collection be imagined differently? What memory about art and culture was being engaged? When I returned to the museum in 2005, the guestbook had gone, and the museum felt more abandoned than before. Cats were lying about, and the guardian was setting up chairs for a private family picnic in the garden. Paint had started to peel off parts of the interior wall, and the space felt desolate. Who was visiting the collection anymore? In the introduction to this book I mentioned Ali Amahan's provocative comment about memory: "I am not interested in national museums of the Third World. Memory that is useless is useless to preserve."[105] What memory is useful, and what is useless to preserve? What memory is useful, and for whom?

The decay of the national museums and their potential to be more than empty symbols in modernization politics has been recognized, critiqued, and acted on by artists and curators in Morocco since the country's independence. By drawing attention to the decay of the museum, these actors have not only drawn attention to a missing cultural architecture but also have practiced a critical reading of the decay of promised institutions of modernity. As a reading of Benjamin might tell us, recognizing decline in an institution before the process of its disintegration is visible allows for the emergence of political agency. In reading the national museum's decay, these actors have exposed the grammars and limits of modernity, modernization and authenticity as practiced by the Moroccan nation-state. These actors have been, and continue to be, committed to the creation of a meaningful museum that reflects local practices of art and memory in their many forms and that serves as a truly public institution. The national museums may have decayed and disappeared, but the desire for an inclusive and locally beneficial national museum remains.

Two

Marketplace Museums: Art and Citizenship in Corporate Morocco

Museums in Moroccan Bazaars and Corporate Marketplaces

Although the cultural elite has lamented the lack of meaningful national museums in Morocco since the postindependence period, local markets and corporate marketplaces have reinterpreted the museum for their own purposes and profit. Whether through small medina businesses that advertise themselves as museums or large corporations and financial institutions that create museums and galleries of modern art, the Moroccan marketplace has fully embraced the idea of the museum as a way to generate income, investment, and prestige. In contrast to national museums, which appear as outdated and unsuccessful symbolic models from modernization politics of the 1960s, for better or for worse, Moroccan "market museums" appear well versed in a liberal market capitalism that has dominated recent Moroccan history. Using a corporate logic similar to that which underpins many museums in the West today, these Moroccan "marketplace museums" are attentive to the dynamics of globalization in the culture industry: increased international tourism, traveling blockbuster exhibits, multiple museum locations created through branding, museum gift shops outside the museum, and mail-order catalogues that dislocate or decenter the museum, to name but a few.[1] In Morocco "marketplace museums" that participate in global culture are not large, wealthy, or established art institutions like the Guggenheim, the Metropolitan Museum of Art, or the Tate Modern. Instead they are a much more variegated set of institutions that participate in both formal and informal economies and use the idea of a museum for their commercial ends. Sometimes the idea suffices, and the museum is not even there.

For example, both tourists and inhabitants often refer to the medina marketplace, the suq, as a museum space due to its collection of goods and wares from all periods of Moroccan history. As a UNESCO protected heritage site, the Fez medina is marketed to tourists as a celebration of Moroccan patrimony, and the profit that is to be made from such a designation belongs not only to airlines and hotels but also to local shops and stalls that use the idea of the museum, however superficially, to advertise their wares. Scattered along the main tourist thoroughfares in the medina are a number of printed signs with arrows pointing to various "museums" in order to turn the tourist from the bustling alleys to slightly off-the-track interiors of carpet shops or expensive restaurants. One startling example of this museum branding in the Fez medina is Abdellah Belghazi's "restaurant-museum," which, as the order of the words suggests, is much more of a restaurant than a museum.[2]

Ubiquitous in American and European museums, the museum gift shop and café have become the ultimate sites of consumption all over the museum world. As James Twitchell puts it: "If your museum is really maximizing return on investment, it also has an intimate eatery where viewers, a.k.a consumers, can rest up between rounds. It should have a name like Garden Café and be separated from an assortment of ferns and potted plants by a large slab of plate glass."[3] The Tate Modern has a café of some sort on almost every floor with special "members-only" refreshment areas for those who have contributed a yearly membership fee. The rooftop café and bar in the Metropolitan Museum of Art, with its views of Central Park, is a destination in itself, and some tourists head straight for the elevators rather than the art collections. In the Belghazi space, the visitor is invited to eat in an environment that evokes a museum-quality collection of artisanal riches without any museological practices actually at work. Rather than creating a café in an existing museum, Belghazi has skipped the museum and rather given us a sumptuously decorated restaurant.

Moroccan shopkeepers exploit the concept of the museum for their own practical and more meaningful purposes in their interactions with tourists. This appears to be a practice common to Tunisia as well, the most interesting example of which I came across in Kairouan. In a wide alley next to a mosque, in a heterogeneous commercial street filled with shops for tourists and locals, one shopkeeper has distinguished his souvenir shop from the competition around him by calling his shop not only a "museum" but also the *"Arab* Museum." What is in this Arab museum? Postcards, reproductions of the mosque, lanterns, rugs, and knickknacks such as ceramic ashtrays and "Eye of Fatima" key rings. Its collection is ever-expansive: if the shopkeeper does not have what the visitor wants to see, he can send for it from another store or send the visitor to a friend's shop. Knowing that the Western tourist trusts museums as legitimizing institutions of culture, he attempts to sell his own version of official culture for a handsome price. As an African sculptor of souvenir art once exclaimed: "We discovered what they [Westerners] liked. We made what they liked when we were hungry."[4] In the face of fluctuating prices and the negotiation of value in the North African suq, what "Westerners" like is the opportunity to buy a piece of the exotic medieval landscape around them within the security and authenticity of a museum. And that is the illusion that the local market-place creates in its use of the museum: security and authenticity in value in the face of fluctuation.

What is sold in the "medina museums" is limited to an "authentic" repro-duction of the past (even if this is in the form of a plastic model or canvas painting depicting "traditional" culture, displayed in the fashion of a barely disguised department store). To borrow Stacy Holden's expression, "It pays to be medieval," and I would add, no matter in what form.[5] French art critic Pierre Gaudibert has written:

> One of the great reverberations of the influence of colonialism was in the mas-sive introduction in all the Maghreb of a "pacotille" [shoddy objects] or bazaar

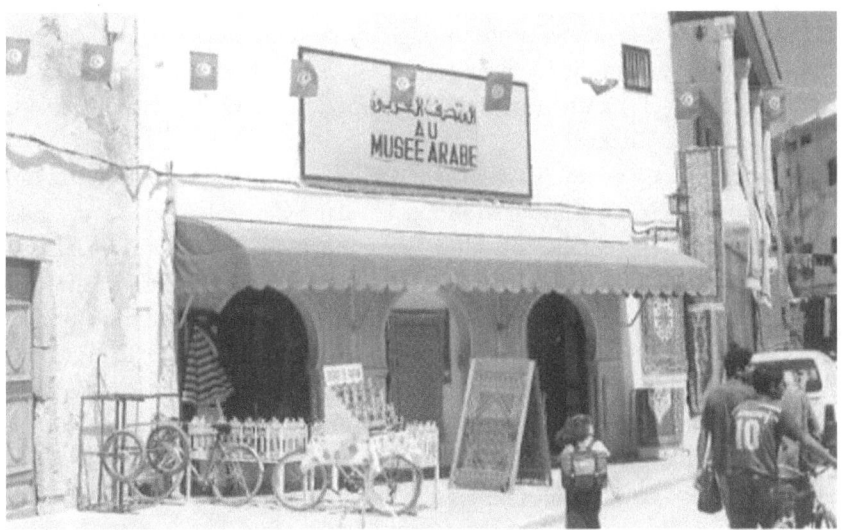

"At the Arab Museum," Kairouan, Tunisia. Photograph by the author, 2000.

orientalism that permitted a mediocre painter to execute commercial visions of conventional visions and scenes. This painting, also termed "the Arab market," has multiplied and widely disseminated oases, gazelles, prostitutes, palm trees, minarets etc.[6]

At the end of the 1960s, Moroccan visual artists attempted to reclaim the metaphorical concept of the "Arab market" from its signification as a marketplace of shoddy crafts and Orientalist depictions to that of a dynamic market for the modern arts that would serve as a parallel if not equal sphere to the Western-controlled discussion, appraisal, critique, and purchase of art. As far as the medina marketplace is concerned, however, their attempts have been ignored. Tourists and shopkeepers are more interested in the conventional scene or the inexpensive reproduction of an ancient Oriental Morocco than in an abstract expressionist canvas that claims universality.

But this does not mean that the marketplace museum has abandoned modern or contemporary arts; it has just located them elsewhere. If one steps outside the medina into the financial environment of the Moroccan corporate sphere, one can see that mini–modern art museums are almost as ubiquitous as medina museum shops. This is not just a thoughtless reproduction of the urban apartheid of the colonial period that separated the medina as medieval from the *ville nouvelle* as modern with a "cordon sanitaire."[7] It is a conscious replication of strategic value. Both the medina and the corporate world have put the "useless museum" to work for them in the logic of their marketplaces: the medina generates profit through the past, the corporate marketplace through alliances with the financial future. Ultimately both museums work to sell the security and authenticity of their products whether they be timeless culture or global finance.

Contemporary art and its display have proved to be a valuable strategy for Moroccan financial institutions to adopt. The bank Caisse de Depot et de Gestion (CDG) in Rabat publishes exhibition pamphlets to accompany its exhibits. Unlike the medina museums, the CDG has price tags on all of its art, and the art is never cheap. In April and May 2000, CDG hosted an exhibit of the work of Bouchta Al-Hayani and produced an advertising pamphlet of his work. Although the cover of the pamphlet shows one of Al-Hayani's paintings, the first page of the publication is a photograph of CDG's modern corporate building. What was really being exhibited? The photograph echoes the colors of Al-Hayani's work—dark purples, yellows, and reds—and the scale of the photograph is identical to the scale of the painting on the cover. This juxtaposition of images begs the viewer to make a mental comparison between the two, linking their modernity. The short texts that surround Al-Hayani's work in the sixteen-page publication come from a slice of the Moroccan cultural elite (novelist Mohamed Loakira, theorist and writer Abdelkebir Khatibi, and novelist and social activist Abdelhak Serhane) as well as Western scholars (Francophone literature expert Marc Gontard and art historian Lydia Harambourg). These textual insertions valorized both Al-Hayani's work and the CDG's interest in it. By describing Al-Hayani as an important painter on the cutting edge of artistic production, the bank secured its own modern image in Morocco and in an international community of finance, convincing and assuring its local clientele in the process. CDG's corporate museum allows it to stage an identity that claims it is grounded in Moroccan society while also a player on the international stage of high finance. Charbel Dagher writes, "The real obstacle [for contemporary art] lies in Arab investors' perception of artistic works as unimportant, with neither the economic value of gold or stock market shares, nor the social esteem of items like jewelry, furniture or fancy cars."[8] But I would argue that Moroccan corporations do recognize the economic value of art and are investing in art in order to boost their image in international finance circles. This dynamic of investment and display is worth a closer look.

Annette van den Bosch has written that "the art museum that emerged in the modern nation-building era is now experiencing dramatic discontinuities in the global era" and that in the case of museums the "transformations of becoming global mean that notions of citizenship and national identity are being re-negotiated."[9] Although van den Bosch primarily refers to national art museums that have to redefine themselves and their collections in light of changing global conditions and realities, in the Moroccan case we can read this tension in identity as at the very core of marketplace museums. What interests me most here is how through modern art Moroccan banks and corporations create spaces and narratives that stage their identity as global, modern citizens of a worldwide economic community all the while negotiating this identity with a performance of national subjectivity.

Due to the forced liberalization of the Moroccan economy in the 1980s, state funding of the arts was reduced as state agencies and bureaucracies struggled to lower the country's debt.[10] Using the language of citizenship and participatory civics, various Moroccan banks and corporations started collecting art to theoretically help the state protect modern art and do the museum work the state could not do. However, if we step into these spaces we can see that collecting modern art has more to do with corporate image, prestige, and public relations than with safeguarding the visual arts for the benefit of the nation-state.

Unlike the medina "marketplace museums," corporate marketplace museums do not sell anything directly but rather narrate the acquisition of wealth and class exclusivity. As John Roberts tells us, the art museum's "direct and indirect function may be to prop up the consumption of art as a sign of class exclusivity and inclusivity (middle-class learning and fashionable taste), but this is not a stable or a unidirectional process." Roberts tells us that the museum is "as subject to external social forces as any other institution even if the impact of these forces will depend on the particular institution, its history and relationship to the national interests of the state."[11] In this chapter, then, I aim to examine the corporate staging of art and subjectivity as it occurs in one of the oldest mini–museums of modern art in Morocco, the Wafabank Space, a gallery and foundation located within the Wafabank headquarters in Casablanca.[12] The use of the word *space* is certainly deliberate, for the museum works to insert a global space into its relations within the restrictive and nationalist sphere of the monarchical state. What is the relationship between the national art interests of a state committed to economic development under the liberal market model and corporate museums committed to creating prestige and ultimately profit for their shareholders? What forces do they exert on one another?

Since Wafabank's gallery opened in the 1980s, financial institutions like the CDG have joined the "corporate art museum" movement to collect and exhibit art while displaying themselves. In the conclusion to this chapter I will explore the dynamics of space and display in two corporate-owned marketplace museums. The 1996 opening of the Villa des Arts in Casablanca and its 2006 sister institution in Rabat show that the North African Omnium Group (ONA) followed Wafabank's lead but ultimately associated itself with the marketing of art through a duplication of the institution and visible imprints on city space rather than through the incorporation of exhibit space in its corporate headquarters. In the Rabat institution, ONA uses technology as the main narrative tool to display its cutting-edge identity, creating an underground virtual gallery that showcases technological advancement in display over art itself. Ultimately an outward commitment to art and the public rhetorically disguises a private drive to power and a display of wealth. The self-reflexive Maroc Télécom Museum also turns to technology and the virtual in narrating its identity. Abandoning art, the Vivendi-controlled Moroccan corporation has created a museum that works to efface the hybrid international identity of the company into a larger national history of Moroccan telecommunications. A permanent collection is linked to a virtual and a part-mobile collection that can be displayed on the Web, in Maroc Telecom storefronts, and in the company's corporate headquarters all over the country.

Wafabank and the Corporate Staging of Modern Moroccan Art

In 1988 the Moroccan minister of culture, photographer-turned-politician Mohammed Benaïssa wrote in praise of Moroccan painting, declaring that it had finally "reached a level of remarkable maturity, that it produces great works and sits at the side of other traditions and cultural sectors that have contributed to enrich the civilizational diversity of Morocco."[13] In the late 1980s and 1990s, members of the cultural elite of the 1960s and 1970s had entered into political structures of power: in the 1980s Benaïssa was minister of culture, and by the late 1990s he was replaced by Achaâri, a poet, who included among his aides in the cabinet the visual artists Aissa Iken and Ahmed Jarid. With their elevation to positions of power in the state, these artists finally held the political authority to legitimize painting as part of Morocco's artistic heritage and create cultural infrastructures to support its dissemination. However, Benaïssa's sincere thanks for the work of Moroccan artists over the thirty years that had passed since Moroccan independence was not delivered at the opening of a long-awaited state-run museum for Morocco's contemporary arts. Instead Benaïssa's remarks were delivered on the occasion of the opening of the Wafabank Space:

> I am overwhelmed with happiness to see pictorial art occupy once again the avant-garde in the promotion of a new type of patronage in Morocco through this important project that is the inauguration of an art gallery in the heart of the Wafabank and through the creation of a foundation. Without a doubt, this exemplary event will incite other institutions and national enterprises from the private sector to afford more attention to the fulfillment and development of the Moroccan Man through his culture and will support his efforts of socioeconomic development. This action will only be the natural re-enactment of a noble tradition of patronage that throughout our history has permitted the enrichment and preservation of our patrimony.[14]

Benaïssa reaffirmed that Moroccan socioeconomic modernity could be supported and developed through modern culture.

As discussed in chapter 1, this rhetoric of culture as a tool of development was not a new one but rather continued in the vein of the Moroccan state's manipulation of discourses of modernization. In his essay "Culture, Museums, and Development in Africa," Claude Daniel Ardouin writes that throughout the latter half of the twentieth century, the terms *culture* and *development* were almost talismanic in the way in which African states used and abused them to immediately signify "ambiguous notions of modernization and progress."[15] Benaïssa's use of the terms "development," "culture," and "the Moroccan Man" spoke to a nebulous project of modernity; however, they were used not to signify state efforts to modernize but rather to highlight the entry of financial institutions into the project of national development. In essence his comments evoked the shift in development policies from state-centered modernization models of the 1960s to market liberalization.

As a man of the state, Benaïssa praised the initiative of Wafabank and legitimized the entry of a private-sector institution into cultural policy. This praise was performed through a rhetoric of authenticity; Wafabank was re-enacting an authentically Moroccan practice: "The initiative of Wafabank comes in time to re-invigorate a civilizational practice that is authentically Moroccan, that we hope to see enriched thanks to the different institutions and enterprises from the private sector."[16] The labeling of artistic patronage as a distinctly Moroccan institution was a strategic move for the state; Benaïssa played to the patriotism of large and wealthy corporations as the state itself lost power, forced to enter what Shana Cohen and Larabi Jaidi refer to as "the now hegemonic model of liberal market democracy [that] posits that economic growth results from both integration into the global market economy and international competitiveness in human capital and industry."[17] As Ahmed Ayoun writes in the periodical *Le temps du Maroc:* "We are witnessing a paradoxical situation in which everyone is speaking about modern culture (politicians, administrators, intellectuals, artists, international organizations . . .) but always in avoidance of the necessary financial effort to accompany these ideas."[18] Ayoun lists the budgets allocated to the Ministry of Culture since 1968 in order to show the fluctuations in funding received by the ministry over the years, emphasizing its instability: 1968–1972, 2.8 million dirhams; 1973–1977, 33.5 million; 1978–1980, 7.3 million; and 1981–1985, 63.4 million. By encouraging the participation of private-sector institutions in a realm of culture that was primarily controlled by the state, the unstable ministry could stretch its budget and delay the construction of a modern art museum, looking instead to the private sector to continue the development of modern state architecture.

By identifying patronage as something distinctly Moroccan, Benaïssa reminded the bank that even though it was a private-sector institution, it was to work for national culture under the auspices of the state:

> In effect, culture cannot be the responsibility of a sole administration, so large is its size. Enriching the culture and the patrimony of a nation is a civilizational project in that it renders the participation of all cultural institutions important and essential—whether it be an art gallery, a library or a museum—in the conjunction

of efforts and regrouping of possibilities for the execution of the High Directives of His Majesty the King Hassan II, Protector of Culture and Arts, in order that diversity of our country continue to be present, marking and reflecting the genius of Moroccan civilization both here and abroad.[19]

The minister touched on all the key points in Moroccan cultural policy. First of all, culture was a "civilizational project" for the entire nation. Second, the state in its limited financial capacity could not do everything; the private sector was just as responsible for the development of culture. However, this did not mean that the state was no longer concerned with the arts and that it would not remain their prime benefactor; Benaïssa was careful to identify the king as not only the "commander of the faithful" but also the "protector of culture and arts." Finally, Moroccan cultural policy was to emphasize the genius of Moroccan civilization both in Morocco and, perhaps most important, abroad. By means of an "authentically" Moroccan system of patronage working in tandem with the state, Benaïssa argued that all these points in cultural policy could be achieved.

Although the institution of patronage was well established in Moroccan culture, it was by no means something as distinctly or purely Moroccan as described by Benaïssa. Patronage relationships between business and art have been traced to as early as 70–8 BCE, to the Etruscan financier Gaius Maecenas (from whom the French and German terms for patronage, *mécénat* and *mäzenatentum,* are derived).[20] In the case of corporate art patronage, art historians have traced its origins to the 1940s and 1950s in the United States. Marjory Jacobson writes:

> The shift from the fortuitous predilection of the individual capitalist to the more seasoned relationship between capitalism and art patronage as a serious substructure of civilization is a late twentieth century prodigy. . . . In a new guise of enlightened self-interest, it has become "the business of business" to support this cultural imperative.[21]

In the United States, the Rockefellers exemplified this transition from a system of individual or family support of the arts to corporate patronage. After the death of his mother, Abby Rockefeller, co-founder of and major collector for the Museum of Modern Art in New York, David Rockefeller decided to continue Rockefeller support of contemporary art through his financial institution, the Chase Manhattan Bank. In 1948 he formed an Art Advisory Committee of the Museum of Modern Art made up of directors and curators to join him and one other bank member in their deliberations on the acquisition of art. By 1959 the art collection was launched with impressive holdings of abstract expressionist art. In looking back on this venture, David Rockefeller wrote in 1984:

The Chase art program attracted much attention and gathered momentum. While there were many who were critical of it, an increasing number of both staff members and customers became fascinated by it, even though they did not like everything we bought. Little by little, other banks and corporations in this country and abroad were encouraged to start art programs of their own. Today, relatively few major banks and corporations are without an art program of one kind or another. I believe that Chase can take pride in having established a trend that has beautified the work places of businesses everywhere and, at the same time, has given important encouragement to contemporary artists.[22]

Art in the bank did much more than just beautify the workplace and encourage contemporary artists: it redefined the image of the bank from a dark-paneled, dimly lit, conservative organization with portraits of men in waistcoats hanging on the walls into a business at the cutting edge, vibrant, dynamic, and full of living art. The trend redefined the relationship between the economic sector and cultural production as more and more corporations invested in art. In the 1980s it was widely recognized that a mature and successful financial organization in a liberal capitalist economy had a responsibility, if not a duty, to support culture.[23]

While the state presented Wafabank's involvement in the arts as an authentically Moroccan commitment to culture in Morocco, Wafabank was just as interested in the development of its own image as a modern financial institution. It was not to due to a sentimental idea of Moroccanness that Wafabank had opted to become a patron to the arts; the very nature and success of its institution as an international bank required that it participate in the global trend.

The first Wafabank publication, *La peinture marocaine au rendez-vous de l'Histoire* (Moroccan painting in a meeting with history), a beautiful glossy-pictured catalogue, emphasized the bank's commitment to the living arts in Morocco. While the title claimed that Moroccan painting had a date with history, the underlying message was that *through art* the bank would establish itself in a history of modern capitalism. Modern art was a means by which the bank could distinguish itself and pledge its allegiance to a global financial community. The book was not for sale but rather was distributed by the bank to both its Moroccan and its foreign investors as a public relations project to show that, like other international banks, it understood the importance of culture.[24]

In the preface to the book, the man then vice president of Wafabank, Abdelhak Bennani, made clear that the opening of the Wafabank gallery was part and parcel of Morocco's progress into the modern world, but he also situated the opening in a larger global context:

Intimately persuaded that this strong entry of corporations into the field of culture is one of the societal phenomena that will bring the most hope for our own society, we have created the Wafabank foundation and have installed in the heart of our corporate headquarters a space of *grand standing* for Art with the ambition of becoming a crossroads of creation and diffusion at the disposal of the City. This only distances us in appearance from our basic activity, the creation of wealth, the production of goods and services; the economic and cultural sectors are and have been so profoundly linked over all time, mutually feeding each other. Thus our steps follow this rhythm: one step in the direction of the market and another in the direction of the City, with one sole objective, to respond to needs and force forward progress.[25]

Like the state and the cultural elite, the bank invested in cultural education and its utility in the drive to progress precisely because it was just as concerned as they were to be invested with the concept of Western modernity. Following Benaïssa's comments, which had linked culture and socioeconomic development under the aegis of a plan for progress, Bennani's remarks emphasized that the gallery "only distances us in appearance" from the creation of wealth. For Bennani and the bank, culture and economics were inextricably linked in the modernization of Morocco. As discussed earlier, this understanding arose not only from modernization discourses but also from the very model and duties of a bank that had been defined in the West. Art in the Moroccan bank thus had a double significance: it linked cultural and socioeconomic modernization efforts in Morocco through the agency of the bank, and it lent prestige to the bank in its public relations with the West.

In providing an essay on the history of Moroccan art for the Wafabank publication, the Moroccan writer and critic Edmond Amran El Maleh was less hasty in his praise of the Wafabank initiative, intimating that perhaps Moroccan artists had not yet received the institution they so desired:

It is appropriate to congratulate without further ado the initiative taken by Wafabank in opening a gallery in the very heart of its corporate headquarters. I was tempted to say, in a humorous vein, that Moroccan painters finally have their bank, something infinitely enviable, but that in this unexpected "hold-up," [English in the original] they find themselves taken as happy "hostages." This is a way of saying that patronage is an initiative that one must hope will develop and diversify itself in the way that the examples of Europe and the United States have given us example.[26]

The inauguration of corporate patronage implied competition for funding, and El Maleh's comments betray an anxiety that the valorization of art would leave the hands of a small artistic group and cultural elite, that aesthetic judgment would be relocated to the banks. The writer feared that artists would have to change their work (its content, its form, and its size) to fit into a corporate world. The autonomy of the artistic field would be compromised by something other—and perhaps more powerful—than the state. El Maleh described the bank's involvement in the fine arts as unexpected and sudden. The idea of holding artists as happy hostages further intimated that this development was out of the artist's control even though El Maleh wrote that his analogy was just "a way of saying that patronage is an initiative that one must hope will develop." This last comment, expressing a hope that patronage in Morocco would develop and diversify in manners similar to what was happening in Europe and the United States in the 1980s, expressed another fear that corporate patronage in Morocco, like the museum and its symbolic grammars of modernity, would be devalued into a gesture to the West, that the bank, not unlike the state, would use Moroccan art for its own political and economic ends.

A year later, however, on the publication of images of the first juried competition by Wafabank, El Maleh's tone had changed from caution to celebration and encouragement:

> It is appropriate to congratulate, in all objectivity, the recent initiatives taken by the Wafabank foundation in the framework of its cultural politics inaugurated by the creation of the Wafabank Space. A sign of new times, the bank is no longer a safety vault, a cash counter, a complex financial machine that is only interested in money. From now on, it will play a non-negligible role in social and cultural development all the while exercising its other functions. The thing is thus understood: it is a practice that is more and more current in the USA and Europe, notably in France these last years. Large corporations and banks multiply their initiatives in favor of the arts and literature in diverse domains and forms: exhibitions, prizes, fellowships. Our country could not remain behind in this movement.[27]

According to El Maleh, Wafabank was living up to its promises to artists, and the first competition had been a great success. The bank had effectively taken over the organization of the contemporary art field, producing exhibits, competitions, and publications that on certain levels of importance overshadowed artist-organized biennial exhibitions and publications. The bank was able to convene for its yearly competitions juries that came from an international cultural elite. In 1989 the distinguished jury consisted of the artistic director of Institut du Monde Arabe in Paris, the painter Farid Belkahia, the writer Mohammed Berrada, and the critic El Maleh. Lahbib M'Seffer, one of Wafabank's chief financial officers and the director of the art program (and also, in a testimony to the rise of artists to positions of political and economic power in contemporary Morocco, a successful landscape painter), explained that the bank always chooses at least one jury member from foreign or Western institutions in order to allow judgment of art to proceed according to global standards in contemporary art.[28]

The discursive tension between the support of the Moroccan arts for patriotic and local reasons and the promotion of the bank's own image in global public relations can be read in the way the bank navigates between its images of Moroccan and international identities through a rhetoric of citizenship and populism. When I interviewed Lahbib M'Seffer in May 2000, he told me that in the 1980s Wafabank had redefined its identity and started to consider itself a citizen with certain duties to its country: "We considered that at a certain moment it would be necessary for banks to play the roles of citizens. We even wrote this into our charter because we see ourselves as both an economic force of the country and a citizen. It is absolutely necessary that we play our role on a national level, especially as the state can't do everything."[29] As a citizen, M'Seffer argued, the bank had a duty to support the arts and guarantee access to them to its fellow citizens.

Although the rhetoric of citizenship is already well established in corporate legal language in the United States, the use of the word "citizen" by the bank director is especially interesting and significant, for the movement from monarchical subject to national citizen is still under debate in Moroccan society. In her article "Moroccans—Citizens or Subjects? A People at the Crossroads," Ann Elizabeth Mayer argues that in the early 1990s the monarchy and its critics had a "sharply diverging vision of the future of the Moroccan polity, differing greatly in their views as to the optimal balance between the monarch's prerogatives and the rights of his subjects, who increasingly seem to think of themselves as citizens of Morocco rather than as King Hassan's subjects."[30]

It might be argued that in contemporary Morocco this turn in identification from subject to citizen has further intensified with the reformist tendencies of the new King Mohammed VI, who appears to be heading the country in the direction of a true constitutional monarchy. The former prime minister of Morocco, Abderrahman Youssoufi, described his first meeting with Mohammed VI: "At our first working meeting session, the king said, 'You must know I'm a democrat.' That's reassuring."[31] In his first speech from the throne, Mohammed VI was even clearer when he said, "We are devoted to the constitutional monarchy, a multi-party system, economic liberalism, regionalization and decentralization, the construction of a state of law, the safeguard of human rights and individual and collective freedoms and the preservation of security and stability for all."[32] He listed economic liberalism as but one of the commitments of the state, but paradoxically it is the one that has most threatened nationalist ideas of citizenship and inclusion. Shana Cohen writes:

During the nation-building period, nationalism and modern institutions inherently promoted internal social cohesion and equalization, if only in name, by citizens. The developing power of the nation-state as an idea and as a political economic system engendered the rise of a modern middle class that saw itself in terms of its function within the nation, the domestic economy, and the scope of state authority. Today, the social power of public institutions, the state and nationalism have shifted to the firm, globalization, and global market capitalism, which together impose an atomistic, nonlocated vision of social order.[33]

Ironically, development policies intended to develop democratic political models in Morocco force the Moroccan state to adopt market liberalization policies that shrink the power of the state and reduce the sense of a unified social order that seeks the participation of equal citizens. The result is grim for a growing disenfranchised population of unemployed youth and marginalized Moroccans: "Their existential anxiety is due not to the loss of legal rights derived from loss of territory and citizenship but to the loss of philosophical purpose and meaning derived from the declining relevance of both territory and citizenship."[34]

Although Cohen and Mayer discuss the legal, political, and economic significance of the terms *citizen* and *subject*, I would like to take a moment to consider the cultural implications of the two terms. Moving from a model of subjectivity in which the state and the king control and dictate culture, the concept of citizenship in the arts implies *participation in* and equal *access to* culture. Citizens, including those in governing positions, bound by a patriotic duty, would participate in the preservation of national patrimony for a public at large. This is what M'Seffer implied in his comments: that the Wafabank gallery was ideally a modern democratic institution, open to all Moroccan citizens. Unlike the medina and state-run museums that cater to tourists more than to a local public, the Wafabank Space, a private-sector space, would, ironically, be the first truly democratic and modern cultural institution in Morocco.

Echoing many before him, M'Seffer stated, "In Morocco, there are no museums."[35] In other words, there are no real public institutions that would, as Carol Duncan claims in "Art Museums and the Ritual of Citizenship," become a link between the state and its citizenry, participating in a ritual affirmation of the social contract between the two.[36] Until the state opens a national art museum that can perform such an affirmation and preserve national patrimony for all Moroccans, Wafabank sees itself as the protector of the contemporary arts. Is this a direct challenge to the king as "protector of arts and culture" by an institution that sees itself not as a subject but as a citizen? On a certain theoretical level, the institution's rhetoric reflects a greater allegiance to international standards of modernity than to the political reality of the country. However, on a practical level, M'Seffer was quick to dispel any threat to the state by saying that as soon as a national museum is opened in Morocco, Wafabank will donate its entire collection of artwork to the state. When I asked if this would happen in the year 2002, in accordance with Ahmed Jarid's architectural plans and projections for a National Museum of Art, M'Seffer was highly doubtful. He knew that the bank's collection is far from being given away.

The adoption of the term "citizen" shows Wafabank's participation in another world order, that of international capitalism and the liberal democracy that feeds it. The bank exists in two worlds, that of the Kingdom of Morocco and that of a global capitalist market economy, and it is in the position to be both subject and citizen. This negotiation can clearly be seen through the bank's exhibition space itself. The gallery is located in the lobby of the Wafabank corporate headquarters in the downtown area of Casablanca. This is the Casablanca of international finance, with wide avenues and high-rise buildings, and the Wafabank building fits into this image with about thirty stories of reflective glass.[37] On entering the building, to the right of the lobby the visitor finds bank tellers and consultant stations; the center of the lobby houses elevator banks and a security desk; to the left of the elevators is the gallery. There is no door to the gallery, but the space is monitored by one of the security guards at the entrance, who allowed me to look at the paintings. So that I might take photographs, Lahbib M'Seffer called down to the security guard to grant me permission; for security reasons, I was not allowed to take photographs of anything but the gallery. This close monitoring and control of space reveals to what extent the bank sees itself as the promoter of security on all levels of interaction with its clients. Their money, their personal safety, and even "their" artwork is secured. However, this concern for security also builds walls between art and its audience, accentuating the fact that the art is not so much for a general public as for a specific clientele.

The physical space of the gallery reflects the modernity of the building as a whole: the floors are marble and the paintings well lit. The paintings that are on display are representative of the short history of Moroccan painting and include works by artists such as Melehi, Chaïbia, and Tallal. The majority of canvases on display are not labeled, pointing perhaps less to the importance of individual works than to their recognized modernity. Primarily abstract, these paintings speak a language of modern art that may be difficult to understand but that is easy to recognize. The first painting that faces the viewer on entry to the space is a large-scale canvas by Tallal, an artist who in the 1960s refused any identity politics for his art and considered himself an international artist above all else. In 1967 he exclaimed: "I am a Moroccan—thus I have no need to paint a mosque or a fantasia to prove it. It is not a nationality or an origin that tells me what to paint. And anyway, I think that Delacroix has already painted everything about Morocco and that there is nothing else to add."[38] His large-scale pictorial representation of two clownlike figures in blue, red, and white, one with exposed breasts, seems a peculiar choice for the first painting to greet the visitor. There are no visual references to Arab, Amazigh, or Islamic culture that would identify it as distinctly Moroccan. However, it is this very aspect of the painting that most closely reflects the desired image of the bank: the bank, like the painting, can accept and refuse definition. Both painting and bank can dissimulate their identities and deterritorialize their images from their Moroccan origins into the explicit cosmopolitanism of an international institution.

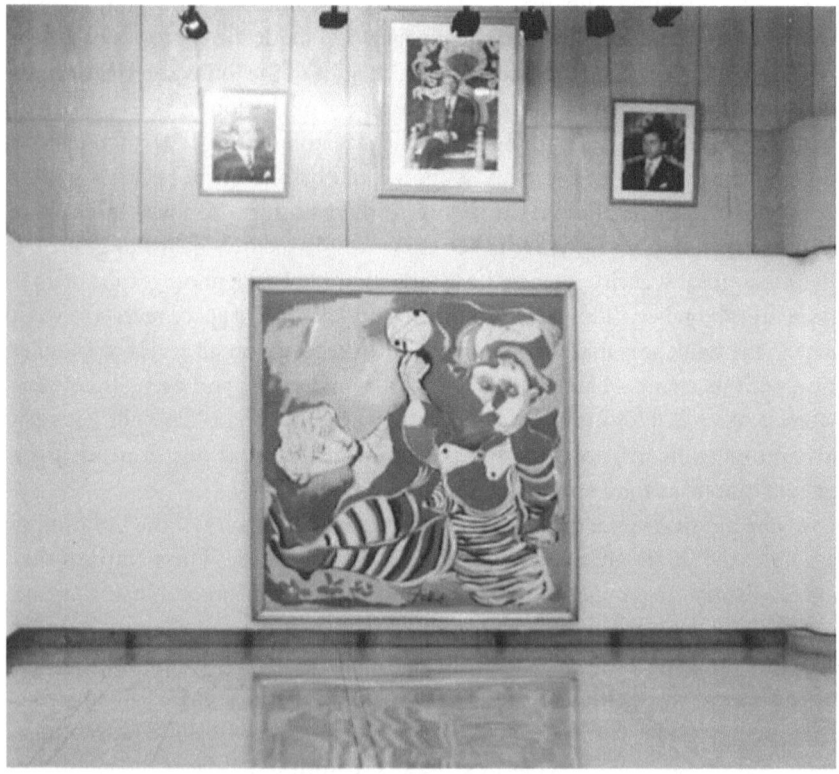

Interior of the Wafabank Gallery, with Tallal painting and portraits of Hassan II (center, above painting) and his sons. Photograph by the author, 2000.

Yet what keeps both the bank and the painting with one foot solidly on Moroccan soil is the photographic portrait of the king that hangs directly over Tallal's canvas. The juxtaposition of a photographic portrait of the late King Hassan II and photographs of his two sons directly over the painting could be read as provocative and potentially subversive; is the king being directly compared to Tallal's clowns?[39] However, rather than associate the figures in the images through analogy, I read the association between the painting and the photographs through the symbolism of the space in which they have been placed.

The most important dynamic in the space is the marked separation between the white walls of the gallery and the darker wooden panels on which hang the portraits of the king and his sons. The use of white cubes to display modern art has been analyzed by Pam Meecham and Julie Sheldon as an attempt to create a pure space free of ideology in which paintings can be displayed on their own merit and with their own messages:

> The presentation of modern art in puritanically regulated white-walled rooms, with strategically placed spotlights and humidity monitors is a familiar part of any visit to the modern art gallery—across the globe. . . . The modern art gallery, without the same obligations to present identity-forming national collections or to serve the redemptive functions of many nineteenth-century philanthropic collections, seemed . . . to provide an ideology-free space.[40]

However, as Meecham and Sheldon continue to argue, although these gallery spaces were not at their inception overtly implicated in discourses of imperialism, social engineering, and anthropology, because their very basis is their rejection of dominant discourses, they have never been free of ideology. The whiteness of the Wafabank Space attests to the desire to create an ideology-free space in line with international conventions for the display of modern art, to construct an autonomous sphere for art, but by its very nature, the space is not free of ideology. The whiteness attests to a desired modernity.[41]

The king is placed outside of this space, but in close proximity to it. In most public spaces in Morocco, the presence of a photographic image of the king serves as a stamp of approval on everything in its vicinity, for the image of the king, not unlike his actual physical presence, lends a certain *baraka* or blessing to everything around it. As Susan Ossman writes in *Picturing Casablanca: Portraits of Power in a Modern City:*

> The quality of *baraka* [grace] had always been attributed to saints, wisemen and sultans. . . . With the advent of the camera, *baraka* was represented with increased frequency through photographs and film. Today photographs of the King are mandatory in public places. In homes too, people often display pictures of authority figures: the King, fathers, sons.[42]

Rahma Bourqia provides an important caveat to this definition, stating, "Although *baraka* is diffused in words, things and places, it is transmitted through the process of polar attraction whereby all forms of it converge around the sacred object."[43] In this modern art gallery, it is not the art but rather the photograph of royalty that is the "sacred object." The elevation of the king's image above all other artwork, above the claims of an ideology-free space, shows how the king, in an elevated benevolence, has given the art, the gallery, and Wafabank his blessing and the gift of state legitimacy. The presence of the king-as-state outside the white cube grants art its autonomous sphere "detached" from politics and religion.

Carol Duncan argues that in a Western state-run art museum, the artwork itself serves as the medium through which the relationship between state and citizen is articulated and affirmed.[44] Through art, its display, and its preservation, the museum performs its duty to the citizen to safeguard national treasures. In the Wafabank case, it is not the art that fills this function; rather it is the image of the king that serves as the medium through which the relationship between the public, the private institution, and the state is articulated. Through the photograph of the king, itself a modern technology of representation, the contractual relationship between all three is affirmed. The paintings in the gallery reflect a certain modernity, a contemporaneity, but it should not be forgotten that their power as symbols of such rests in part, if not wholly, with the state's benevolence and desire to modernize.

The placement of the king's image in the gallery, and not just in the banking area of the building, which would fulfill the mandatory aspect of displaying the monarchy in a business setting, performs an allegiance to the king as the "protector of the arts" and Morocco's leader on the road to modernity. The king is not just an antiquated figure from a feudal past; he has a place in the modern future of Morocco. Thus, although Wafabank sees itself as a citizen in its commitment to the arts as an autonomous institution, it does not stray too far from its position as the king's subject.

If this site enacts a ritual of imagined citizenship and subjectivity, we should return to the question of the gallery's public. The bank considers the space of the gallery public even though it is in a high-security institution. How does this translate into reality? Who is the gallery's public? Lahbib M'Seffer is very proud of the bank's community outreach programs, and in his description of these actions his rhetoric becomes almost populist in nature.[45] First of all, when the bank is invited to sponsor an exhibit abroad, as it has done in both France and Spain, it insists that its participation is contingent on the exhibit's traveling to Morocco. Furthermore, the bank will not publish any exhibit materials unless the exhibit has come to its space. This policy has led to several free exhibits of high quality in the Wafabank Space, such as an exhibit of Picasso's work in 1993. I would argue that these types of exhibits have less to do with bringing elite European art to the Moroccan masses than with the bank administrators' savvy knowledge of the importance of corporate sponsorship for blockbuster museum exhibits—exhibits that in the United States serve as vehicles of aesthetic pleasure and consumption for middle-class audiences. On a much smaller scale than that of such exhibits in the United States, Wafabank mini–blockbuster exhibits are intended to attract the same type of bourgeois audience despite rhetoric to the contrary. According to M'Seffer, these exhibits, as well as the results of the annual painting competition, have openings that attract seven to eight hundred people. When asked about the makeup of the crowd, M'Seffer described the public as journalists, cultural figures, government officials, and lovers of art. This depiction does not sound too different from Protectorate museum audiences or accounts of attendees of bourgeois gallery openings in the 1960s press.[46] How does Wafabank really go beyond the cultural elite and the bourgeoisie in its creation of a public? M'Seffer claims that those who come into the bank to perform financial transactions all benefit from the gallery: "When a transaction lasts twenty minutes, instead of waiting, clients wander into the gallery and sometimes even become impassioned for what they see."[47] But who is this client with twenty-minute transactions? Surely not the average Moroccan, who lives near or below the international poverty line.

The exclusion of the average Moroccan in light of the bank's professed commitment to Morocco and its culture as a *citizen* among citizens is problematic. Does this mean that only those with "money in the bank" can become citizens entitled to their country's artistic patrimony? Does it mean that those who are not permitted to enter the space of the bank will remain forever subjects? In order to attest to its participation in the values of modernity, the bank has espoused a rhetoric of democratizing and developing modern art for Moroccan citizens. However, in order for its rhetoric to have meaning, the bank has essentially delimited the meaning of *citizen* to *member of the bank*. Thus, like any other modern institution, it is able to ensure that all "citizens" have free access to the latest artistic creations in the country.

The politics of exclusion present in the corporate museum of the 1980s reflected the market liberalization and widespread inequalities in Moroccan society of the time. James Ferguson writes that neoliberal order has brought

a different understanding of modernity in which, no longer promised as a telos, it has come to be simply a status—a standard of living to which some have rights by birth and from which others are simply, but unequivocally, excluded. As understandings of the modern have shifted in this way, the vast majority of Africans denied the status of modernity increasingly come to be seen, and may even see themselves, not as "less-developed" but simply as less.[48]

For Wafabank, limiting its definition of *citizens* to those elite and cosmopolitan Moroccans who had already acquired a level of wealth on the same scale as elites in Europe and the United States enabled it to ignore the majority of Moroccans, who were excluded from this privileged status; they were less developed and hence purely "less."

The "lesser" Moroccans excluded from the citizenship of the bank struggled with basic material needs. In 1981 and 1984, just years before the opening of the art space, downtown Casablanca witnessed "bread riots" brought on by a brutal drought and severe International Monetary Fund policies that had shaken the country. As Susan Slyomovics describes the 1981 Casablanca riots: "Although protestors demonstrated to maintain subsidies on staple goods . . . demands to the government encompassed the right to education, affordable housing, and employment opportunities."[49] In the gallery, freedom of expression was conveniently protected for a global citizenry, while freedom of speech was curtailed outside its walls. Slyomovics tells us:

> To describe those post-independence years [during the reign of Hassan II from 1961–1999], Moroccans assign the names *zaman al-raṣāṣ* and *al-sanawāt al-sawdā* in Arabic, in Moroccan Arabic *liyyām l'kḥla* (in French, *les années de plomb* and *les années noires*): "the years of lead," phrases evoking an era of grayness and lead bullets, and "the black years," the times of fear and repression, and *les années sombres*, the gloomy years of forcible disappearances, farcical mass political trials, and long prison sentences for large numbers of people who from a variety of political positions voiced opposition to the regime and became prisoners of conscience.[50]

Although the social, economic, and political reality for the large majority of Moroccans was grim, for the bank's fellow citizens, a defined public of Moroccan bourgeois and international investors, images of modernity as presented in art increased the confidence they felt in the economic future of *their* modern Morocco and in the economic prospects of Wafabank.

The model of corporate patronage in the bank converses with trends in the United States and Europe, and the presence of modern, Western-style artwork serves to convince and placate the bank's Moroccan public that their financial institution is similar to those in the West. As Moroccan historian Abdallah Laroui wrote in *The Crisis of the Arab Intellectual* in 1971, "Today's Arab society is heterogeneous: different epochs, temporalities, and humanities are placed side by side therein."[51] For Laroui, the crisis of the Moroccan intellectual lay in the fact that the narrative of modernity in which modernizers had invested, for better or worse, could not support the idea of heterologies and heterogeneous time. For Wafabank, this appears not to be a concern. Rather than being haunted by questions of hegemony, it accepts that Moroccan history, like global history, is moving in different directions and at different speeds. While rhetorically it pledges an allegiance to the development of Morocco through culture, in practice it services a small group of people who are moving in the same circles. To this restricted "modern" public, the bank can affirm the values of modernity.

In articulating the reasons for opening a gallery in its corporate headquarters, Wafabank invoked a discourse not only about the place of contemporary painting in Morocco but also about the cultural identity of a kingdom claiming to be a democratic nation. Negotiating between its image as an international citizen and that of a loyal subject, Wafabank has developed strategies through which it is possible to imagine and stage both by practicing a politics of exclusion. In between these identities, we may find Moroccan artists and their art. In Edmond Amran El Maleh's words, they are still "happy hostages," though it is uncertain for how long.[52]

Beyond Wafabank: Corporate Art Institutions and Museums of the Corporation

At the beginning of the twenty-first century, corporate "market museums" appear just as anxious to narrate shared visions of the future with international clients while rhetorically proving their commitment to the Moroccan state, and they build on the Wafabank example. This trend can be read in the ways in which the largest Moroccan financial conglomerate, ONA, and multinational conglomerate Maroc Télécom have created museums that focus on the link between transnational and virtual technologies and local civic responsibilities in order to narrate their positions between global citizenry and local subjectivities.

ONA is a holding company that is active in banking, insurance, mining, information technology, and the fishing and food industries. It boasts the Moroccan royal family among its shareholders and presents itself as an enlightened corporation that, like Wafabank, takes its local identity seriously. (In fact, the ties between Wafabank and ONA are more than theoretical: in 2004 ONA increased its shareholdings in Wafabank and initiated a merger between Wafabank and Banque Commerciale du Maroc, creating the Attijariwafa Bank.) Since 2005, "citizenship" has been one of the main rubrics at the company's Web site, where investors can see what concrete civic actions have been taken by the firm.[53] When ONA started thinking about art in 1996, it created a space that reflected the company's plural and hybrid identities and linked its global and local interests.

In 1999 ONA opened the first Villa des Arts in Casablanca under the direction of Sylvia Belhassan, a key promoter of contemporary arts in Casablanca and Rabat. Belhassan, a Swiss national married to a Moroccan, seemed to incarnate and animate the hybrid spirit of the space. The museum, housed in an art deco villa built by a Casablanca businessman in 1934, soon developed into the premier location for contemporary art in Casablanca, with well-received exhibits from both Morocco and abroad that not only focused on cutting-edge visual art and installations but also rethought the relationships among contemporary visual art, design, and traditions of artisanal production. The Villa des Arts was located not in corporate headquarters but rather on the edge of a park, making the space itself much more accessible to the general public. Art was no longer so obviously restricted to a citizen-customer clientele such as that at Wafabank, CDG, or other financial institutions; however, it would be a mistake to think the space was not conducting the same work of dual allegiance as were those institutions.

The art space performed a hybrid mixture of the local and the global, and this occurred not only in the galleries and exhibits but also on the level of institutional cooperation with other museums. The first exhibition organized by the museum was titled The Disoriented Object in Morocco, and Belhassan succeeded in borrowing objects from the Musée des Arts Décoratifs in Paris. Likewise, for an exhibit on contemporary textile arts, the Villa des Arts worked with the Reina Sofia Museum in Madrid. Finally, someone was reversing the direction that Moroccan arts had traveled over the past century. Moroccans would no longer have to travel to Europe to see the art achievements of Moroccan culture. Although the ONA Foundation was responsible for most of the funding of such exhibits, Belhassan also managed to win financial support from corporations and companies outside Morocco. The exhibit Casablanca Architecture 1900 to 1960 was co-funded by the French energy company EDF. Though it focused on Moroccan arts, Belhassan invited international artists to display their work in order to start transnational conversations and collaborations. As Beat Stauffer notes, "Nothing of the kind had existed in Morocco hitherto, and it seemed self-evident that such a place would also take an interest in developments beyond the country's borders."[54]

However, in 2004 the tension in negotiating between international and national identities finally became visible when Belhassan resigned from the Villa des Arts amid pressures to create more conservative Moroccan-centered exhibits in the corporate space. As she confirmed to me in a 2007 interview, while the gallery worked to produce interesting exhibits of local artists, "ONA's powers-that-be said that the energetic arts administrator was too 'elitist,' that the exhibitions were too expensive and—above all—that too few Moroccan artists were having their work shown. Following the terrorist attacks in Casablanca, demands were also made that more be done for young people in the *banlieues*."[55] The corporation thought the space had become too international, too elitist for its national image. And when the international threatened the local identity of the corporation, it saw fit to get rid of the international director.

Belhassan told me that her work to bring talented progressive Moroccan artists to the public had been misrepresented as elitist.[56] She stressed that her resignation had been due to a lack of curatorial freedom following extended disputes with corporation executives who wanted tighter control over exhibits. Since her departure, the Villa des Arts in Casablanca has undergone a period of structural instability. Although it is still open and hosts exhibits, it has disappeared completely from ONA's press packets. Rather than rethink the institution and its commitments on a fundamental level, the corporation has created a second version of the Villa des Arts in Rabat. Although this new Villa des Arts stresses its commitment to Moroccan art and the city of Rabat, it is much more conservative in its exhibits, more luxurious in its physical space, and perhaps not surprisingly less accessible to the Moroccan public than its counterpart in Casablanca.

In December 2006, ONA opened the Rabat Villa des Arts. In its press releases the corporation defined contemporary arts (visual, theater, musical, and literary) as part of the core identity of the holding company and recommitted itself to its global identity but with a twist. The inaugural exhibit presented the works of Moroccan painters living in diaspora, and the symbolism of recognizing Moroccan culture beyond the borders of the state fits well with the type of global identity that works well *in* the nation-state. The weekly independent newspaper *Le journal hebdomadaire* declared the new arts complex "more than a space, a concept."[57] And ultimately, close examination of the complex beyond its nationalistic gestures reveals that the Villa des Arts in Rabat is more about appropriate image than about socially engaged art, more about exclusivity than about public access, and more about distinction and wealth than about the civic development it advertises.

The space has all the qualities of a professionally run affluent contemporary art museum: two galleries, a virtual gallery, an outdoor café, workshop spaces for outreach art programs, a library, glossy maps, marble restrooms, an outdoor auditorium, and even visitor feedback forms handed out by the guard at the visitor entrance when one exits the space.[58] These forms ask standard marketing feedback questions divided into four sections: (1) Analysis of the Public: questions on the visitor's nationality, sex, profession, age, and city of residence; (2) Analysis of the Visit: questions such as "Was this a first visit?" "If not how many times have you visited the Villa des Arts?" and "How did you find out about the activities of the Villa des Arts (program, posters, press, Web site, television)"; (3) Analysis of Activity: questions such as "Did you come to take a walk on the grounds, see the current exhibition, visit the virtual museum, the multimedia library, attend a talk/debate, participate in a children's workshop, see a performance, have a cup of coffee?" and "Would you like to be informed of activities?" "By mail or e-mail?"; (4) Analysis of Services Provided: questions such as "Were you greeted at the entry?" "Were you given directions?" "Were you given a program of activities?" "Were you given a map?" "Did you do an individual tour?" "If so, would you have liked to take a guided tour?" "Did you take a guided tour?" and "Were you satisfied with the tour?" These questions are followed by a small space for comments. The feedback form speaks the language of customer appreciation that today's corporations use so well, and yet its very questions reveal who the intended public is meant to be. The fact that the very first question asks the visitor about

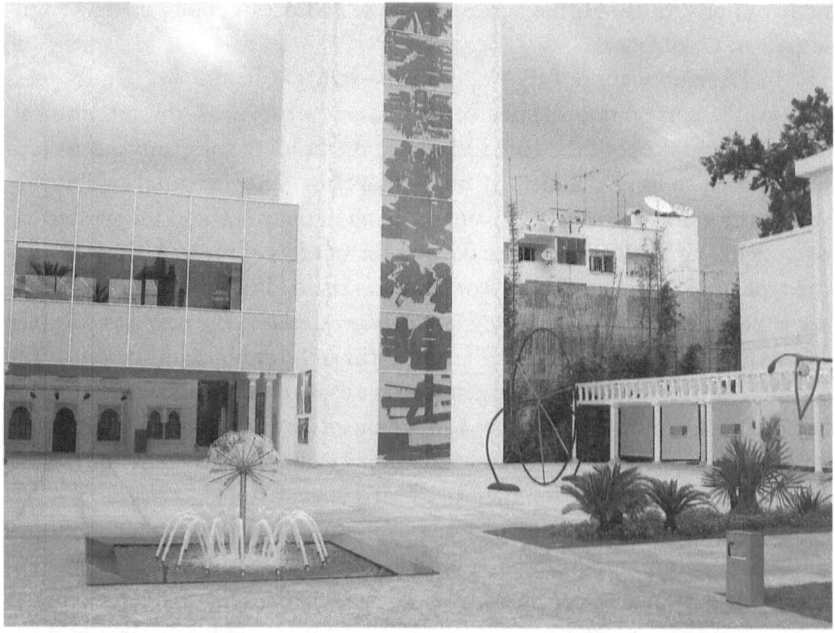

Villa des Arts, Rabat. Photograph by the author, 2007.

his or her nationality shows that while rhetorically committed to the national, the space is primarily concerned with international tourists or, more accurately, the foreign clients or dignitaries who inhabit and work in the surrounding neighborhood.

To a larger extent than Wafabank with the Wafabank Space, the holding company has managed to create a mini–national museum to prove to the international finance community that it is committed to art in an appropriate and well-endowed fashion. Through the art museum ONA has created a highly polished national space in which to entertain foreign dignitaries—in short, an embassy of art that is distinct from the city around it. This dynamic was made clear on my first visit to the space, when it was closed for a high-security private function. On another visit I introduced myself to the only other visitors present: the wife of an official in the Italian Embassy and her family visiting from Italy. In the summer of 2007, the two galleries of the Villa des Arts—the Villa du Parc and the Galerie sur Cour—hosted an exhibition of Canadian artist Dominic Besner's paintings, which were shown with the contemporary creations of Moroccan caftan designers Mohamed Lakhdar, Albert Oiknine, and Karim Tassi. While I was visiting the exhibit, a museum administrator gave a guided tour to a Canadian diplomatic delegation, stressing not only the correspondences between Besner's work and the caftan creations but also the happy cohabitation of Moroccan traditional art with international tendencies by noting the juxtaposition of the canvas paintings with the painted ceiling and tiled fireplace of the 1929 art deco villa. Likewise an outdoor photography exhibit stressed the unity of vision between Morocco and other nations. The foreword to the exhibit, titled Four Continents, Three Photographers, One Vision, claimed that the two Moroccan and one American photographers "encourage us—through these images—to explore on our own the thoughts and feelings that bind us together as one unique vision." This unique vision is never defined but claims a shared humanity in a new global order.

Although the museum broadcasts its wealth and shared values with foreign dignitaries and investors through art, on my last visit to the space, a humorous nonofficial narrative took place in the Galerie sur Cour that spoke of local exclusion. One particularly chatty security guard gave me his own interpretative tour of the Canadian's paintings focusing on the eye motif on the various canvases and ultimately creating a narrative that spoke of male desire, isolation, and the possibility of love. Although this reading of Besner's work was certainly possible, it did not take a psychoanalyst to see that the young man was talking about himself. I asked him if he liked working at the villa, and he said it was a definite change from his previous security post at the ONA-owned upscale supermarket Marjane (51 percent ONA, 49 percent Auchan), from which he had just been transferred. After a short career protecting one type of commodity, he was now charged with another. In both the supermarket and the gallery, he experienced a certain type of isolation, distanced by his modest salary not only from the bourgeois goods he was protecting but also from the type of people who might visit.

Despite rhetoric to the contrary, the Villa des Arts is a space of isolation that is coded through distinction. This fact can be read through the physical interaction of the museum with the surrounding neighborhood. First of all, ambient music is piped in all around the grounds of the villa, sonically transforming the space into a distinct place within the city grid, but although strains of this soft music occasionally waft out onto the sidewalk, the sidewalk is not transformed into a space of reflection and art for passersby. Although the villa's decorative metalwork on the sidewalks around the gallery and the gilded street signs seek to show how the ONA gallery is invested in beautifying the city around it—renovating "the street" so to speak—this renovation stops past the building's footprint and walls, when the level, clean sidewalk becomes broken again with potholes and littered with food wrappers. Through the renovated streetscape it has created, the Villa des Arts displays its role as a responsible resident of the city on a purely superficial level. In fact, we could even argue that through its interventions in public space, the institution actively colonizes the immediate space around it in order to build a larger perimeter of exclusivity around the villa. Although the intended goal may be to beautify public space with the exteriorization of art onto the street, the practice actually does the opposite: it reveals the poverty of the city's public utilities and resources in contrast to the villa's (unattainable) wealth.

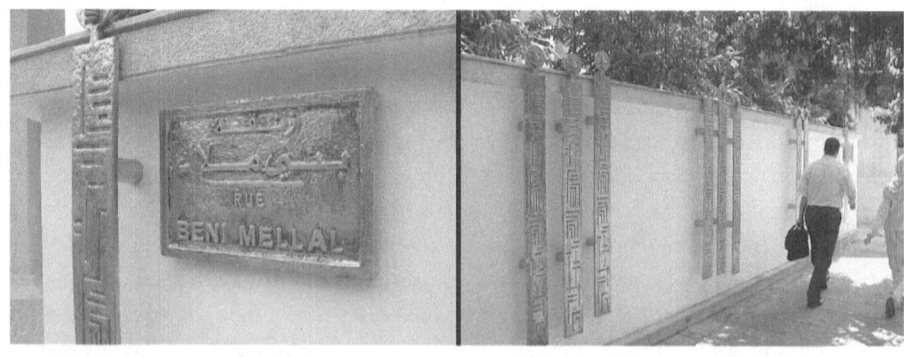

Exterior walls of the Villa des Arts compound, Rabat. Photograph by the author, 2007.

This practice of claiming inclusivity while performing distinction is visible in another space within the Villa des Arts: the virtual gallery. Built in a type of underground bunker, the virtual gallery boasts interactive digital floor projections, eight flat-screen monitors that change images every few minutes in order to exhibit twelve hundred artworks that ONA either owns or has displayed in its collections, and two digital documentation booths (one on traditional arts, the other on the modern and contemporary) where, without touching any screen but by simply pointing to a projected menu, one can navigate various regions, histories, and object biographies. The virtual gallery is open to the "public" only when there is a large enough group (usually about six people), and even then public access is limited due to the strictly guided character of the visit. In order to see the art and the archives of digital documentation, one is constantly monitored while hearing a closely followed script that stresses the forward-thinking nature of the space, ONA's commitment to documenting patrimony, and its cutting-edge technology. Both times that I visited this space, the guides were extremely friendly and appropriately conversant in the technology of the space but knew next to nothing about the art itself. Although visitors were encouraged to interact with the technology— stepping on the interactive digital floor projections or choosing information to access in the documentation booths—this interaction was monitored and observed. The digital documentation booths were difficult to operate, and they did not allow more than one person to access them at a time. Needless to say, no one was talking about or even looking at the art. Physical artwork had been replaced by digital slides and the accessibility of the art diminished even further.

The museum uses technology as its narrative tool in order to articulate a cutting-edge image of the corporation. In so doing, the ONA Villa des Arts takes literally Tony Bennett's definition of museums as "technologies of progress."[59] The museum is not a metaphorical technology of progress; it is all about technology. And although this technology purports to emerge from the digital revolution that has swept the world, it also reveals the unequal reach of the revolution and access to its benefits. The Villa des Arts claims to support the arts in a civic fashion, but ultimately the arts function to underline its own image of power and wealth.

The Maroc Télécom Museum that opened in Rabat in 2001 also appears anxious to display identity through technology, but to different ends. Although marketing campaigns for the company have focused on concepts of transnational communications such as crossing borders and becoming nomadic, the museum presents Maroc Télécom as solidly national.[60] Its majority stockholder is the multinational corporation Vivendi; however, 49 percent of the company is owned by the Moroccan state. The museum's mission statement underlines the corporation's national image by stating that the museum's purpose is to "protect our national patrimony in telecommunications and thus confirm the engagement of our company to work in the national cultural domain in order to diversify and enrich the field."[61] The museum claims that it is the first and only museum of telecommunications in Morocco (strategically ignoring the National Postal Museum, which also includes telecommunications in its collection), and it insists that through the history of telecommunications in Morocco visitors will appreciate and discover important moments in a larger Moroccan history.

Both the physical museum and its Web version offer hands-on exhibits that interact with technology, and the educational outreach that it has done is seemingly unequalled in the Moroccan museum world. The museum creates temporary exhibitions in its Maroc Télécom stores, and it has created a virtual replica of itself at the museum's Web site and on CD-ROMs that it distributes to schools and various libraries around Morocco. In December of 2003, it even organized a "Muséo-Bus" that took the museum "team" to the Ouhoud School grounds in Rabat to give presentations on the collection and demonstrate the virtual museum on CD. If Moroccans cannot visit the museum, the museum will go to them. Unlike Wafabank, which restricted its "citizens" to members of the bank, or ONA, which seems intent on using combinations of national and international artwork to court international clients and foreign dignitaries while proclaiming its work to beautify civic space, Maroc Télécom reaches out to the largest possible national audience.

What conclusions can we draw from such "marketplace museums," which are eager to efface or disguise their multinational identity in favor of diffusing a narrative of national belonging? And what can we think especially in light of processes of economic liberalization in the country? What the Maroc-Télécom Museum and the ONA Villas des Arts appear to tell us is that although the nation-state seems to be losing power to forces of globalization, in reality the power of the state has far from disappeared. In their work on globalization in Morocco, Shana Cohen and Larabi Jaidi note that although from all appearances NGOs, corporations, and other nonstate organizations appear to be gaining prominence and power in Moroccan society, "the state in Morocco has also used these associations to implement policy and assert its power, directly and indirectly."[62] Economic and political liberalization is not guaranteed and relies on the benevolence of the state; although corporations may have greater freedom to practice in the marketplace, the breadth and space of this freedom is still negotiated with the state. Arjun Appadurai has argued that in today's version of "modernity at large," the nation-state is in "terminal crisis."[63] But as corporate marketplace museums have shown, this has not come to pass in Morocco, where through art and institutions of memory, corporations remain cautious to balance their identities as global citizens and local subjects. Meanwhile, their museums reflect the continued atomization and fracturing of Moroccan society.

Three

A Private Cabinet of Curiosity: The Belghazi Museum and Its Politics of Nostalgia

Where do objects of outrageous memory go? What place is there in national museums and corporate collections for the curious and the historically bizarre? In 1979 art historian E. H. Gombrich bemoaned the scientific didacticism and lack of creativity of the modern museum:

> I have a gloomy vision of a future museum in which the contents of Aladdin's cave will have been removed to the storeroom and all that will be left will be an authentic lamp from the period of the Arabian nights with a large diagram at its side explaining how oil lamps worked, where the wick was inserted, and what was the average burning time. I grant that oil lamps are after all, human artefacts and tell us more about the lives of ordinary people than the precious tinsel of Aladdin's cave. But must I receive this improving instruction while I support myself on my tired feet rather than sitting snugly in a chair and reading about the history of domestic illumination?[1]

What would he have thought of the Belghazi Museum, a Moroccan museum that functions as a cabinet of curiosities and calls itself not an "Aladdin's Cave" but a near relative, an "Ali Baba's cave"? The Belghazi Museum would offer Gombrich not only a chair to sit in but lunch as well. The owner of the museum would be happy to open drawers and cabinets of objects at his behest and tell him stories of both light and tinsel. The Belghazi Museum has not removed the contents of Ali Baba's cave to the storeroom but rather organizes its collection as a storehouse of marvel and wonder. As the journal *Al Maghrib Culture* reported in an article provocatively titled "La mémoire retrouvée"

(Memory regained): "Mr. Belghazi has opened a space to regroup all those 'marvels': some 5000 objects occupy this place bumping into each other, placed into proximity with each other, almost superimposed upon one another. A mixture of genres, styles and centuries."[2]

The history of the modern museum is narrated by scholars as a linear transformation of the institution from monastic collections to Renaissance cabinets of curiosity to nineteenth-century Enlightenment and national museums to twentieth-century corporate-marketed and alternative diverse community museums. Throughout this history we can read the institution of the museum as becoming more and more public as it opened itself to a wider variety of more heterogeneous visitors. So what does it mean to reverse this path and to return today to the intimacy and idiosyncrasy of a cabinet of curiosity? Is it a postmodern self-reflexive play with museum history as has been described in work on the Jurassic Museum and other contemporary art institutions?[3] Or is the return less playful, a neoliberal return to a cultural architecture that, although more open socially than the monastic collections that preceded it, was never truly public? More important, what does a cabinet of curiosity mean in a Third World context? By returning to an arguably premodern cultural architecture, is Belghazi's museum a critique of the failed model of the national museum that seeks to democratize culture as the path to modernity in Morocco? Or is something deeper at stake that has more to do with nostalgia and the uncertainty of the future?

When Abdellah Belghazi founded the Belghazi Museum in 1996, he argued that the national museums were structures foreign to the Moroccan landscape and that his museum was the first private institution for cultural preservation and the encouragement of the Moroccan arts. The organizational logic of the museum separates ground-floor public spaces from upstairs private displays and invites only those willing to pay a hefty sum into the "heart" of its collection. This logic reflects the exclusionary dynamics of class relations present in Moroccan society and accepts their divides. Calling his private collection an Ali Baba's cave, Belghazi narrates a story that reclaims riches from public bureaucracies and restores them to rightful owners and also interiorizes art into a private space of appreciation and wonder. To a certain extent, Belghazi reveals the hypocrisy present in Moroccan national museums that claim to hold art for the people but that do not really allow for its appreciation and care; however, he does not offer a better public model in return. Rather, his path to the preservation and display of patrimony suggests a model that will exclude the majority of the Moroccan population in favor of privileged guests and private patrons, claiming that not all cultural riches should be for everyone to see.

On the level of display, a two-tier model for access to culture sits firmly in place. Engagement with the past through narrative machineries functions differently on the two floors of the museum. While the ground floor engages in modern display dynamics that suggest that the past has been amply mastered into scientific and rational logic, the cabinet of curiosities that dominates the second floor is founded on literary tropes and undisciplined stories. The cabinet feeds on a certain nostalgia for the past, when now national treasures could be held in one's hand and not maintained behind sanitized glass, when stories about objects were told and not typed on labels. This nostalgia appears to return to fictions of a pre-Protectorate, premuseum past in Morocco when individual families collected objects for their pleasure and had control over their histories—when Morocco was not overrun by international forces of colonialism and globalization. This return inside, to the home and the family, points to a fear of a future in which life will not be ensured. Fictions of a premodern Moroccan time nourish a sense of security when the present and future seem so precarious.

The Belghazi Museum is not a historical reproduction of a cabinet of curiosities, but what Belghazi calls the "heart" of his museum definitely takes the form of a cabinet of curiosities and shares characteristics with its Renaissance predecessor for different reasons and with different consequences. The cabinet of curiosities as an institution has been amply studied in its historical context in Germany, France, and Italy, and particularities of cabinets from the sixteenth to the eighteenth century as they were transformed into Enlightenment museums have been carefully analyzed and noted.[4] I will not rehearse that history here, but I do want to highlight three particularly interesting roles of Renaissance cabinets that are relevant in the context of Belghazi's twenty-first-century Moroccan cabinet: the cabinet as a stage of authenticity (the collector as the collection and the singularity of the object), the cabinet as the interiorization of knowledge (visible and invisible objects and the politics of controlling display), and finally the cabinet as a palace of memory (the literary logic of collections based on stories told by the owner or guide). Focusing on the Belghazi Museum's interpretation of these dynamics, this chapter examines the Moroccan cabinet's staging of a premodern identity as a nostalgic turn from the insecurities of modern life in Morocco. Ultimately, what I aim to accomplish here is to read Belghazi's museum as part of a larger conversation with existing museums in poorer countries in the postcolonial world, a conversation that questions the need to accept the history of the Western museum as a natural path for its own development and also questions the path of modernization that Moroccan culture has seemingly accepted. While other art institutions have accepted the dynamics of modernization and globalization, Belghazi's museum does not entirely follow the trend; in fact, the museum is convinced that it is participating in the liberation of culture from those very forces. Arjun Appadurai argues: "For many societies, modernity is an elsewhere, just as the global is a temporal wave that must be encountered in *their* present."[5] For Belghazi, the global and the modern may just be a passing wave that his cabinet will weather until a better moment in Moroccan history arrives.

Staging Authenticity in the Belghazi Cabinet

In order to distinguish itself from the medina marketplace museum and state-administered national museums, the Belghazi Museum creates a performance of authenticity that at once transforms the private collection into a *personal* one that emphasizes the rarity and singularity of its objects through theatrical unveilings and ultimately converts the anonymous visitor into a privileged guest in a private home. The trope of the family is applied throughout this performance. From the ownership of the objects to the service that the museum provides for the patrimony of an extended national community, the museum stresses that its form is an organic manifestation of a Moroccan family.

In emphatic contrast to the foreign genesis of the national museums in Morocco, Abdellah Belghazi narrates the birth of his museum through the genealogy of his family.[6] Belghazi's great-grandfather, an astronomer, was the first in the family to collect valuable navigation tools, and this love of science and beauty was passed down in the genes. The museum press packet states:

> The Belghazi Museum is first of all the realization of an old dream, that of a family of artist-embroiderers from Fez, direct descendants from the "Lions of the Zarhoun Mountain," ancient and uncontested masters of Arab-Islamic art. A family that has never ceased to nurture a passion for art objects, preserved for centuries, then passed down from generation to generation, until our days.[7]

One of the most important manuscripts in the museum is a seventeenth-century mathematical study by Belghazi's great-grandfather Bnou Ali Bnou Ghazi Al Othmani, and the valuable collection of Jewish caftans and religious objects comes from his wife's side of the family. By emphasizing the personal nature of the private museum, Belghazi insists that his collection is more authentic than the distant culture displayed in public museums. Susan Crane tells us that "cabinets were intensely personal and private by nature" and that "the object and the collector were defined in terms of each other."[8] This is definitely the case in the Belghazi Museum. Reiterating that the collection is the fruit of familial labor and that objects never left the family's hands for over five generations of ownership, the museum is named for the family and defined by its history. This quality is further highlighted by the family's actions to protect their collection during the French Protectorate and resist French efforts to define and institutionalize Moroccan culture. Authenticity is thus staged through a narrative of continuity in family ownership of objects, artistic and scientific ability, and resistance to external control of culture. Not only have the Belghazis been actively collecting art objects from within Morocco; they have also worked to collect Moroccan objects from abroad, bringing objects back home and back into the family, so to speak. Belghazi narrates this repatriation of art as testimony to a commitment to his family and, extending the trope, to the nation at large.

When Belghazi opened the museum ten miles outside of the capital city of Rabat, and ten miles away from the national museums, he brought with him the opulence of both his ancestral home and the hidden riches of the Fez medina into the woods of Bouknadel and created a contemporary palace that is called alternately the Belghazi Museum and the Dar Belghazi Museum, *dar* signifying home in Moroccan Arabic. This home for Moroccan culture is not in the symbolic heart of the nation, the capital of Rabat, and its topography of national museums. The Belghazi Museum does not participate in the state-administered space of culture; rather it declares that museum world a failure and rejects it for a more inclusive but personal vision of national art. First, unlike the national museums, the Belghazi Museum has united material culture from all of Morocco's ethnicities: Amazigh, Arab, and Jewish art intermixed under one roof. In the national museums, there is no trace of Jewish culture in the exhibits, and Amazigh cultural production is often separated from other art and poorly represented if at all. Second, unlike the national museum system, Belghazi has committed himself to the collection of Moroccan painting and sculpture as a part of national heritage. This art (including works by Chaïbia and Ben Allal) is mixed with other precious objects on the second floor of the museum, which also has a small exhibit room that functions as a conference hall—a place to talk about the future. Even the exterior of the building is concerned with an inclusive representation of time periods from Moroccan architectural history and seeks to combine various valorized architectural styles into a large concrete structure. Traditional Merenid doors serve as an entryway to the courtyard of the museum, and on the building itself there are Merenid wooden doors, a trace of green tiling also from the Merenid period (1270–1465), and Kufic Qur'anic inscriptions mixed into stucco walls. In the garden, two iron horses by a nineteenth-century artist from Meknes stand in proximity to Abdellah Belghazi's own contemporary sculptures. The eccentric material mixture of genre and historical period on the exterior of the building is a fitting reflection of what is to be found on the inside. Is this private museum more national than the national museums? Is its collection more "authentically Moroccan" than those of its state-run counterparts?

While the collection may boast that it is more national than those of the national museums, public access to the objects is certainly not as inclusive. The only section of the museum that is open to the general public and is the focus of tours for schoolchildren is the ground floor of the building, and entry is not free. In fact, for the majority of Moroccans, the fee of forty dirhams is completely prohibitive. On this floor, Belghazi has created a standard and passable museum of ethnography that is not dissimilar to the national museums in its display practices. Four large rooms house objects representative of the Moroccan arts and include Arab, Amazigh, and Jewish textiles as well as carved doors, copulas, chests, and musical instruments. The objects are behind glass in display cases, and for the most part they are clearly labeled in French and Arabic. When I visited the museum on several occasions in 2000, in the first display case there was a sign in French declaring: "Dear Visitors, We apologize for the lack of information on certain articles. The Museum administration is currently effectuating the creation of these technical labels for the galleries."[9] Through comments like these, Belghazi conveys to his public that he understands what a modern museum is about: clear organization and contextualization of objects. On this floor, displayed items are primarily organized by material and theme. For example, there is a display case on the development of Arabic script in Morocco that juxtaposes metal engravings with leather book bindings and pages of Qur'ans in order to give context to the use of writing. The didactic quality of this methodology, while not entirely complete with explanatory labels, is nonetheless very clear and well researched. There is no disarray, and for the most part there are no random objects. Here exhibition practice follows standard museum conventions. This is not the part of the museum that *Al Maghrib Culture* described as the rich but chaotic mixture of objects. In fact, this floor almost functions as a cover for what is upstairs. If anyone wants to see a "museum," there it is.

For an additional (and negotiable) fee of 160 dirhams (approximately sixteen dollars), the visitor is granted admission to the upstairs of the museum. Once the price is decided, with mutterings like the magical "Open, Sesame!" the anonymous visitor enters a magical storehouse of treasures and is transformed into a privileged guest of the family. Alternately called the "reserve" and the "heart" of the museum in press materials and by the staff, this vast space houses about 70 percent of Belghazi's collection. It is overwhelmingly impressive in its size and variety of objects, including Amazigh textiles from the eighteenth century, gold and silver jewelry, carpets, astrolabes from as early as the eleventh century, woodwork, musical instruments, and a large collection of objects from Jewish material culture. While some objects are in cabinets behind glass, others reside in drawers or cupboards, hang on walls, or lie on top of each other on the floor. And while there are no stuffed animals, the display cases in the first room of the second floor resemble cabinets of curiosity: chests, cabinets, and drawers that are opened for the visitor by the owner or guide. Thus the second floor of the Belghazi Museum takes the visitor on a trip back in time and museum history to orchestrate Belghazi's personal and authentic collection. Amir Ameri has written that the Renaissance cabinet was preoccupied with the authenticity and singularity of its objects: "The bafflingly heterogeneous body of objects encountered in these cabinets appears to have one thing in common. Rare, singular, or wanting of life, the objects of the cabinet eschewed reproduction."[10] The Belghazi cabinet is organized precisely through tropes of the rare, the one-of-a-kind, and the wonderful, and Belghazi emphasizes this by pointing his visitors to objects that can be described in superlatives, such as one of the *oldest* existing genealogies of the Prophet Mohammed; the *smallest* Qur'an in the world, measuring only 27 mm in width and length; and the *longest* embroidered belt in the world, a nineteenth-century belt of silk and gold that measures twelve meters in length. Here nothing is labeled; the superlatives are oral and are part of an authenticating performance in which Belghazi retrieves objects wrapped in velvet or nestled in special silver boxes and explains their significance. When I visited the museum, the genealogy of the Prophet was produced from a vault in a small room off the main hall, and Belghazi slowly drew out the process of retrieving the object while predicting how astonished we would be. The object's singular value and power of authenticity thus comes not only from its identity and how it came into the collection but also from how it is presented. And this extends to the collection as a whole. Even the printed presentation of the museum in press coverage and catalogues performs its role as part of the cabinet grammar of the superlative and the original: the Belghazi Museum is the *first* and *only* private museum in Morocco, the Belghazi has the *largest* collection of Jewish material culture, etc. One article has even described the museum as the "largest museum in Africa."[11]

The effect that this performance of presentation creates is a fundamental change in the identity of the visitor. No longer is the visitor an anonymous spectator, a member of the public at large; rather he gradually adopts a more individual identity that is structured through a relationship to the Belghazi family.

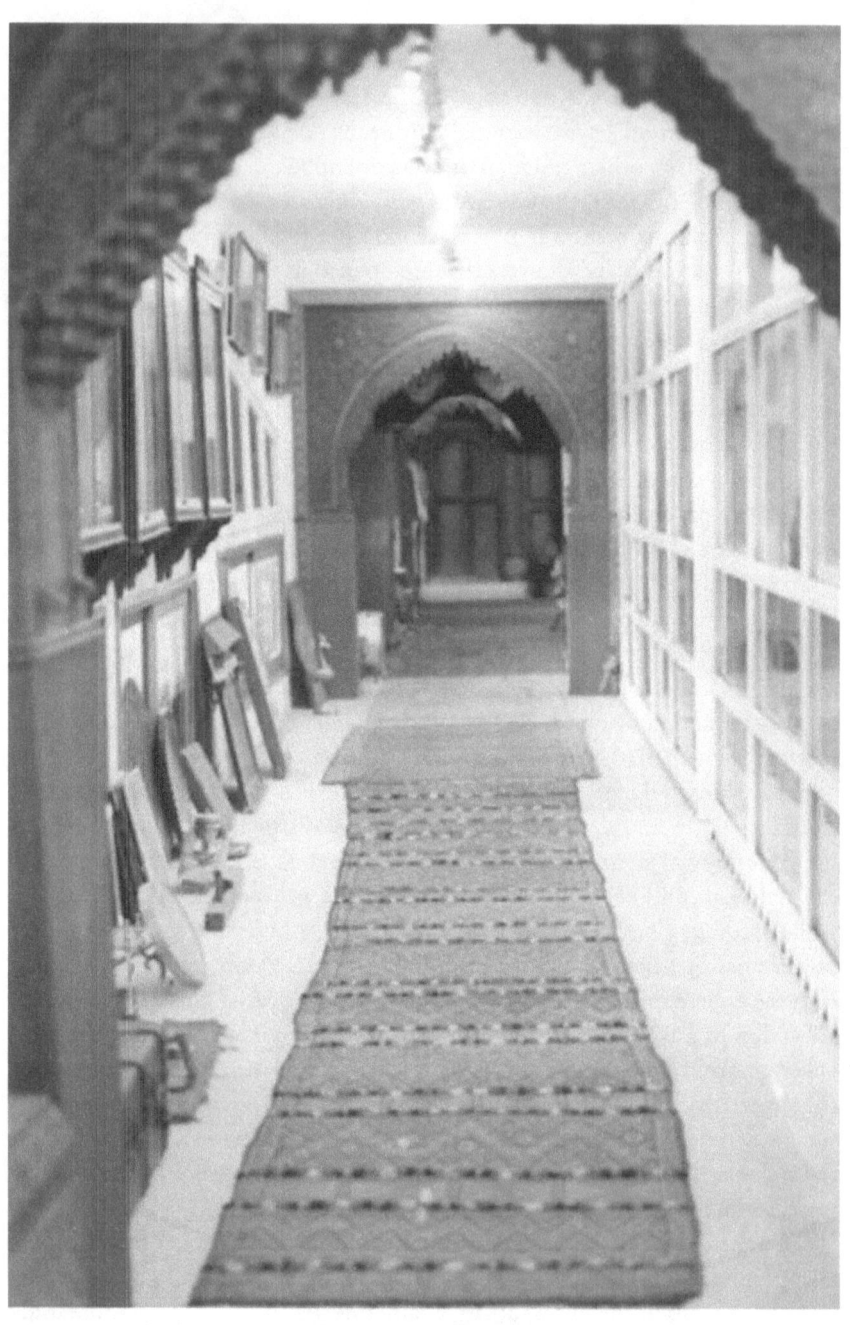

The "heart" of the Belghazi Museum. Photograph by the author, 2000.

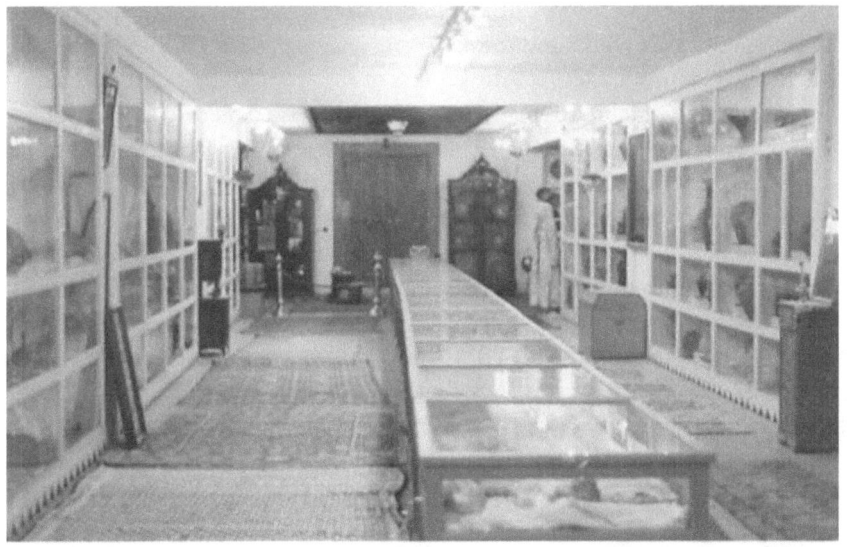

The Belghazi Museum and its cabinets. Photograph by the author, 2000.

The visitor becomes a privileged guest as drawers and cabinets are opened at her behest. The change in status from visitor to guest is further heightened by the fact that the entry fee includes a lunch served by Belghazi's cook and maid. Visitors can choose among four different dining areas of different styles in the main room, which gives the illusion that one is actually dining on museum pieces. The tables were carved by Belghazi, a skilled craftsman, and once the meal is over, he is happy to sit down for a cup of tea. The consumption of culture takes on a new shape in these walls; not only is one allowed to touch art, but the effect created is that one is actually living in it, sitting on it, and indulging all one's sensory pleasures. As mentioned in chapter 2, the Belghazi ancestral "palace" in the Fez medina takes this practice even further and advertises itself as a "restaurant-museum," returning the idea of the museum as a public art institution to its aristocratic roots, in which a privileged few partook of the heights of culture. The visitor as guest alters the viewing experience in the museum from a rational, educational, and predictable practice to an experience of individualized wonder, delight, and surprise.

While in the national museums artwork loses its utilitarian function, the Belghazi museums attempt to reinfuse both space and art with contextual significance: a pillow is meant to be leaned on, a wooden table eaten from. In reversing the modern idea of art as something inherently nonutilitarian, Belghazi attempts to take the Moroccan arts out of the purely aesthetic realm valued by the Western art world and restore their "original" significance. As Barbara Kirshenblatt-Gimblett tells us, the process of contextualization in the contemporary ethnographic museum aims to bring "dead specimens 'to life' through the theater of installation."[12] In the Belghazi Museum, it is not just the object that is installed but also the viewer. This construction of "original" identities for both Moroccan art and its viewers (or users) works to efface a history of French intervention in and interpretation of Moroccan culture. Through the reordering of objects and their replacement in a "premodern" or "pre-colonial past," Belghazi attempts to give his collection a seamless uninterrupted Moroccan identity secured in the idea of the family. The enactment of the trope of Moroccan hospitality further enforces this idea: the copious amounts of food brought out by the maid, the never-ending tea service, even the opening of cabinets and the display of objects, adds to the construction of Moroccanness in the museum.

The Power of the Invisible: Rescaling the Museum and the Politics of Prestige

The focus on an intimate relationship between the owner-guide and visitor—privileged guest in the Belghazi Museum is not just an effective marketing ploy to attract tourists who want a more intimate (however staged) experience of Moroccan culture. It is also an attempt by Belghazi to rescale heritage management from monolithic museums and national narratives back to the human. It is through human interaction that objects acquire and divulge their meanings, not through the faceless bureaucracy of a Ministry of Culture. And thus, to a certain extent, the Belghazi Museum seeks to liberate Moroccan culture from Eurocentric museologies in Morocco that, while seemingly democratizing access to culture, have ironically precluded a direct relationship between objects and humans. As Christina Kreps argues in her book *Liberating Culture: Cross-Cultural Perspectives on Museums, Curation, and Heritage Preservation,* the hegemony of Eurocentric museology works to "not only mask diverse approaches, but also undermine the rights of other people to exercise control over the management and care of their own cultural heritage."[13] Belghazi claims that he has the right to exercise control over his own collection; however, his "liberation of culture" from models of the national museum in favor of personal control of cultural artifacts is a serious concern for those who wish to ensure access to the collection and administer state control over collective practices of patrimony. For if objects are made visible by their owner, they can also be made invisible.

In writing of the Renaissance cabinet, Amir Ameri discusses its politics of authenticity and power through the control of objects and their place. He argues that rather than being placed on display, "the objects in the cabinet were not meant to be seen," and that although dignitaries and cognoscenti were allowed access to the collection, "for the most part . . . the cabinet was secluded, and inaccessible to the public. The impetus behind the collection was not to make oddities, rarities, and singularities visible, but to render them invisible."[14] Thus Ameri concludes that what was preserved in the cabinet was not only rare and singular objects, but also an institution

> that kept the rare and the singular out of circulation and out of the places to which it did not belong. The spatial control exerted over these authortic objects may well be what made the cabinet suitable for the occasional display of sovereignty to foreign dignitaries. On display was not so much the objects in the cabinet, as the spatial control exerted over them—i.e., the collection.[15]

In other words, the cabinet was as much about displaying control over property, power, and prestige as it was about collecting the elements of a wondrous world. Paula Findlen notes that in the case of Italian cabinets of curiosity, "collecting was not just a recreational practice for sixteenth and seventeenth century virtuosi; but also a precise mechanism for transforming knowledge into power."[16]

Like the cabinets described by Ameri and Findlen, the Belghazi Museum engages in a spatial control of access to the collection and uses this power to set its value and prestige. First of all, although the museum is mentioned in guidebooks to Morocco, it is by word of mouth that its celebrity among tourists has spread. After all, the museum is not in an urban environment and is difficult to reach by bus if one does not have access to a car. But as those who have experienced the collection are quick to proclaim, it is definitely worth the trip. The difficulty of access gives added value to the authenticity of the experience; one has to expend extra effort to gain an exclusive look at Moroccan culture, and one is rewarded with an excess of objects, stories, and food. In the museum, spatial control is exerted on the level of display—what is visible, what is invisible, what is explained, and what is kept silent. By not revealing all his objects and keeping certain pieces invisible, Belghazi maintains control over the identity and value of his collection. The absence of documentation and a published catalogue gives credence to the idea that there are still more objects in his collection that perhaps more privileged guests might see or that might be only for the eyes of his blood relatives. Understandably, the lack of visibility of his collection and the challenge that it poses to national patrimony is troubling to the Moroccan state. Who is entitled to see what? And what is the museum hiding? Is it selling objects? What is it collecting? Ambiguous and uncertain answers to these questions feed a dynamic of exclusivity, create an anxiety of control in the Ministry of Culture, and disrupt its mission to secure public access to Moroccan patrimony and dictate cultural projects. By determining the extent of (in)visibility in his collection, Belghazi has been able to leverage funding and special considerations from the government while maintaining control over the location of *his* Moroccan culture, ultimately appropriating some of the state's power to decide where objects of national value belong.

As in the Wafabank Space, Belghazi has been careful to maintain a certain visual protocol vis-à-vis the monarchy. In the "heart" or "cave" of the museum, Belghazi has hung a photograph of Prince Mohammed VI before Hassan II's death strolling with Belghazi through the collection, as well as other photographs of Belghazi taken with dignitaries. The museum has been officially recognized by the state as the first private museum in Morocco, and Princess Lalla Meriem was present at its opening in 1996. This royal patronage and state sanction do not, however, enable a comfortable coexistence of state-controlled and privately owned patrimony. Although celluloid testaments to cooperation between state and private efforts in the preservation of Moroccan art continue to hang on a wall in Mr. Belghazi's office, the relations between the museum and the Moroccan Ministry of Culture have grown progressively strained. Since the museum's opening in 1996, a number of quarrels have occurred between the museum and the ministry over the control and preservation of objects. The ministry has accused Belghazi of illegally exporting art objects to the West for sale.[17] In turn, Belghazi has accused the ministry of failing to offer him needed financial support for the preservation of valuable objects. Belghazi claims that the ministry is a bureaucracy more concerned with personal advancement and prestige than with art: it is simply jealous and bitter that his museum houses more objects of worth than the national ones. In response, the former director of museums in Morocco, Ali Amahan, has called Belghazi a charlatan.

As the Belghazi Museum acquires more objects and gains prestige, the national museums appear as empty and hollow monuments with few pieces and even fewer visitors. Not only does Belghazi's museum challenge the national museums' prestige; it disrupts the state's efforts to symbolize a movement toward Western modernity by reversing the history and purpose of the museum from a crucially democratic modern infrastructure of the state to a private, personal, and idiosyncratic space of exhibition. The treatment of the "heart" of Moroccan culture as a cabinet of curiosities strikes fundamentally at the idea of the narration of nation-state through modern and scientific means and is inherently at odds with the politics of modernization and development in the Third World. Perhaps most significantly for the state, Belghazi's museum not only challenges the idea of culture for modernization purposes; it also creates multiple narratives of Moroccan culture that question and render unstable the narratives of the state.

The Belghazi Cabinet as a Memory Cave

As scholars tell us, in Renaissance cabinets of curiosity the collection was as much about the stories that brought the objects to the cabinet as it was about the objects. Objects were not labeled or arranged in an order that was clear and logical to the modern eye. Stories tied the collection together and created spaces that were almost cacophonous with the possibility of meaning. Barbara Stafford has described the curiosity cabinet thus: "Crammed shelves and drawers, with their capricious jumps in logic and disconcerting omissions, resembled the apparent disorganization of talk," where objects "'chatted' among themselves and with the spectator."[18] In the Belghazi Museum, undisciplined stories and the disorganization of talk open the possibility of stepping outside supposedly logical and rational narratives of culture created by the discourse of the nation-state. History is not unidirectional toward the present, and this can be seen in the museum in the way contemporary painting is hung next to eighteenth-century calligraphy and objects of various periods brush against each other. Rather than constructing a narrative walk toward the present, Belghazi's museum forces the visitor to stop, sit, and interact with a disorganized group of artifacts. And as if the cacophonous talk of heterogeneous objects were not sufficient, the Belghazi Museum has adopted a literary text of fantastic proportions from *A Thousand and One Nights* to serve as the organizing metaphor for the collection.

When Mr. Belghazi joined me on the second floor, he and his assistant both proclaimed the Ali Baba quality of his collection. This is an image that has served Belghazi well. His press packet has grouped several articles by journalists that describe the museum as "a palace straight out of *A Thousand and One Nights*"[19] and "a true Ali Baba's cave. Almost 4000 objects on a surface of 7000 meters squared."[20] Another journalist writing for the newspaper *Al-Bayane* exaggerated the analogy even further: "As soon as you pass through the imposing doorway, you find yourself in the cave of Ali Baba multiplied in riches to the hundredth power."[21] By engaging with a marvelous tale of epic proportions, the museum opens itself to another universe of meaning through a body of literature that emerged from a golden era of Arab storytelling and empire.

The tale functions on two levels: on the one hand, it creates an easily recognizable, if not stereotypical, image of wealth and prosperity to attract foreign tourists in search of Arab authenticity. On the other hand, the use of the tale also speaks to a deeper dynamic of nostalgia that turns to the medieval riches of the past to disguise the poverty of Moroccan life today.

Before I examine these two functions more closely, a quick look into the story reminds us of its details and reveals the many striking parallels between fiction and the reality created by the museum. In the Burton translation of *The Arabian Nights,* the description of the cave says that it was

> a large cavern and vaulted, in height equaling the stature of a full-grown man and it was hewn in the live stone and lighted up with light that came through air-holes and bulls-eyes . . . the whole room filled with bales of all manners of stuffs, and heaped up from sole to ceiling with camel loads of silks and brocades and embroidered cloths and mounds on mounds of varicolored carpets besides which . . . coins golden and silvern without measure or account, some piled upon the ground and others bound in leathern bags and sacks.[22]

The Harvard Classics translation provides a similar scene of excess, describing the cave as "a well-lighted and spacious chamber, lighted from an opening at the top of the rock, and filled with all sorts of provisions, rich bales of silk, embroideries and valuable tissues, piled upon one another, gold and silver ingots in great heaps and money in bags."[23] This great material wealth, stolen by a sinister band of forty thieves and hidden in a cave, is discovered by a poor wood-cutter, Ali Baba. Through the intelligence of his maid, Ali Baba is able to outwit the robbers and keep these goods.

In Belghazi's modern interpretation of the tale, he is the poor woodcutter (though not exactly poor, Belghazi is in fact a trained wood-carver); his personal assistant, the charming Miss Nazat, uncannily plays the maid; and the forty thieves are simultaneously the French administration and the current Moroccan Ministry of Culture, both of which have attempted to control and dictate culture in Morocco. Belghazi, like Ali Baba, sees himself as the owner of great treasure, and, as already discussed, he is eager to narrate the legitimacy of this ownership at great length, both orally and in print. In many respects, Belghazi performs the story he has adopted to serve his institution well, but just as his museum's construction of a seamless Moroccan identity is a suspicious fiction, so is the tale from *A Thousand and One Nights.*

Belghazi attempts to create a consumable image of wealth and prosperity for foreign tourists through a widely known "Oriental" tale of riches. And "Oriental" is key here. As Edward Said discusses in *Orientalism,* European scholars in the eighteenth and nineteenth centuries fashioned an imagined geography that encompassed the entire Islamic world in a veil of exoticism.[24] Through the creation and maintenance of ethnic stereotypes, Orientalist scholarship permeated every realm of daily life in Europe, furnishing images of the exotic other for advertising and logos.[25] Although their translations were accomplished by the most respected scholars, the stories of *A Thousand and One Nights* inflamed the popular European imagination. In 1909, the editor of the Harvard Classics translation of the tales wrote of their immense popularity in European culture:

> In the two hundred years of their currency in the West, the stories of the "Nights" have engrafted themselves upon European culture. They have made the fairy-land of the Oriental imagination and the mode of life of the medieval Arab, his manners and his morals, familiar to young and old; and allusions to their incidents and personages are wrought into the language and literature of all the modern civilized peoples. . . . Many more phrases and allusions of every-day occurrence suggest how pervasive has been the influence of this wonder-book of the mysterious East.[26]

The tale of "Ali Baba and the Forty Thieves" in particular falls squarely into the creative discourse and imagination of Orientalism. The Middle Eastern origins of the tale have been a subject of debate, with some speculation that the tale may have been the work of the eighteenth-century French Orientalist Galland, who inserted it into the Arabic body of the Arabian Nights.[27] Ali Baba appears to be the ultimate construction of the Orient for its others. The currency of the name flows from East to West and back again, a popular signifier and construction of riches, luck, wealth, and ethnicity.

One need only search for Ali Baba on the Internet to find how widespread this epithet is today, when it is used to add a connotation of wealth, luck, and exoticism to business establishments. A Tunisian student has set up a Web site called "Ali Baba Online" to offer his services, and one should not forget the plethora of restaurants, bazaars, and carpet shops that affix Ali Baba to their names.[28] Mireille Rosello claims:

> Today Francophone people of North African origin, regardless of their nationality, have the option of playing with stereotypical images. Instead of resisting the schizophrenic splitting of audience created by the denouncing of stereotypical voices (I, as a listener, denounce you, the speaker, as a creator of stereotypes), they not only pretend to go along with the stereotype as truth, they also offer a perfect performance of who they are supposed to be.[29]

The student, the guide, and the restaurant owner can defuse the negativity of the Oriental stereotype "Ali Baba" and use it to their advantage in order to present themselves as more "authentically" Arab. And this authentication of ethnicity is something desired by a West that, according to Rey Chow, in its postcolonial, postmodern condition is rethinking the problem of the native and his "endangered authenticity."[30] Through Ali Baba, through the Western construction of the Orient, Belghazi ultimately gives the Western tourist a Morocco that is more authentically Oriental and exotic than Morocco itself; his is the Morocco that is *supposed* to be.

Belghazi's primary use of the story is to attract tourists to his authentic and exclusive Moroccan institution, but there is another reading of the museum's use of the tale of Ali Baba that I would like to offer that focuses less on the tourist and more on the existential conditions in Morocco today. Read next to contemporary stories of disenfranchisement, poverty, and struggle, the Ali Baba tale, and the museum as an Ali Baba cave, effectively erect protective spaces of memory that use nostalgia to shield Moroccan culture from the realities of the present. The universe of the cabinet of curiosities allows the family and its visitors to travel through all periods of Moroccan history without having to step out of a space of riches and be confronted by the difficult realities of life in the present, in which, according to World Bank data, 19 percent of Moroccans lived under the national poverty line during the 1990s and unemployment rates vacillated between 15.8 and 22.9 percent. Like Ali Baba's cave, the Belghazi Museum is set apart from the city; it is out in the woods, distant from shantytowns and shut off from difficult conditions of life for the urban poor. And let us not forget what Ali Baba does with his riches in the tale. The Burton translation reads: "In after days, he showed the hoard to his sons and sons' sons and taught them how the door could be caused to open and shut. Thus Ali Baba and his household lived all their lives in wealth and joyance in that city where erst while he had been a pauper, and by the blessing of that secret treasure he rose to high degree and dignities."[31] The Harvard Classic version succinctly reads: "He was the only person in the world who had the secret opening of the cave, . . . [and] all the treasure was at his disposal. . . . Some years later he carried his son to the cave and taught him the secret, which he handed down to his posterity, who using their good fortune with moderation lived in great honour and splendor."[32] The potency of the tale's ending lies not with Belghazi's advancement in society, but rather with the issue of hoarding wealth and shutting the door.

This dynamic of protecting oneself in the interior of a cave while the rest of the world slouches simultaneously to and from a promised modernity is aptly described in another literary text, this time by a contemporary Moroccan writer and journalist, Idriss Al-Khoury. In the 1994 short story "Youssef fī baṭn ūmhu" (Youssef in his mother's womb), Al-Khoury recounts a mother's conversation with her unborn son. While the entire family prepares for his arrival with great celebration, preparing food, washing elegant dishes, filling the house with delicious fragrances, Youssef, quietly sitting in his mother's womb, decides that he would rather not be born. The family and his mother wait impatiently for his arrival, but no sign of birth is imminent. Finally the mother asks her child why he must tarry so long:

> When will you come out?
> When I see fit.
> But the matter is not in your hands.
> Then when God wants me to.
> I want you right now.
> But I am afraid.
> Of what?
> Of the world and of my unknown future.
> There will be a place for you in this world, a place for you to sit in school.
> I doubt that, I fear that I will be one of the outcasts.
> No, they will welcome you, they now have new classes open all over.
> And if the reporters on television made a mistake?
> No, there is not much of a chance of that.
> Let me sleep.[33]

Youssef's concern about his future and the world into which he will be born articulates itself through the possibilities of education and advancement. What is the point of being born when there is no chance of fulfillment, no chance of an education, and no chance of a job? Youssef would rather remain in the warm and cavernous womb of his mother than go out into his dark and dismal future. His mother tries to assure him that all will be well, that there is a place in the world for him; however, Youssef is never quite convinced, and in the closing lines of the story, as he is being born, he asks himself the following question: "Shall I stay? Will there be a place for me in school, a bed for me in the hospital, a seat for me in an office?"[34] On entering the world, young Youssef can only imagine leaving it.

Al-Khoury's story is an indictment of state neglect in the area of socioeconomic modernization. In today's Morocco, he asks, what is the point of being modern? It appears as though the Ali Baba cave is asking the same question. Sheltered from the outside, Belghazi's cabinet-cave serves to nourish and protect his vision of Moroccan culture through nostalgic tales of past glory while the country traverses what the museum sees as temporary but unsettling waves of modernity and globalization.

The Cabinet in between the Global Universal and the Local Community

The cabinet of curiosities has recently resurfaced in the worlds of the Western museum and art as a fundamentally liberating approach to the display of culture precisely because of its ability to render established and authoritative scripts of culture unstable. Artists and curators are attracted to the form in order to create real and virtual exhibits that are not organized through hierarchies of logic or established narratives but rather group objects and art through intimate and personal definitions of wonder. The attraction of contemporary cabinets is that *anyone* can collect objects of marvel, not just established authorities. The Brooklyn art installation "Wunderkammer: Wonderworks," which was displayed in September and October 2000, used the concept of the cabinet to expose the similarities between the cabinet as a mode of organization and contemporary communications and networking technology. In their curatorial statement, Geraldine Erman and Eve Andrée Laramée wrote: "By re-examining the pre-modern model of the wunderkammer, we hope to shed some light on artists' post-modern concerns with collecting, indexing and archiving the Wonderful."[35] Collecting images from the Web and creating universes that connect objects from across the world and time through personal aesthetics is an activity that arguably anyone can do. The blog of the *Proceedings of the Athanansius Kircher Society* is one such venue; there people post pictures of and information about wondrous and curious objects, images, and events that range from pictures of hundred-year food to underwater art installations.[36] Contributors post images and comments, and others reply with diverse levels of discourse, creating a model of conversational machinery that defies hierarchies of knowledge. Internet cabinets of curiosity have the potential to become models of a civic conversability that Tony Bennett has urged the contemporary museum and its curators to consider.[37]

In the Moroccan context, however, it appears as though the function of the cabinet is the opposite. Belghazi's museum claims to liberate culture from hegemonic narratives of the nation-state, but the conversational model that his cabinet sets in motion is exclusionary rather than open for exchange. Rather than opening itself up for access to the public at large, the Belghazi cabinet adopts an elitist model that controls access to its collection and renders much of it invisible to local communities. Although contemporary Internet cabinets appear democratic and populist—anyone with Internet access can visit at any time—the Belghazi cabinet controls its viewing public and the stories it tells. In its nostalgic return to an institutional model that protects personal wealth and familial inheritance, the concern of the Belghazi Museum appears to be the future of memory rather than the future; it rejects Andreas Huyssen's suggestion that it is time to remember the future and leave obsessive machineries of memory.[38] Shana Cohen has written of the challenge for the contemporary Moroccan subject not to withdraw from the future into the nostalgia of protective memory when faced with the challenge of a global neoliberal order that has dislocated meaning:

> Mahmud Darwish's (1988) isolated, confused narrator asks, "I am not a citizen here and I am not a resident. Therefore, where am I and who am I?" The narrator then concludes, "You realize that you are present philosophically, but you are absent legally." For young Moroccan men and women, the statement becomes "You realize you are present legally, but you are absent philosophically." Any theory and strategy of politics for the global middle class must confront this absence, and not as a nostalgic return but as an embrace of the challenge the global market economy presents to the subject.[39]

In Belghazi's museum he has embraced the challenge of the global market economy by operating a private institution of art and deciding the location of culture, the identity of his public, and the profits to be made. But the politics of his cabinet of wonder have certainly not rejected nostalgic returns.

I started this chapter with questions, and it is with questions that I conclude. What can we surmise about the place of a cabinet of curiosities in a twenty-first-century postcolonial context? Is the Third World cabinet the product of a process of economic liberalization that has disabled the state's capacity to collect and protect art and handed culture over to those who can afford it? Is the reappearance of the cabinet a symptom of the deepening divide between those who have and those who have not? What are its implications for national patrimony? In her review of a South African exhibit at the 1998 Johannesburg biennale titled "Who's It For?" Jen Budney asks the key questions facing African art today: "Whose story is being told, whose history, whose religion, whose meaning, whose future, not to mention who gets to participate in the making of institutionalized culture and which audience benefits and how?"[40] These questions for the future of African art are relevant to the future of the Moroccan museum. Whose story is being told in the museum, who gets to tell to it, and who benefits?

While the Belghazi Museum hopes to shield Moroccan culture from the uncertainties of development and globalization in Morocco, the cabinet also aims to protect Moroccan art from the insecurities and inequalities of the museum world. At a time when major museums such as the Louvre, the British Museum, and the Metropolitan Museum of Art claim to be universal and proclaim their rights of ownership under the banner of globalism, local museums around the world struggle to protect and conserve their culture from the forces of globalization and global power. In 2002 eighteen European and American art museums issued a "Declaration on the Importance and Value of Universal Museums" arguing that their museums "serve not just the citizens of one nation but the people of every nation."[41] But who has access to these collections? Not those people from the global South, who cannot cross borders as easily as artwork and whose cultural heritage remains under threat from international debt, poverty, and lack of institutional resources. Urging museums and their scholars to reconsider the contemporary museum from a *different* global angle, Saloni Mathur has written, "The issue of collection and preservation of universal cultural heritage . . . should be measured against the contemporary *destruction* of cultural heritage in Afghanistan and Iraq, in the form of looting of the Iraq National Museum in Baghdad and *its* repercussions in the international arena."[42] Rather than celebrating certain large museums' ability to collect universal culture, we should be attentive to the politics of exclusion and destruction that occur simulataneously. As Geeta Kapur writes on the subject of Third World art and neoliberal economic order: "What we are doing under the tutelage of the IMF and the World Bank involves not only anti-poor, proconsumption policies but also the virtual surrender of national sovereignty—operable only on the basis of a welfare state."[43] It is in this light that Belghazi's jealous guarding of his fortune and his museum's repatriation of art *to* Morocco takes on political relevance. Why donate objects to a national museum system that might not be able to protect them? Why allow Moroccan art to be located only elsewhere, such as in Paris at the Institut du Monde Arabe or the Musée du Quai Branly? Historian Abdallah Laroui insists that Europe "still possesses the only true Arab, Islamic, African and Asian museums."[44] And while the Gulf States engage in an ambitious project of building museums for the Middle East, the repatriation of objects from European museums back to the Middle East after their completion is by no means ensured. In fact, if the "Declaration on the Importance and Value of Universal Museums" prevails, it is possible that objects might travel only as loans to the Louvre franchise in Abu Dhabi.

    The closing of Belghazi's cabinet doors thus arguably protects the objects of wonder and their memory from a dangerous moment in history in which, much as during the Protectorate period, Morocco does not stand on equal ground with Europe and the industrialized West. Protecting culture by making it disappear from public view may be a valid strategy and has been used in Iraq and Afghanistan, but the disappearance of objects during periods of instability does not reassure proponents of public culture that they will not disappear more permanently, reappearing only in auction houses and on antiquities black markets. Both the Belghazi Museum and the Ministry of Culture are equally suspicious in this regard. The Moroccan government has suspected the Belghazi Museum of selling objects on the black market, but as Amina Touzani has written, the absence of an exhaustive national inventory of patrimony and the lack of surveillance and monitoring of restoration by the government also result in illegal sales of patrimony.[45] What is most needed at the present moment in Morocco is the creation of a meticulous, transparent inventory of the objects in all national, corporate, and private museums. The Moroccan public at large may remain alienated from all three types of institutions for a long period to come, but at least art will be on display through a museum of documents. When material museums fail, we must look to alternative methods of collection, preservation, and display.

Part II

Tactical Architectures of Art

Discursive, Ephemeral, and
Nomadic Museums

Four

Imaginary Museums
and Their Real Phantoms:
Exorcising Monumental Discourse

What would it mean to create a museum of art that houses discourse rather than objects? And positions on art and the modern rather than modern art itself? For many in the museum world, this would be the ultimate travesty, the betrayal of the object, and the end of art as Hegel predicted. In the Discursive Museum, a 2001 symposium held in Vienna, artists, museum curators, and scholars discussed the future of art in a context in which the material object is rapidly vanishing and being replaced by installations that are ephemeral or cannot "endure the test of time," in which museum visits are more about the large and exciting architecture of the space rather than about the intimacy of its contents, and in which constant talk replaces silent contemplation of art.[1] In his opening remarks, Peter Noever stated: "The museum as a place for communicating art is a space where various forms of verbal expression encounter each other. Progressively, it is also a place where such forms are born. . . . One could even say that the museum is a specific configuration of discourses."[2] However, many of the participants seemed to ask the question, "Must the museum be so verbal?" Scholars such as James Cuno and Hans Belting argued against the discursive and the ephemeral in favor of museums that ask the public to meaningfully engage in art, to physically visit a place that is not virtual, "exciting," or fast-paced in order to slowly and quietly reflect on art objects themselves.[3] The title of a dialogue between artist Gerhard Merz and art historian Herbert Molderings went even further, provocatively declaring: "We'll Stick with It: Any Interference in the Soundlessness, Timelessness, Motionlessness, and Lifelessness of the True Museum Is Disrespectful."[4] Over two months, participants in the symposium met in the empty central exhibition hall of the MAK Museum (Museum for Applied Art), an institution dedicated to the display of applied and contemporary arts. As participants sat in the beautiful space, what was conspicuously missing from the discussion was the possibility or even the necessity of a discursive museum precisely because there might not be a building, a physical museum of art, or a space in which to hang visible art to be a source of inspiration to the public. What was missing from the discussion was the notion that discursive museums might be indispensable in places where real museums do not exist.

In many places around the world, the art museum exists as a void, and discourse is the only trace of the institution. In describing the lack of a museum of art in Peru, Gustavo Buntinx writes: "This is a radical absence: the theme here is not the deprived museum, disadvantaged by inadequate resources, but the greater deprivation provoked by the very lack of a museum—our grand museum void."[5] As I describe at the begining of this book, the very first statement that is often made by Moroccan artists, intellectuals, and curators on the subject of Moroccan museums is that they do not exist. At no point was this void as deeply felt as in the postindependence period, when Moroccan artists and intellectuals labored for, petitioned about, and discussed the necessity of a museum of art in Morocco. Through these discussions they succeeded in creating their own imaginary museum, a discursive museum that housed not art objects but issues of great debate on art and culture: What did it mean to create modern art? Is Moroccan art the same as Islamic art? Should the artist work in service of the nation? And how does one participate in universal art movements without sacrificing the particularities of local Moroccan cultures?[6]

Faced with a lack of material infrastructures, artists turned to the immaterial, to discursive spaces they could control and fashion without major monetary interventions and spatial considerations: journals and newspapers. Although the state had been active in presenting a veneer of modernity through art, the discursive museum was the opposite of superficial in its treatment of modern culture. It served as a materially invisible but theoretically profound reconsideration of modern art in Moroccan society by suspending, repositioning, dissecting, and re-presenting dominant narratives. Barbara Kirshenblatt-Gimblett describes the potential of the museum to serve as a utopic space for thought: "While all utopian worlds are built out of other worlds, only better, the museum literally takes the world apart at its joints, collects the pieces, and holds them in suspension. Identified, classified, and arranged, objects withdrawn from the world and released into the museum are held in a space of infinite recombi-nation."[7] I argue that in *writing* and *speaking* about modern art in Morocco through their discursive museum, Moroccan artists suspended and repositioned the monumentality of dominant discourses both in the West and in Morocco, discourses about such things as Orientalism, Islam, univeralism, local nation-alism, and neobourgeois materialism. Artists performed this relocation not merely to dismiss or mock the contents of such discourses but rather to dimin-ish the authority of dominant discourses by inscribing their own narratives. In so doing, they attempted to create a space for Moroccan art that would in-crease their own agency in controlling, developing, protecting, and disseminat-ing modern Moroccan culture. This pedagogic dynamic appears most clearly in the local press, where public transcripts on art were formed that linked the acquisition of wealth to the acknowledgment of art as another source of cul-tural capital and encouraged the bourgeois Moroccan to replace his or her idea of facile entertainment with cultural betterment.

In her study on art worlds in twentieth-century Egypt, Jessica Winegar tells us, "Of all the activities that went into art-making in Egypt, none was more prominent and widespread than discourse. . . . [Artists'] view of themselves as intellectuals and cultural elites with advanced discursive powers led them to privilege discourse among all of their activities."[8] This is certainly the case in Morocco as well, where artists of the postindependence period *spoke* of seem-ingly everything permissible. Discursive interventions occurred across long stretches of time. Michel Foucault wrote, "We must be ready to receive every moment of discourse in its sudden irruption; in that punctuality in which it appears, and in that temporal dispersion that enables it to be repeated, known, forgotten, transformed, utterly erased, and hidden far from all view."[9] Through journals, newspapers, and meetings, artists and intellectuals contributed to the discursive museum at different moments, inscribing, repeating, forgetting, and transforming the shape of their institution. But if one thing animated their project the most, it was the hope that discourse would bring forth a new soci-ety and the discursive museum, a meaningful place for Moroccan arts.

Art historian Toni Maraini describes the 1960s in Moroccan art circles as a period of hope and excitement that a new society could be formed through an engaged and modern art:

> My friends spoke of the artistic situation in Morocco, of the country's cultural
> provincialism, of its anomalies, of the burden of a Fine Arts administration
> inherited from colonial times, of neocolonialism. . . . They were conscious of
> the historic role of their generation. They had numerous projects and a work
> schedule in order to shake up and change the (in)existent structures. . . . We

were animated by that which the "project of modernity" claimed as the most lib-erating and dynamic.[10]

The project for modernity awakened in the cultural elite a desire to push the limits of their culture, to break through reified representations of Moroccan arts created by dominant discourses in both the Western and the Arab-Islamic worlds. In 1966, the poet Abdellatif Laâbi wrote: "Something is preparing to happen in Africa and in other countries of the Third World. Exoticism and folklore are becoming unsteady. Nobody can predict what this 'ex pre-logical' thought will give to the world. But the day when the true speakers of collec-tivities make their voices heard, it will be like an explosion of dynamite in the rotting arcades of old humanisms."[11] Laâbi exclaimed that what was once termed premodern or "prelogical" thought by colonial powers would return with a vengeance to disrupt not only colonial narratives of exoticism but also local dominant discourses that sold Moroccan culture as folklore. A new Moroc-can art that espoused the liberating tenets of modernity—democracy, educa-tion, and freedom of and from religion—would replace outdated systems of thought, "old humanisms" that continued to oppress collectivities and silence voices.[12] This generation of Moroccan artists actively committed to the spread of literacy, mass education, secularism, and the liberation of art into an auton-omous institution independent of religion and politics. In fact, as Shana Cohen writes, this generation "pursued a model of nation and self with as much or more fervor than Al-Fassi himself. Their movements, predominantly Marxist and communist rather than Islamist, strove, as radical movements of this period did, to reduce poverty, eliminate elite privileges and create a government of 'the people.'"[13]

However, the explicit adoption of and commitment to discourses of moder-nity by this postcolonial elite often placed them in a position of ambivalence and anxiety or, as Buntinx terms it, "a *syndrome of marginal occidentality:* the anxious desire to belong to a model condition that is felt as one's own but unreachable at the same time."[14] While artists sought to decolonize Moroccan art from relationships of dominance with the West, they often continued to rely on Western narratives and structures to support their actions. Although their work espoused modern aesthetics, its legitimization rested in the great metropolitan centers of capitalism and aesthetic modernity: Paris, London, and New York. Despite this dislocation, the Moroccan cultural elite remained committed to a project of modernity. And in this sense, they performed the central problematic of the postcolonial condition as described by Ngugi Wa Thiongo in *Decolonising the Mind*.[15] While intellectuals focused on a political

decolonization of art and its institutions, on a deeper level they worked to decolonize the fundamental structures of thought that guided their work. Moroccan intellectuals were deeply engaged in this problem, and in their discourse we
can read the often painful negotiations to forge a new voice, a new narrative,
to "enter modernity" at will.[16]

In writing of the dilemma of Latin American writers committed to modernity, Carlos J. Alonso suggests, "While arguing for the adoption of the ideology
of modernity and its values, Spanish American writers also moved simultaneously to delimit a space impervious to that rhetoric as a strategy to address the
threat with which the discourse of modernity unremittingly confronted their
discursive authority."[17] The delimitation or clearing of space in the discourse
of modernity that Alonso describes is not dissimilar to Homi Bhabha's notion
of a writing that occurs somewhere between mimesis and mimicry: "What
emerges between mimesis and mimicry is a *writing,* a mode of representation,
that marginalizes the monumentality of history, quite simply mocks its power
to be a model, that power which supposedly makes it imitable."[18] A writing
of Western modernity from the periphery, in its partial and incomplete repetition of modernity as ideology and practice, diminishes its discursive power
and leaves spaces for negotiation. In describing this dynamic in the work of
North African Arab avant-garde writers, Andrea Flores Khalil suggests, "These
texts consciously 'speak' the language and engage these notions as part of their
intellectual genealogy, pointing to their colonized identity and criticizing the
hypocrisy that at once rewards and stigmatizes it."[19]

This chapter explores how Moroccan intellectuals and artists deeply committed to modern art cleared spaces for negotiation of their position within
the discourse of modernity and its aesthetic manifestations and in so doing
created a discursive museum that meaningfully framed their work and provided a refuge for utopian thought. In what follows I trace appearances and
disappearances of discourses in the various rooms of the discursive Moroccan
museum and in its larger public transcripts. What obsessively underlies all discussion in this museum is lack, the painful presence of that which is missing:
state support, recognition by the art market, local knowledge and support of
cultural production, and, most of all, a meaningful *material* museum, which
is always phantasmagorically positioned elsewhere and only imagined at home.
Whereas the participants in the 2001 discursive museum sat in an empty institution in Vienna and talked about the lack of art in art museums, the participants in the Moroccan discursive museum of the 1960s and 1970s produced
art and discourse in the absence of a physical museum to house their work.

Entering the Discursive Museum

The majority of texts that build the discursive museum that I outline here appeared in several major cultural journals: the bilingual (French and Arabic) *Souffles/Anfas* (1966–1972), founded by poet Abdellatif Laâbi; *Lamalif* (1968–1988), founded by Mohamed Loghlam and Zakya Daoud (a.k.a. Jacqueline Loghlam); and *Integral* (1971–1978), founded by painter Mohamed Melehi. The articles that comprise the museum include manifestos about culture, literature, and art; critiques of cultural institutions and foreign cultural centers; analysis of artwork and literary texts; and many poems. The contributors to these journals were diverse but used a common vocabulary of progressive, often Marxist reform and cultural decolonization based on shared theoretical language from thinkers such as Frantz Fanon, Aimé Césaire, and Albert Memmi. Moroccan poets and novelists such as Abdelkebir Khatibi, Mostafa Nissaboury, Idriss Al-Khoury, Tahar Ben Jelloun, and Mohammed Berrada wrote literary and analytical pieces alongside non-Moroccan writers from the Middle East and former French colonies such as adonis, Etel Adnan, Nazim Hikmet, René Depestre, and Malek Alloula. With art historians such as Italian Toni Maraini and Syrian Afif Bahnassi, Moroccan artists discussed contemporary artwork and architecture. They wrote critical pieces on cultural policies and practices in Morocco, as well as in the Maghreb and the Mashrek, including pieces on art scenes in Iraq, the work of Egyptian architect Hassan Fathmy, and documents detailing the formation of pan-Maghreb art associations. All of these texts about art and literature did not exist in isolation from local and world politics but were deeply imbricated in the political world around the writers. To greater and lesser degrees, the journals published sociological analyses of class in Morocco, articles about agrarian reform, and statements about contemporaneous events in the Arab world, including pieces expressing support for Palestine.

The museum that I will guide you through is ultimately about visual modern and contemporary art, and I would argue that reading about art in the journals often simulated visiting an art museum. For example, in addition to reviews and photographic essays on artists, the journal *Integral* published a glossy reproduction of one artwork in each issue for its readers to frame and hang on their walls. For the reader this dynamic was not unlike that of taking a poster or postcard home from the museum to remember the art experience, participate in the collection of valued art, and cultivate his or her taste in a personal, private space. Journal covers were designed by various artists, producing yet another space for the display of art that could circulate through

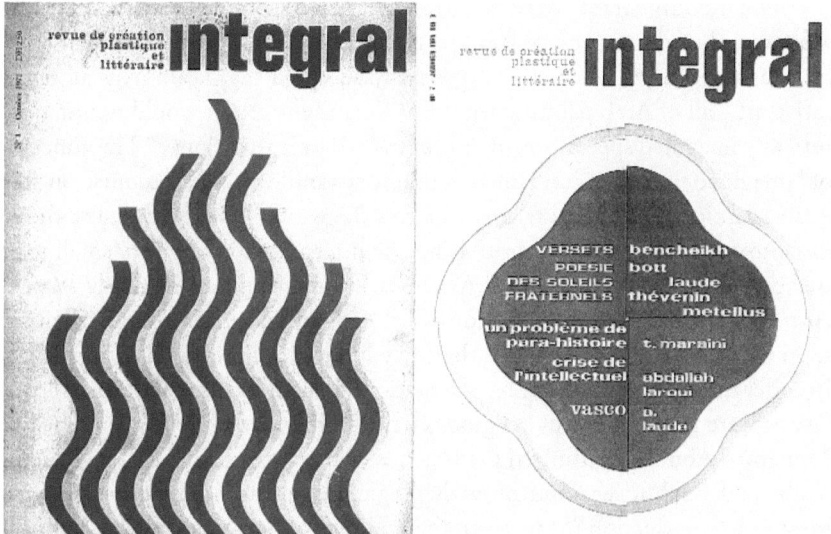

Integral journal covers by Mohamed Melehi. Left, October 1971; right, January 1974.

many hands. The critical frame of the journals functioned as did the critical practice of valorization in a museum. It staged modern Moroccan culture and ultimately educated and disciplined its visitors. Let us enter into its rooms.

Writing Modern Art in the Room of Islamic Art

From the outset, Moroccan visual artists were doubly marginalized. With both local and international definitions of Middle Eastern art tied to a limited pre-eighteenth-century definition of Islamic art, there was no space for contemporary painting, sculpture, and photography in either real or imagined musuems. In the discursive museum, the first room that needed to be cleared for modern art was the room of Islamic art as it was conceived in both national and Western museums. Modern art by Moroccan artists was marginalized in both Morocco and the West by several dominant discourses on Islamic art, including religious readings of prohibitions against figuration in art, popular interpretations of religious proscriptions, and Orientalist scholarship on Islamic art as an ahistorical and minor field. All these discourses provided resistance to claims of legitimacy and authenticity made by contemporary Arab canvas painters by buttressing the notion that the aesthetic identity of the Middle East and North Africa remained firmly entrenched in religious proscriptions on figurative art.

The monumentality of such representations of Middle Eastern art struck a blow at the authenticity of Arab painting and the authority of its painters. As Mohamed Aziza wrote, if it is generally accepted that Islam bans all figurative art, "all of Arab painting would be 'inauthentic' as it would not be tied into any imagined specific norm of the Arab-Islamic tradition."[20] The concept of "imagined norms" is fundamental to understanding how a discourse on the Arab-Islamic tradition in art arose. I stress the word "imagine" because these discourses derived their authority from the interpretation of a very small textual base in sacred Islamic texts.[21] As Oliver Leaman argues in his study *Islamic Aesthetics*, "Although the destruction of images may have been given a religious rationale, that does not establish that they in fact had a religious rationale."[22] In order to clarify the issue of representation in Islam for its practitioners, two fatwas were pronounced by religious clerics in the 1920s: the first, by Sheikh Mohamed Abduh, legitimized the practice of fine arts; the second, by Sheikh Mohamed Bakhit, legalized on a theological level the use of photographic means of reproduction.[23] However, the majority of both academic and popular discourse on the issue of representation in Islam returns to the hadiths and does not consider the more recent fatwas.

Islamic art history as an academic discipline formed in Europe was dominated by Orientalist ideas of Islam and the arts of its world until the 1960s and the scholarship of Oleg Grabar. Until this point, with few exceptions, the long history of the arts in the Islamic world, in the Middle East and North Africa, was treated ahistorically by scholars, who were more interested in formal studies of objects or in producing static generalizations about Islam and the "Arab people" than in addressing historic and geographic developments in the art of the region. Islamic art was placed as a categorically atemporal "other" in an evolutionary history of art that valorized European figurative experimentation as the epitome of advancement. The majority of early and mid-twentieth-century scholars agreed that Islamic art was primarily abstract and concerned with the divine, and in order to illustrate the universality of Islamic art as a nonpolitical ahistorical religious aesthetic (primarily consisting of calligraphy, arabesques, and floral decoration of objects), these scholars, while not denying the existence of other forms of art in the Islamic world, ignored it. The primacy of a discourse on Islamic art as a religious art that is uninterested in the secular world neglected a vibrant and political history of patronage, communication and commentary through form, and a tradition of figuration represented in objects such as manuscript illuminations of history and poetry, miniatures from those depicting such religious themes as the birth of Mohammed to those depicting picnic scenes in gardens, and finally, though later, a

Persian tradition of Qajar canvas paintings in oil.[24] Art in the Middle East was not all about timeless religion; rather the arts were deeply tied to the dynamic societies in which they were produced. They responded to change and presaged development.

Although today's academic scholarship on Islamic art has done great things to move away from this understanding of the art of the Middle East, popular and religious discourses around the Middle East often support pre-1960s academic discourse. While attitudes vary according to geographic location, gender, political affiliation, and education, many men and women in Morocco are quick to argue that art in the Islamic world is solely a celebration of the divine and that figuration is banned by the hadiths. The insistence of the Moroccan public on identifying their art as nonfigurative artisanal production based on their concept of Islamic art continues the colonial valorization of the craft industry and strikes at the very heart of Moroccan painters' claims to be representatives of a Moroccan cultural identity. When the majority of Moroccans believe that figurative art is banned by Islam, Moroccan painters must constantly explain and justify why their art is legitimately Moroccan and not Western.

Staking a claim for the legitimacy of their art in the Islamic world, Moroccan artists had to constantly engage with both academic and popular discourses that threatened their position. One example of such engagement is a lengthy article in the Moroccan cultural journal *Integral* that traced a genealogy of Arab painting from the present to the thirteenth-century Iraqi illuminist Al-Wasiti. At the beginning of the article Syrian art historian Afif Bahnassi declared: "For certain people, to speak of Arabic painting immediately implies re-posing the problem of the existence of representative art. This problem has been resolved a long time ago, and no longer does anyone believe that the practice of painting was prohibited in Islam."[25] But the problem had not been resolved for the Moroccan general public; in fact, to this day this discussion has continued. In his 1996 book *Esthétique et art islamique,* Moroccan scholar Moulim Al-Aroussi writes: "The image exists and moreover, with force. And yet despite this, we do not cease in posing the problematic on the possibility of figurative representation in Islam."[26] In reframing the definition of art, Moroccan painters had a double task presented to them: to establish the authenticity of Moroccan painting in the Islamic world and to establish the authenticity of Moroccan modern culture in the West.

Writing Modern Art in the Room of Naïve Art

In their interactions with Europe, Moroccan artists spent much discursive time not only establishing that their canvas painting was legitimate in a tradition of art in the Islamic world but also establishing that their work was authentically modern. In doing so, they had to contend with Western discourses that placed their work on the threshold of modernity and with art markets that valorized Moroccan unschooled painting and folk art over academic modernism. Paternalist attitudes and neocolonialist rhetoric from French critics unremittingly threatened the painters' claims to modernity and caused artists to address their exclusion from global aesthetic preoccupations. The discursive museum worked to clear the presentation of Moroccan art from patronizing narratives that maintained Moroccan art was young and naïve.

In the early 1960s, canvas painting in Morocco was labeled as a young art by critics and journalists, reflecting its relatively short history vis-à-vis canvas painting in the West but also its dynamism, boundless energy, and projects for change. Yet despite the youthful energy of their movement, and precisely because of its youthful history and institutions, Moroccan modernists remained trapped in a semiotic game emanating from the West that simultaneously encouraged their efforts and labeled them as underdeveloped. One French journalist of the 1960s exclaimed: "Moroccan painters are in the stage of an infant, feeling around before it can see, but at least the child is born!"[27]

On August 5, 1965, the Moroccan French-language newspaper *L'opinion* started a conversation about painting in Morocco that would occupy Moroccan art journalism for a decade to come. With more than thirty years of fine arts training and more than nine years of independence, Moroccan artists started to publicly discuss their place both in the international art world and at home. The conversation, titled "Young Moroccan Painters, Where Are We?" opened with a letter from the painter André Elbaz urging the Moroccan cultural elite to legitimize canvas painting as an integral part of Moroccan national culture and urging the Moroccan government to regard all Moroccan art as a national patrimony to be supported and protected. The deeper questions implicit in Elbaz's complaint were these: How could one decolonize canvas painting when the very form, the medium of expression, was seen by both Moroccans and the French as a colonial import whose sole market existed in the Metropole? How could artists emerge from a neocolonial relationship that persistently disenfranchised their own cultural authority? Elbaz ended his letter with an appeal: "Who will answer this challenge?"

The first response was published on August 11 and came from France. Over four days, French art critic and then curator at the Museum of Modern Art in Paris Pierre Gaudibert provided a history of Moroccan art and the development of canvas painting, a narrative frame. He made the following promise: "The Maghreb having become politically independent can lean on its traditions without becoming stuck in the repetition of the past, opening itself to international currents, without abdicating its originality." Gaudibert urged Moroccan painters to enter aesthetically into international modern art movements with the implied promise that there they would find a freedom of expression embraced by the rest of the world. His closing statement revealed the paternalism running barely below the surface of his advice: "[The creation of an infrastructure to support the arts] would amplify a movement that would place it [Morocco] in first place on the African continent."[28] Who would place Morocco first among African nations? From where did this legitimization spring? Gaudibert's words reveal the continuation of a Western developmentalist agenda that would modernize African culture through a framework of legitimization that compared nations and instilled a competitive drive for recognition and reward from the West.

But few Moroccan painters understood Gaudibert's comments in this way. These artists saw Europe and its art as spaces of freedom from the repressive political environment in Morocco, and, as for a great number of writers, ironically the site of freedom was within the borders and culture of their former colonizer. Many took refuge in the Western valorization of their work, for Western critics, unlike Moroccan critics, could "recognize" their worth through established disciplines and institutions of art history and aesthetics.[29] This position of seeking praise and legitimization from France was strongly critiqued by Moroccan writer Edmond Amran El Maleh: "The Moroccan painter is protected (the protectorate after all protects the personality) and is received according to structures already instituted a long time ago. . . . Even when he plays the *enfant terrible,* he is the recognized runt, revindicated by the holy mother of the Occident."[30] El Maleh critiqued the paternalist or maternalist attitude of the West as a continuation of colonial relationships of power and warned painters that the monumentalization of Western authority would maintain those infantilizing structures in place.

Although Gaudibert encouraged Moroccan artists to follow contemporary trends and enter the Western world of modern art, the French art market throughout the latter half of the twentieth century was more interested in developing a different Moroccan art: the naïve. Naïve art as an artistic genre refers primarily to the work of unschooled painters; in Morocco it started in the last years of the Protectorate and continues to flourish today as a valorized art form. Moroccan unschooled artists often represent daily life in Morocco in startlingly bright colors, playing with perspective and form and incorporating techniques from the popular arts onto their canvases. For example, the paintings of Fatima Hassan Al-Farouj are often inspired by henna patterns and Amazigh textiles;

the subject matter of these paintings is highly ethnographic, with their titles explaining daily scenes such as those of bread making. In the 1960s, for Moroccan academic painters and modernists who for the most part had rejected figurative art, the art market's valorization of the ethnographic was a bitter echo of Orientalist art and its fascination with the exotic other.

Moreover, the very term "naïve" was extremely problematic; no one failed to understand its developmentalist and evolutionary implications. When the book *La peinture naïve au Maroc* was published in Paris in 1985, the epigraph was a quote from Baudelaire's commentary on the Universal Exposition of 1855: "I have come to seek asylum in an impeccable naiveté."[31] The "primitive" and "pure" cultures he wrote about gave Baudelaire sanctuary from the ills of his modern world. The book's repetition of Baudelaire's words 130 years later hailed Morocco as pure, untouched, and timeless and its art, unperturbed by the burdens of knowledge, as faithfully reflecting the subconscious of its culture.

In the 1960s, it was precisely the use of terms such as "primitive," "pure," and "timeless" to describe Moroccan culture that Moroccan modernists saw as most dangerous to their projects for a national modern culture. In 1967 the Moroccan cultural journal *Souffles/Anfas* published an edition devoted to the state of contemporary art in Morocco. One of Morocco's academic artists from the Casablanca school, Mohammed Chebaâ, addressed the decolonization of Moroccan art through the question of aesthetics and genre in painting. He wrote:

> Schematically after independence, there was a colonial politic that wished to impose "naive art" as the sole form of expression in Morocco, a naiveté that corresponded to a local mentality and sensibility. What they wanted to affirm was that an under-developed country can only produce an art which is under-developed. They wanted to deny under-developed countries the right and the capacity to participate and contribute to universal art movements, deny the artist of these countries intellectual weight and modern aesthetic preoccupation.[32]

For Chebaâ the path to the decolonization of Moroccan culture lay in the firm refusal of the Moroccan arts to be associated in any way with anything but the modern. Although Chebaâ disputed the infantalization of Moroccan painting, his position was nevertheless based in an evolutionary discourse of modernity that placed cultural production on a scale from less to more developed. Unschooled and illiterate artists discovered and exploited by European dealers could not be seen as part of a modern national arts movement. According to Chebaâ, the practice of a power relationship that maintained Morocco in a subordinate position vis-à-vis the West directly denied modern Moroccan painters the freedom to participate on a global level, to participate in "universal art movements." Chebaâ argued that naïve painting followed the thematic agenda of Orientalist painters. Through an artistic vocabulary valorized for its authenticity and "truth," naïve painters continued to transmit a certain touristic image of Morocco that included the kasbahs, colorful markets, and scenes from everyday life. According to Chebaâ, the task of the Moroccan painter was to create a canon of signs and symbols that broke free from those Orientalist vocabularies of representation.

However, in his espousal of universal modern aesthetics and rejection of naïve art, Chebaâ performed in the same "theater of refusal," the same discursive space of marginalization, that he criticized.[33] Instead of changing the terms through which naïve art was seen, instead of removing naïve art from a teleological narrative, he further engrained the work of naïve painters in a discourse that maintained their identity as underdeveloped, and only one step underdeveloped from his own. Furthermore, in rejecting naïve art so vehemently, Chebaâ rejected another type of Moroccan artist: the female artist. Although academic painting during this period was dominated by men, many women participated in art as unschooled painters. Chebaâ's inherent exclusion of women simultaneously points to the primarily male nationalist model of the decolonizing world and to the heroic masculinity of abstract expressionist art.[34] How does one include work by women in the discussion of modern art in Morocco when these women artists had been doubly marginalized by the art movement and by leading men in their society?

This question caused many in the arts scene to struggle to rephrase and alter their rhetoric when describing the work of untrained painters. Thus one can find a number of articles that expound the innate genius of certain unschooled painters while defending them as everything but participants in "naïve painting." Among these painters it is interesting to note how the figure of Chaïbia was treated. An illiterate middle-aged woman and the mother of one of Morocco's most talented academic painters, Tallal Hussein, Chaïbia became one of Morocco's most famous naïve painters. In 1966 Zakya Daoud described Chaïbia's call to painting in a *Lamalif* article titled "A Promising Painter": "One day, Chaïbia had a strange dream, the subject of which was painting. The next morning, moved by this dream, she went to Marrakesh, and there she bought several pots of the most ordinary paint. That same day she painted, encouraged by her son Tallal and his friends Cherkaoui and Elbaz."[35] Daoud described the almost mystical and definitely spontaneous awakening in which the painter, attuned to her deepest subconscious, accepted the challenge to paint it.

This narrative is distinctly similar to certain European perceptions of Moroccan art as spontaneous and primitive in its relationship to subconscious forces, an art in which one can see the soul of the people.[36] But Daoud, as though she had Chebaâ's admonition in mind, continued: "However, the strangest thing in Chaïbia's case is that she isn't a naïve painter, or at least, she is much more than that. She mixes the naïve with the abstract." In a gesture to the academic painters of the time who were immersed in an abstract expressionism, Daoud claimed that Chaïbia's legitimacy as a Moroccan painter lay in her adoption of a certain and specific form of abstraction. However, Daoud could not hold to this rhetoric for long, and by the end of the article she had returned to a vocabulary of valorization echoing Western attitudes: "Chaïbia, more than any other painter, is endowed with the artistic talent of the Moroccan people because [in her work] she has reinvented everything without ever having read or seen or learned."[37]

What is important to note here, however, is that Chaïbia was not just a passive pawn in an art debate. Chaïbia's own narrative of her work as an artist, translated by Fatima Mernissi and first published in 1985, shows that she used Western valorization and support to better her own standing in a society that did not give her the means to express herself: "What could an illiterate woman do for a living? What do you think? I was a maid, a house maid. I cleaned houses and floors. . . . I felt I had to do something."[38] Even once she was established as a successful artist, Chaïbia lamented the lack of attention given to her in Morocco:

> On March 8 1984, we were invited to celebrate the Year of the Woman at the Ministry of Culture. I went but nobody paid attention to me. The same year I was invited to France. One hundred and seven women from all over the world were invited as artists. They chose one of my paintings to make a poster. It touched me very much. An artist like me needs that. *Educated women have to take care of us who did not have an education.* There must be a joint responsibility between women who are lucky enough to go to school and those who were not. An educated woman has to help the others, otherwise how can we change society? Morocco will not advance if those who have privileges forget the others.[39]

Although artists from the modernist elite bemoaned Chaïbia's success as a negation of their own efforts, Chaïbia criticized her marginalization as an uneducated woman in both Moroccan art circles and Moroccan society at large. She posed a larger question: Who has the right to participate in art and by extension in the production of cultural patrimony? Modern culture was not only male and expressionist.

The issue of naïve art goes to the heart of an argument over legitimacy and the control of cultural capital in Morocco, revealing the anxiety of the cultural elite about maintaining hegemony over contemporary cultural production, controlling its development and its direction. For Chebaâ, naïve painting as an aesthetic choice robbed the young painter class of its claims to global legitimacy and tied Moroccan arts in a neocolonial relationship with the West. Naïve painting challenged the idea that education was necessary to express oneself and participate in global culture. For Chebaâ's generation of artists who had struggled and worked their way through European institutions, the idea that the "illiterate" could control the arena of cultural production and represent the goals of an independent Morocco was a step backward in their progress toward modernity. However, in critiquing and devalorizing naïve art for its "native informant" status and its neocolonial and anthropological relationship with the West, Moroccan modernists often refused to recognize to what extent their own relationships with modern art were imbricated in uneven political and economic power structures. As Moroccan writer and theorist Abdallah Stouky commented, "In general the Moroccan artist is literally colonized by the West to the point at which he can only affirm the universality of his cultural past through the judgment and manipulation of the Other."[40] Although Moroccan modernists rejected the idea of naïveté and the identity politics that elevated and valorized unschooled art, they did not appear to reject their own "youth" and identity as subjects of Western narratives of art. In asking "Young Moroccan Painters, Where Are We?" they continued to locate themselves within a teleology of progress, deferring the larger and more problematic question: "Moroccan painters, why are we still seen as *young?*"

Writing Modern Art in the Room of the Nation

Postcolonial studies of art such as the work of Geeta Kapur on Indian art and Jessica Winegar's work on Egyptian art worlds have shown how discussions of modern art among artists were often set in the discursive frame of the nation. Kapur describes nationalism as a "foil to western universalism," and Winegar argues that the nation provided a sense of rootedness for artists' identities that were unremittingly questioned by the politics of international art markets. She writes that in Egypt "the historical constitution of the field of visual arts through colonialism, and its cementing through the institutions of nationalist socialism, necessarily linked visual art practice to national ideology" and that "the nation became the dominant frame through which the majority of art world people made sense of the transformation."[41]

In the Moroccan discursive museum, many artists believed that their work was fundamentally a deep transformative engagement in the decolonization of art and the creation of a national culture. However, at the same time, many felt that the nation as it was being defined postindependence by the government and conservative forces in society ultimately stifled their freedom on the level of expression and aesthetic choice. Artists thus used modernist discourse strategically to distance themselves from the demands and limits of a conservative nationalism led by politicians such as Al-Fassi who advocated a cultural return to an Arabized past and argued for an Arabization of social and economic structures such as education and law.[42] Artists performed what postcolonial critics such as Partha Chatterjee term anxiety: "a persistent complaint at being excluded from or discriminated against in the matter of equal access to the supposedly universal institutions of knowledge" but with a difference.[43] For institutions of universal modernity were not the only exclusionary forces; in many respects the nation was just as discriminatory and repressive. Many argued that the path to artistic freedom should be articulated *through* a cultural specificity that was rooted in the idea of the nation at large and its multiple practices and local histories of art. In order to have freedom in art and redefine national culture, the most expansive definition of the nation had to be created. As the manifesto of the Association for Cultural Research declared in *Souffles* in 1968, "We can thus use the term national culture in our counter-offensive to aggression, as an agent of detachment from dominant Western culture and as a framework for clearing out, deepening and re-edifying our own cultural givens."[44] Abdelkebir Khatibi repeated this committment to a critical definition of national culture in *Integral* in 1973 when he wrote: "In order to lift any ambiguity from the expression 'national culture,' one must insist on the fact that this historic project should be a contestation of values and institutions upon which the power of the dominant classes and imperial allies are founded. This is why we speak of a progressive national culture in the service of oppressed and exploited cultures."[45]

Moroccan artists performed their double bind between exclusionary grammars of the nation and the universal through a variety of discursive negotiations on the concepts of the individual artist, the nation and universal aesthetics. In 1967 Chaïbia's son, the academic painter Hussein Tallal, stated in the cultural journal *Lamalif:* "I am a Moroccan—thus I have no need to paint a mosque or a fantasia to prove it. It is not a nationality or an origin that tells me what to paint. And anyway, I think that Delacroix has already painted everything about Morocco and that there is nothing to add."[46] While Tallal's passport and place of birth identified him as Moroccan, artistically he saw himself as belonging to an international community with the freedom to paint his own individual vision. A facile nationalism that consisted of representing daily life in Morocco did not interest him, and he saw this aesthetic trend as merely continuing the pictorial representation of Morocco as structured through Orientalist painting.

His imagined museum was one in which art could be free from political pressures to create a certain type of heritage or folkloric propaganda.

Tallal recognized the extent to which French painting, especially the work of Delacroix, had been interested in documenting all things "Moroccan." Through image and object collection French art scholarship had attempted to narrate the essence of a Moroccan nation and to establish a canon of images through which Morocco could be defined. Couched in Tallal's declaration was the question of to whom this opus belonged. By participating in ethnographic aesthetics would he, as a painter, merely add to the reification of his nation by the West? Among his contemporaries, in his own work—oil paintings of distended clowns and children in bright, almost primary colors—he takes the least from a distinctly Moroccan visual vocabulary. In the painting *Cirque,* for example, Tallal presents two clowns whose forms betray a preoccupation with decay and alienation, silence and loneliness. The clowns, entertainers, are presented as entrenched in their own thoughts, distant from each other though in the same frame. Tallal's subject matter came from within, intensely personal and intensely pained. His neoexpressionist style had less to do formally with a distinctly "Moroccan" visual vocabulary that emerged from local cultural practices than with contemporaneous painters Francis Bacon and Jean Rustin.

Most artists did not advocate a rejection of national identity, but at the same time, they did not want the primary descriptor of their professional identity to start with the word *Moroccan*. In a 1967 piece in *Lamalif,* André Elbaz wrote: "I am not a Moroccan painter. I am Moroccan and I am a painter." Elbaz agreed with Tallal that national identity and artistic vocabularies should not be conflated. He did not want his work to be recognized or judged through an abstract geographic signifier of identity that could simultaneously give or take value away from his work. Art held captive to identity politics was exactly that, captive: "Art should touch the universal and not a nation. It is necessary to have liberty in art."[47] In claiming that art should touch the universal, Elbaz tried to extricate Moroccan painting from the position of an object in both nationalist and international market discourse, claiming that art as an autonomous sphere should be able to cross national boundaries freely. We can read here the struggle of artists to refashion the rules of what Olu Oguibe has termed the "culture game" in which non-Western artists are marketed through an otherness that gives value to their work through identity politics while simultaneously keeping them at the margins of the international art market.[48]

In Elbaz's words, we can see the emergence of a discourse on autonomy in art, one of the central tenets of cultural discourse on modernity.[49] This tenet was further articulated by Mohammed Benaïssa, the photographer who would become the mayor of Asilah in the 1970s, the minister of culture in the 1980s, and then in the 1990s the minister of foreign affairs, the position in which he currently serves. In 1973 he wrote: "We must be able to decolonize vision."[50] In this he argued not only for a decolonization of art from reified representations of Moroccan culture but also for a decolonization of art from politics. Benaïssa believed that photography as an art had to distance itself from French colonial photography and its impositions of moral narratives and judgments. However, it was also imperative that it avoid becoming an apparatus in new nationalist documentations of Morocco. Photography had to become independent of politics and history. Standing behind his words, in his work from this period Benaïssa delved into questions of form, light, and image construction rather than focusing on ethnographic or human subjects. However, as his political career attests, being an artist interested in formalist aesthetics did not preclude participation in the project of the nation-state.

We can look at Tallal, Elbaz, and the young Benaïssa as representatives of one strand of discourse, in which the decolonization of Moroccan art did not mean the reworking of an opus of colonial images or an ethnographic nationalization of vision but rather the freedom to focus on questions of form and "beauty" that *claimed* independence from politics and history. They did not want to be simply "Matisse's grand-sons."[51] In distancing art from religion, colonialism, and Moroccan Arabizing nationalism, these artists articulated a new path for individual and national development. In a 1966 article in *Lamalif,* Zakya Daoud, the journal's editor and chief art correspondent, described an exhibition of student work at the newly formed fine arts school of Casablanca that attempted to articulate this new nationalism through formalist aesthetics:

> In their first written statement, they [the students] say: "the world cannot live without art," "art is inseparable from life," "art is the true witness of the civilization of a country," "I want to practice this art that I have seen since my childhood in order to live in a different world," "art elevates" and "art will be my companion." These awkward sentences, in lines awkwardly traced in French while the majority of students had their start in Arabic, are pierced with a fervor, a need for work, to escape, the desire to attach oneself to something, to have a "companion," the end of a childhood, the beginning of a new nationalism: the practice of art and the beautiful.[52]

Daoud proposed a nationalism based in the "practice of art and the beautiful," with art and its practice as a vehicle for building both the nation and the individual. The students described their commitment to art through a prism of self-actualization (art as a companion, art as a means of escape, art as a means of work and a measure of worth), and Daoud transferred this description into a discourse on the actualization of the Moroccan nation. According to Daoud, through the production of beauty as an apolitical concept, Morocco would move away from the reifying discourses of colonialism, neocolonialism and political nationalism.

But does a movement toward formalist aesthetics necessarily decolonize art or extricate it from relationships of dominance? How is it possible to divorce the aesthetics of modernism from politics when its very formalism makes a political statement? In Daoud's comments we can already discern the problem with treating art and beauty as separate and autonomous from political relationships of power. In describing how the students' comments were "awkwardly traced in French," she unwittingly pointed to the crux of the issue: In whose language are questions of beauty articulated? And how are modernist aesthetics exclusionary? Why did discourses on art occur haltingly in French, while the majority of students spoke Arabic? In claiming that their work belonged to a "universal" aesthetic, many in the cultural elite struggled with how the term *universal* itself redrew unequal power relations with the West and excluded them as latecomers to a European tradition.

In the same 1967 issue of *Souffles* in which Mohammed Chebaâ argued for artistic freedom to participate in modern universal aesthetics, Toni Maraini argued that these issues were not only questions of style and language—for example, naïve art versus academic abstraction—but rather that they posed the dominant cultural and societal issues of the day. The choice to paint in an international style had to be about more than simply the decolonization of the arts through an imagined escape from politics. Moroccan painters could not just participate in an international modernity; they had to intervene in the discourse and create a specific Moroccan modernity:

> The intervention of painters (in the discourse of modernization) is necessary in order to propose, whether on the level of the every day technological object (the industrial plan) or whether on the level of the means of collective communication (graphic art, advertising, calligraphy, photography), an appropriate and healthy aesthetic. Their work is not only situated on the level of individual creation, but rather their work inscribes itself into the framework of a collective visual education.[53]

In this statement Maraini called the individual artist, who is both Moroccan and an artist, to social commitment in a collective vision. She warned against a modern international style of architecture and public art that remains culturally anonymous. The artist, whether more interested in the future or in the past, must acknowledge responsibility in the creation of a new modern culture that is historically and culturally specific. Otherwise, he or she will remain at the edges of the universal.

Writing Modern Art in the Room of the Universal

One response to the ambivalent position of Moroccan art in universal movements was to claim that abstraction was distinctly Moroccan. Some artists
argued that abstraction in visual languages came not only from a gradual decon-
struction of representational art in light of technological revolutions or from
a desire to empty art of its power to create master narratives through representation in reaction to the totalitarianism of the 1930s and 1940s; abstraction
came from Europe's interaction with the Middle East and Africa. These artists
used dominant discourses that posited abstraction as central to Islamic and
African art to legitimize their participation in international languages of abstraction, arguing that their arrival at modernist aesthetics was the result of a long
tradition in art and not the result of a superficial adoption of Western forms.
High modernism was not just European; it was authentically Moroccan. A
discourse on the Islamic roots of abstraction enabled artists to shift the location of "universality" in art away from the West and to distribute its capital
more equitably to Third World participants. By declaring abstraction a distinctly Moroccan practice, the Moroccan cultural elite tackled their position
of ambivalence vis-à-vis their peripheral position in international art circles.
In describing the dynamics of Egyptian modernism, Walter Armbrust has argued
that "Egyptian modernism allows for Europe as a cultural catalyst, but insists
on continuity between present and past: no rejection of tradition, and there-
fore none of the uncomfortable dislocation of European modernism."[54] I would
argue that uncomfortable dislocation was at the core of the modern art experience in Morocco, but that in fact "attempts to pair images of locally recognizable authenticity with Western cosmopolitanism" was one way to appropriate
space within exclusionary universals.[55]

Although artists such as Tallal, Elbaz, and Benaïssa looked to break with
the past, Melehi adopted, at least on the level of rhetoric, a modernism that did
not break with "tradition" but rather narrated present avant-garde art as solidly
linked to past cultural production as lived and recognized in every life. In 1971
Moroccan writers Abdelkebir Khatibi and Tahar Ben Jelloun responded to
Maraini's critiques of culturally *unspecific* international abstraction by producing articles claiming that the Moroccan movement of abstract painting was intimately tied to Moroccan cultural specificity. Their pieces appeared in the
inaugural issue of the Moroccan arts journal *Integral,* and both articles commented on the painter Melehi's work as an example of Maraini's call to social
commitment in the arts.[56] Ben Jelloun started his article with the valorization of
the fine arts in general: "What is the ability of the work of art if not to change

the fundamental structures of our imagination to the same extent that the economic revolution is changing our social structures?"[57] According to Ben Jelloun, modern art, like the modern economy, serves as a vehicle in the development of modern structures of thought. He argued that Melehi's work, in its abstraction of Moroccan reality, forces a change in the structures of thought through which Moroccan reality is experienced:

> The work of Melehi through its structure, forces a visual activity, an activity of re-creation rather than mere perception, a change of our aesthetic categories. . . . Here we must realize that Melehi's preoccupations essentially emerge from a Moroccan or Arab concreteness. On an aesthetic level this corresponds to other things than the gated kasbahs or exotic souks. It is not folklore. It is an empire of signs and forms existing by themselves and joining the most elevated level of visual research.[58]

Ben Jelloun tried to position Melehi in between two worlds, taking the best from both. While Melehi's act of creation takes place within the most elevated international standards of visual research, the base for his work is always a Moroccan material reality. Ben Jelloun argues that Melehi forces the viewer to change his or her vision of art in order to understand his work. If the viewer is from the West, the change would be from understanding Moroccan aesthetics as those of Orientalism, folk art, and naïve painting to understanding them as those of complex abstraction. If the viewer is Moroccan, the change would be from an understanding of abstraction in art that is based in an Islamic past to an understanding of abstraction situated in the international present.

One can only note how incredibly abstract Moroccan material reality becomes not only in Ben Jelloun's descriptions but also in Melehi's work. Melehi's visual style has remained remarkably stable over the span of his career and focuses on repeated waves in different bright and unnatural colors. This is not the figurative depiction of a medina, nor is it an older form of abstract expressionism. His choice of both palette and geometric forms is intimately tied to the international art scene of the 1960s and 1970s, visually echoing developments in what critics labeled "op art" and postpainterly abstraction.[59] So where can we read Moroccan specificity? Where is it located? In an analysis of Melehi's work, Khatibi provided a response: "There is no pause. There is no concession to figurative seduction, even if the waves seem to draw themselves from afar. Nothing trembles except the sign. . . . And it is through this worrisome necessity that ancestral memory finds itself: the work of Melehi joins to a certain point the abstract art of Arabic culture. But this is due to an appropriation, not an artifice."[60] For Khatibi, cultural specificity in Melehi stems from the appropriation of an entire tradition of abstraction into a world of semiotics in which modern or contemporary signs disturb and revive ancestral memory. The contemporary, modern world in which Melehi is invested is the visual means through which he interprets the Arab past. In abstracting certain images from ancestral memory, he turns them into signs that circulate and gain value and meaning through a new international memory.

The analysis of Melehi's work performed by Ben Jelloun and Khatibi shows how cultural discourse on modern art in Morocco navigated Western ideas of universality in visual art. Both Ben Jelloun and Khatibi appear in these citations as thinkers committed to the path of modernity in Morocco; however, this commitment to modernity caused them to embrace certain problematic teleological maps. By this I mean that in their descriptions of "tradition" and "ancestral memory" in Melehi's work, Ben Jelloun and Khatibi treated Moroccan culture as primary fodder for a technologically advanced visual language. Not unlike the dynamic present in Picasso's decontextualization and appropriation of African masks for his modern canvas, Melehi's work, as well as Ben Jelloun and Khatibi's interpretation of it, have presented a similar treatment of Moroccan popular and ancestral culture.[61]

In his 1972 article "Reflections on the Dialectic of Modernity and Tradition," journalist Abdallah Stouky traced a history of the colonial and neocolonial art world in Morocco and concluded:

> To turn around in order to regain possession of one's past is a rich political and cultural attitude but only if it is to regroup, revalorize and take inventory of the past in order to place oneself in a dynamic modern culture. . . . Traditional patrimony is one dimension of the Moroccan artist while modernity is another. It is up to him [the artist] to find the geometric link between the dimensions.[62]

Stouky called on the artist not to slip either into the world of international abstraction or into the recreation of the past but rather to find geometric links between the two that avoid a straight teleological line. He urged Moroccan painters not to abandon their modernist ambitions but to deny Europe and the West an exclusive right to their terminology. In urging them to reposition "universality," Stouky asked artists to think about the creation and manipulation of authenticity in art. How could a distinctly Moroccan visual vocabulary be created without succumbing to Western-style valorizations of popular and ancestral culture as folk art and without simply appropriating their grammar as raw materials for more technologically advanced abstraction?

For Farid Belkahia, a painter and then director of the École des Beaux-Arts in Casablanca, this challenge was answered by disrupting teleologies of practice in art education to reconfigure relationships between popular arts and academic abstraction. As Cynthia Becker writes, "Rather than teaching his students European artistic techniques based on three-dimensional representations of the human body and objects from nature, . . . he had them study indigenous Moroccan artistic forms such as Amazigh carpets, jewelry, calligraphy, and metal work techniques."[63] Nada Shabout describes the work of the Casablanca school in similar terms, writing, "They not only hoped to break away from academic teaching practices and naive painting but also to eradicate the distinction between craft and fine art that had been inherited from the West in order to reconcile the past with the present."[64]

Writing Modern Art Out of the Bazaar Museum

Stouky declared that the Moroccan artist must "create modern work and not succumb to the song birds chanting the authenticity of the bazaar."[65] By the "authenticity of the bazaar" he referred primarily to the marketing of "traditional" Moroccan arts for tourism under the Protectorate and their valorization by the postcolonial Moroccan state. He critiqued how the bazaar, the marketplace, dictated the terms of authenticity and value, and he asked artists to think about the location of authenticity in culture and who controlled it. An earlier article in *Lamalif* had expressed a similar point of view:

> We must preserve certain works that are systematically being bought by foreigners who are knowledgeable of their aesthetic and pictorial worth, but for this one must start to furnish a national market. . . . These revendications must be expressed energetically because at this moment our artists are becoming expatriates. Their native soil is ungrateful while foreigners offer a nurturing market.[66]

In answer to these calls, Moroccan artists started to redefine the term "Arab market" from its signification as the production of crafts and reified traditions to that of a dynamic art market that would serve as a sphere parallel if not equal to the Western-controlled discussion, appraisal, critique, and purchase of art.[67]

If in the 1960s Moroccan artists were looking almost exclusively to European art markets for legitimization, by the 1970s they had turned toward the incorporation of a culturally Arab sphere with a shared history. In the late 1960s, Abdellatif Laâbi had proclaimed that "the Arab world has always constituted a culturally and spiritually unified entity . . . with a common patrimony and cultural destiny."[68] In 1974, Chebaâ warned of the need for contemporary arts to surpass their current state of feuding terminologies and aesthetics and enter into a *political* reality that required unity. This need for unity, according to Chebaâ, was the direct result of recent political developments in the Arab world, notably the lack of unified support for the Palestinian cause. And we can see here, in his call to social commitment, how Chebaâ himself had come a long way from 1967, when he had advocated complete freedom and autonomy for the individual artist. At the end of his article, Chebaâ exclaimed that Morocco needed a new arts movement:

> The new artists will be driven by the bias of culture to become more and more conscious each day of their social insertion and will make their decisions based on their ties to class. Thus there will no longer be any egoistic painters, living on the lie that they have created from their underhanded artistic work. There will be painters that will live and feel the permanent palpitations of their community; that is, through their cultural insertion into society, painters will find once again the reason to exist as a **human-painter**.[69]

In questioning what Arab cultural unity meant, Chebaâ argued for social introspection and a new humanism. Located firmly within a local community, a new culture would solve the dilemma of the Arab man torn between the past and the future. These words of Chebaâ bring us back to the manifesto of the poet "adonis," whom I cited in the introduction to this study. In order to surpass a state of simulation, the Arab intellectual would have to question the deepest structures of his mind and fundamentally change himself.

When Abdallah Laroui published *The Crisis of the Arab Intellectual,* the book came as a painful critique to many in the Moroccan elite, but ultimately his argument was not dissimilar from Chebaâ's: change in the Arab world would have to occur on the level of the individual and his community in a radical reworking and liberation of thought. In the introduction Laroui explained that the book was not merely a critique of Arab culture in general and that of Morocco in particular, for the failure to extricate itself from a colonial relationship with the West or the grip of a reified Arab past. He wrote: "The main concern of the Arab intellectual is how to make his contribution to public life more effective. This book attempts to answer this ever relevant question."[70] The question, reformulated, regarded progress. How could Arab society move forward rather than remaining in relationships of the past?

In order to address this question, Laroui analyzed how tradition was manipulated in the hands of a political elite. Working within a Marxist model, he argued that the traditionalization of culture is a form of alienation: "There exists another form of alienation in modern Arab society, one that is prevalent but veiled: this is the exaggerated medievalization obtained through quasi-magical identification with the great period of classical Arabian culture."[71] Though Laroui primarily defined cultural production as the written arts, in the visual arts the Moroccan state was equally interested in protecting and sanctifying classical Islamic arts and disseminating their importance. But a more provocative indictment to read in Laroui's words is that of the contemporary arts themselves and their claim to legitimacy through an Islamic tradition of abstraction. The claim to legitimacy is made through Islamic arts because it can be accepted in a climate in which a revival of Islamic culture is a priority. Although movements advocating a turn to the "modern" use the past to justify their claims, Laroui writes that a political elite will always claim the superiority of tradition to modern culture. This is not the path to change. As he maintained:

> The political elite directing the national state, the traditional or modern intellectual elite, the civil or military bureaucracy, the technocratic stratum etc.—none of these groups, all of which belong to the petite bourgeoisie, wishes for or seriously imagines a victory of the modern over traditionalist thought. No one would like to see modern rationality over step the limits of the factory, the public bureau, or the office. . . . Modern culture is thus a means, a tool, an ideology subordinated to traditional culture, where the latter is propounded as an intangible value. These points permit us to explain the permanence of traditionalist thinking.[72]

The model that Laroui proposed to the Arab intellectual to break through traditionalist thinking is one of rigorous and thorough critique: continued efforts to free culture from the past and to reanimate that which has been reified for political ends:

> All too long has the Arab intellectual hesitated to make radical criticisms of culture, language and tradition. Too long has he drawn back from criticizing the aims of local national policy, the result of which is a stifling democracy and a generalized dualism. He must condemn superficial economism, which would modernize the country and rationalize society by constructing factories with another's money, another's technology, another's administration.[73]

Laroui wrote this book in 1971 looking back at the events of the 1960s. He was seeking revolution, a decolonization not only of Moroccan culture but of socioeconomic reality itself. The discursive museum should be opened to and become a fundamental part of Moroccan society at large and not merely the domain of intellectuals and a social elite.

Opening the Discursive Museum to Public Transcripts

During the 1960s and early 1970s, Moroccan intellectuals navigated discourses that constantly positioned them between the West, a reified nationalist Arab past, and a nebulous Moroccan modernity. The cultural elite whose words I chronicled earlier were intensely committed to the idea of modernity as a means to leave an "underdeveloped" or "timeless" identity. In writing modern art, artists attempted to delimit spaces in dominant discourses in which they could stake claims to cultural modernity and solidify their discursive authority. Perhaps not too surprisingly, these discursive institutions replicated many of the dynamics of exclusion and discrimination present in actual museums and art markets: on a local level, they regulated who could enter the conversation on cultural modernity and how their work could be seen.

In many respects, and despite their best intentions, artists and intellectuals of the 1960s and 1970s saw the Moroccan public at large as ever-undifferentiated masses that needed enculturation in order to participate in culture. As Abdellatif Laâbi put it in the 1980s, for the cultural elite, interacting with the Moroccan people was a form of tourism; many intellectuals, he argued, have "an exterior vision of popular culture and look upon it with a neo-touristic or auto-exotic gaze."[74] The Moroccan public was figured as a monolithic bloc condemned to never make the transition from understanding craft to appreciating art by themselves. While Abdellah Hammoudi argues that a "master-disciple" authoritarianism is inherent in Moroccan society, elite condescension toward nonelite Moroccans mirrors the French colonial condescension and politics of exclusion that artists and intellectuals fought against in their own relationships to the art market.[75] Although education was seen by the Moroccan cultural elite as crucial to the development of taste for the fine arts and painting in general, the education of the Moroccan public at large was by no means smooth.

The process of controlling access to art and culture, and ultimately protecting elite hegemony, can be read through newspapers, television programs, and even cinema. In their work on popular culture in Egypt, Walter Armbrust and Lila Abu-Lughod both show how establishment-controlled media developed ideologies of enculturation that educated the public while protecting a certain elite domination of culture.[76] Likewise, Jessica Winegar has written that in the case of Egyptian visual art, in order "to achieve this particular elitist modern, they engaged in strategies of 'containment' of the lowbrow and especially of the middlebrow." Discussion and discipline of popular taste "was one of the main exercises of power in which artists engaged, and was in large part shaped by their own ambivalent position on the margins of the petite bourgeoisie and intellectual life, and by their subordination to economic and political elites."[77] The Moroccan cultural elite of the period engaged in the enculturation and discipline of the Moroccan population, in particular the growing urban bourgeoisie, that historically antagonizing agent of projects of aesthetic modernity. In order for this population to understand their work, they would have to make the transformation from what Pierre Bourdieu has called in the French context the "naïve spectator" to the informed viewer. Bourdieu tells us, "Like the so-called naïve painter who, operating outside the field and its specific traditions, remains external to the history of art, the 'naïve' spectator cannot attain a specific grasp of works of art which only have meaning—or value—in relation to a specific history of artistic tradition."[78] Having freed themselves from the marker "naïve" through complex discursive negotiations, artists were not so quick, however, to liberate their public of such a marker, and we can read this control and renegotiation of cultural capital in the national press.

In his work *Domination and the Arts of Resistance: Hidden Transcripts,* James Scott defines a public transcript as a script that is read and written in the public domain and a site in which knowledge is transmitted between groups of people. Scott argues that the public transcript transmits not only knowledge but also the power relations embedded in the production of said knowledge:

> In ideological terms the public transcript will typically, by its accommodationist tone, provide convincing evidence for the hegemony of dominant discourse. It is precisely in this public domain where the effects of power are viewed, relations are most manifest, and any analysis based exclusively on the public transcript is likely to conclude that subordinate groups endorse the terms of their subordination and are willing, even enthusiastic, partners in that subordination.[79]

For Scott the public transcript includes documents such as colonial and state reports, government publications and newspapers, and academic publications that participate in the solidification of dominant discourses by providing images and evidence of their legitimacy and by displaying the "willing" subordination of other discourses.

If we look at the major Moroccan national newspapers from the postindependence period, we can read directives, images, and evidence of the importance of modern art as well as exchanges of opinion between the cultural elite and a growing bourgeois public in which the public becomes a willing if not an enthusiastic partner in its subordination. Newspapers stressed the importance of viewing modern art as part of modern life, and in so doing they attempted to define taste in and for art. In the 1960s, three major Moroccan daily newspapers, the French-language *L'opinion* and *Le petit Marocain* and the Arabic-language *Al-'Ālam,* printed articles on art and culture daily. Each newspaper had a cultural section located toward the back of the paper, written for the most part by intellectuals, writers, and arts journalists. The three newspapers differed but slightly in both their approaches to presenting culture and what "culture" meant. This was due in part to the specific urban demographic of their readerships, identified by place of residence and political opinion.[80]

While artists and critics provided evidence of the legitimacy of their vision of modern Moroccan culture, newspapers published letters of critique from the general public. These letters were never a serious threat to the discourse on the dominance of the artist; in fact, public critiques were often surprisingly trivial. By publishing these critiques, the "public" transcript retained its image of public participation while maintaining its discursive authority vis-à-vis a new bourgeois class and their definitions of modernity.

In its treatment of culture, *L'opinion,* the newspaper of the ruling political party, Istiqlal, focused on the visual arts more than the written. In so doing, the paper showed a commitment to modern visual culture. Not only did it list all gallery openings and expositions, but it also published reviews and critiques of the art scene in Morocco. The newspaper encouraged its readers to attend these openings and stressed how important visual art was for Moroccan culture and for the Moroccan public. In an article on an exhibit of Moroccan painter Kacimi, one journalist exclaimed, "It is with joy that lovers of painting in Rabat learned of the exhibit of the young painter Kacimi that took place in the Maison de la Pensée. Painting that is significant and modern."[81] In this article, not only was Kacimi's painting identified as "significant and modern," but, by extension, modern art and a taste for it were signaled as means through which a modern identity and social distinction could be cultivated. Some artists enjoyed their relationship with the emerging bourgeoisie and did what they could to profit from the situation. As Abdelhak Sekkat wrote: "Young Moroccan painters, in order to give a certain importance to their work, asked for elevated prices in selling their work as if the monetary value of a piece was a guarantee of its worth."[82]

The newspaper encouraged the development of a taste for art not only through extensive listings but also through rhetoric. Titles were written in the imperative: "Admire This Work of Art!"[83] and "Read This!" the title of a serial column by the writer "Ben." Imperative structures such as *il faut* (one must) permeated the texts: "One must visit this exhibit to understand the work accomplished" and "Artists and amateurs of painting do not forget to visit this exhibit. You will be welcomed!"[84] In one case, the article even attempted to persuade the public to forgo a day at the beach in order to visit a gallery: "Whatever it might be, this week you should delay one of your departures for the beach or escape from your office to admire his work."[85] Rather than going to the beach, an activity open to any Moroccan, the reader was called to distinguish himself from the crowds and partake of higher forms of culture. This insistence on guiding the readership to the art gallery not only delineated the requisites for acquiring cultural capital and the prestige associated with it but also can be read as a thinly disguised act of discipline for the emerging leisure class. Even when articles revealed a frustration with this public, they continued to affirm the importance of the art exhibit: "It is useless to encourage our readers to come and admire the magnificent work of the thirty-six artists represented. Let us hope that exhibit exchanges can be made in Morocco so that the public can better acquaint itself with the present art."[86] The public should not only better its acquaintance with art but also better itself.

Many articles in *L'opinion* attempted to engage the reader in dialogue, and, testifying to how heated that debate could become, a formal space was created for readers' responses under the heading "Our Readers in Anger."[87] While this space was open to any and all subjects and appeared in different sections of the newspaper, it often made its way into the cultural pages, where the sources of anger and the topics engaged were often surprising. On April 10, 1965, the following anonymous letter was published:

> Decidedly, in the television program "Arts and Letters," painting is very fashionable. All the subjects presented by Miss "Arts and Letters," if I may call her that, deal exclusively with painting exhibitions. Maybe this is to inspire us to take the vocation of an artist-painter. Painting is indeed an art that should merit our attention, but once again these programs on painting must be agreeably and properly presented, which, unfortunately is never the case![88]

This angry reader had already acquired a certain amount of social distinction. He watched television programs on art and literature and recognized the importance of modern culture. The opening of his letter might lead us to think that it would present specific ways in which the larger Moroccan public should be educated in order to understand the value and significance of Moroccan painting. However, the reader critiqued the presentation of the subject matter solely on an aesthetic level: "I have to say that Miss 'A and L' is not cut out for this genre of program. She is not photogenic. As soon as she appears on the screen she starts stumbling and stuttering. . . . To judge by the interviews she conducts so ingeniously with artist-painters, she gives the impression of a timid and shy beginning-grade school-teacher asking questions to a student."[89] The reader was more concerned with the presenter of the program than with the subject matter itself; for him, "Miss 'A and L'" did not correspond to an appropriately professional image of a television presenter. What models of propriety was the reader using? And what spectrum of positive and negative femininity was he engaging when he simultaneously desired the image of a beautiful woman and derided the presenter for being too submissive in her interactions with modern culture? The letter raised the larger issue of how modern culture should be presented and engaged in the media, but in its personal attack on "Miss 'A and L,'" it stumbled into complex articulations of desired gender roles in modern Moroccan society.

"Miss 'A and L'" answered the reader's letter with a defense of her conduct, redeploying the gendered vocabulary of the reader's attack. She refers to herself submissively in the third person and defines her position in a passive tense:

> As Miss "A and L" has pointed out several times, she would only simply wish to be the voice through which a being, that usually expresses himself through the paint brush, could make himself known. A voice that is sometimes naïve, admittedly, reflecting the simple and pure emotions of an art that is even more touching. . . . Long live painting on television and long live painters!"[90]

Her reply was less concerned with art than with articulating her position as a woman in modern Moroccan society, a position that she identified as being as new as painting. "Miss 'A and L'" defended herself by engaging gender descriptors such as naïvité, simplicity, and purity as *valorized* categories of the feminine and of art itself. Although this exchange might have opened up a more profound conversation about the role of women in the arts or about models of disseminating modern culture to the general public, it remained entirely superficial where art was concerned. Although the reader certainly threatened the discursive authority of "Miss 'A and L'" and opened a fascinating window into gender negotiations among the urban bourgeoisie during the 1960s, the public transcript on modern art in Morocco remained fundamentally unengaged.

Another letter by an angered reader complained of the oversophisticated and florid writing of journalists covering the arts. The reader in question had read an article in the newspaper *Le petit Marocain* about the painter Miloud and had written a response to *Le petit Marocain* that they failed to print. He appealed to *L'opinion* as a legitimate newspaper that knew the responsibilities of the press to publish his letter, and they printed it in the space headed "Our Readers in Anger." The letter described the incomprehensibility of the prose used by the Moroccan art critic:

> Wanting to say too much, and too well, he says nothing clearly. This question of form is more grave than it appears. For the confusion in written expression encourages an intellectual confusion. Finally to what ends can an article of this genre serve? Not for the public, who is already too abused by it, nor to painting, for which it has more serious consequences. The function of a critic in essence is not to praise without end, but to help the artist to see clearly by giving him an intelligent point of view.[91]

When we read this letter in conjunction with the previous one, we can see the problem of choosing the correct tone and style with which to address the

Moroccan bourgeoisie. While one presenter supposedly infantalized both painting and the public, another critic confused issues through an overly sophisticated rhetoric that communicated little. The angered readers posed the right
questions: what is the function of a critic, and what form should critics use to
communicate with both the artists and the public? Although they said little
about the art itself, these letters attested to the formation in 1960s Morocco
of an art public with differing levels of education and distinctions of taste.

The letters sent to *L'opinion* often targeted the very question of the identity
of the Moroccan art public. In one such letter, the reader Lekbir Chihab, a reg-
ular correspondent to the paper, wrote to ask who was the public of national arts:

> I am writing to you this time with a very important question: the public for
> Moroccan literature. . . . Is the problem the lack of a public capable of tasting and
> savoring our real national literature? Illiteracy, poverty, do they render us impo-
> tent vis-à-vis the creation of a true national literature and of a diligent encour-
> aging public? . . . Without arts and without letters, there is no progress!"[92]

Although Chihab specifically targeted literature in this letter, the question of
the public for art and letters was the same. Through semantic choices, Chihab
addressed a fundamental issue facing Moroccan culture: taste. Who possessed
the taste for the arts? Who possessed the ability to savor Moroccan national culture? Although he questioned how an illiterate and poor public could understand the value and worth of the arts, he reiterated the importance of the arts
in terms of progress and modernization. In advocating mass education and in
addressing the question of poverty in Morocco, Chihab distinguished himself
both from the urban poor and from the status-conscious bourgeoisie to join
forces with the progressive artist.

The newspaper *L'opinion* was a national paper that was run by the political party in power. It had a cosmopolitan and relatively elite public readership,
and its correspondents were writers and intellectuals in their own right.[93] *Le petit
Marocain* was a regional paper based in Casablanca, and its audience was primarily the new bourgeoisie that was taking shape in commercial Casablanca.[94]
Le petit Marocain covered cultural events, with a heavy focus on the visual arts,
and, like *L'opinion,* it insisted that the public become involved in culture with
prods such as "The Casablanca public is called to attend this conference."[95]
But unlike *L'opinion, Le petit Marocain* had a very specific audience; the newspaper, owned by the French banker and businessman Yves Mas, functioned as
a society paper, and in so doing defined its public as status-seekers. This was
one of the main critiques of the paper by Abdellatif Laâbi, who in 1966 published a piece in *Souffles* criticizing both the paper and its readers. He wrote:

We leave them [the reading public] the indescribable columns of *Le petit Marocain*. Coffee with cream, crossword puzzles, the summary of sports events and the daily horoscope have never hurt anyone. For these "intellectuals," there are of course issues of family planning, the Karsenty galas and the ciné-club. But to all these routine and constrained readers of *Le petit Marocain* we wish a bad appetite.[96]

According to Laâbi, the audience of *Le petit Marocain* was interested only in crossword puzzles and daily horoscopes; in other words, they were a leisure class with few pressing concerns. Their financial situation was stable, and their largest problems were which galas to attend and how to plan their families. But what was so indescribable to Laâbi *about* the cultural columns of this newspaper? It was precisely *what* the newspaper articles described.

The majority of articles on art in *Le petit Marocain* did not describe the content of exhibitions. Rather, they listed the people in attendance at the exhibitions. The newspaper blatantly treated culture as a commodity: art varied in value depending on the marketplace and the society of people surrounding it. Although this may have been a disservice to the artists of the time, it gives the historian a glimpse of the Casablanca social scene and the identity of the Casablanca art public, for the articles in *Le petit Marocain* were essentially lists of names. One article in particular had three lines of text and then seventy names of people in attendance; another included twenty-four names, yet another twenty-eight.[97] So who attended these exhibits? The majority of the names listed were French and Italian, testifying to the continued presence of a European community in local cultural affairs. Other names included those of Moroccan cultural ministers and government dignitaries. The art scene had become a good opportunity for the Casablanca economic and political elite to be seen, and in modern and progressive surroundings.

Although the French-language papers reported extensively on activities in the realm of the visual arts, the Arabic daily *Al-'Ālam* preferred to focus on the written arts and traditional cultures in general. *Al-thaqāfa,* the Arabic term for culture, has wide connotations, its meaning ranging from culture in general to art and tradition. In this sense, the paper carried over different concepts of cultural worth formed on a linguistic divide. But although *Al-'Ālam* did not give primary focus to the visual arts, as did its French counterparts, it did not completely abandon them. Almost every Friday, the paper ran a section titled "Al-'Ālam al-fani" (The world of art). The interviews with artists and essays on both European and Moroccan art were similar in style and tone to those in *L'opinion,* which is to say a mixture of the didactic and the laudatory. However, on May 2, 3, and 4, 1965, *Al-'Ālam* published a long feature article titled "The Springtime of Art in Settat" in which the critic went beyond the usual treatment of contemporary art in Morocco.[98] The opening lines were almost celebratory as the journalist introduced the exhibit: "The municipal hall in the town of Settat opened its doors in welcome of its artist visitors: graphic artists and sculptors, Moroccan and French, and welcomed with them all lovers of art." But barely out of the first paragraph, the author warned the reader that his article would not be one of pure adulation: "In the exhibition hall the artists presented their work in bouquets of both painted and chiseled artistic production. From these bouquets some [flowers] had bloomed, some were at the height of their maturity, some were covered with a thick layer of dust, and some had wilted and withered or were in the process of doing so."[99] The writer chose the flower, a proven device for the representation of beauty in both European and Arabic traditions, to enter into a discussion of aesthetics. It is interesting that the writer chose such an organic metaphor for an art that was seen as artificially imposed in his country. What is most important, however, is the writer's opposition to the discourse that Moroccan painting was just a young art. This critic presented what others called the "youth" of the Moroccan arts in its many different stages of development. And in his view, a view that I have not seen elsewhere, the work of some unnamed artists was already past its pinnacle and had withered and died.

Although using this metaphor of decay was an innovative way to treat the Moroccan arts, the most provocative and significant statement followed. The writer asked what spectators really got out of such an exhibition. He described the public as composed of curious and friendly spectators who had come to follow different developments in art. But, as he wrote, "Many of them left the exhibit with nothing except for disdain, for most of them only saw confusion inside the costly and precious frames, a confusion called art."[100] Here the writer gave us a glimpse of public reaction, though no specifics as to the composition of the art public itself.

Although one could read the initial analogy of Moroccan painting and sculpture as existing in different conditions of development as a positive indication of the success of the art in taking to its new soil, the presumably Moroccan public at the exhibit read this as a failure. Not only did the work presented at the exhibition lack a sense of unity, but most of it appeared either amateurish or stale. Furthermore, in writing that some paintings had less value than their frames, the writer critiqued the idea that as long as it was packaged and presented in a costly fashion, any painting could be worth something. What is interesting in his statements is that the critic was ultimately concerned with "good taste" in art. What the public should consume rather than bad art in costly frames was good art, and the newspaper was there to help the public make these distinctions.

The author of the article did not let this criticism color the entirety of the feature. Over two days he examined the work of three male painters and one female painter and finished by encouraging the newspaper's readers to come out in support of the abundance of exhibits and artwork in the country: "Truth be told, all these artists, with their varied experiences and [personal] quests, turn Moroccan art into a mirror of a new and daring soul, and a taste which is gradually spreading and taking hold. Hurray for these artists! And please [give us] more exhibits like this one, young folks!"[101] The conclusion of his article, the phrase *yā shabāb* (young folks), has several significations. Not only can the term *shabāb* be used to address young people in general, but it can also have a proletarian connotation, often signifying solidarity between working people. The use of the word *yā* is a direct interpellation of the readership, the audience and artists. And thus it is very interesting to find the terms *yā shabāb* and *dhawq* (taste, savoir faire, sensitivity) in the same three lines. In this moment the writer specifically addressed the Moroccan public at large and not just the bourgeoisie or the cultural elite, addressing it by name. In so doing he emphasized the importance of that which had been traditionally cultivated by the elite and now was *potentially* within the majority's reach: taste.

Newspapers such as *L'opinion, Le petit Marocain,* and *Al-'Ālam* all participated in valorizing the visual arts, and although they were more conservative than the progressive art that they presented, they supported the cultural elite's discourse on the importance of modern art for a modern Morocco. Published critiques of art by readers and writers alike remained on a superficial level that never threatened or truly engaged the transcript on Moroccan painting. Public transcripts in the press were involved in educating the public and disciplining them to become the ideal audience for a museum that would one day no longer be imaginary by turning art appreciation into a public activity that built social distinction, and in turn creating new public spaces (albeit censored) for art. The newspapers thus succeeded in creating a public transcript that ultimately supported the discursive museum and rarely called into question its fundamental discourse.

Conclusions

How do we understand the work of the discursive museum in hindsight? Was it just the work of artists who struggled to escape their identities as "comprador intelligentsia"? Kwame Anthony Appiah writes, "Postcoloniality is the condition of what we might ungenerously call a comprador intelligentsia: of a relatively

small, Western style, Western-trained, group of writers and thinkers who medi-
ate the trade in cultural commodities of world capitalism at the periphery."[102]
On one level this certainly fits the description of Moroccan artists who built
their discursive museum in order to escape constant marginalization at home
and abroad. But as I hope I have shown through the many negotiations internal to the imaginary museum, Moroccan artists argued for their relevance in
the world at large. They were not only concerned with their position in Western art markets but were committed to being a transformative force in Moroccan society, providing a critique of the restrictions of a nationalism that was
fixated with the past, and arguing against a superficial modernity that attracted
those in power. Art historian Rasheed Araeen writes:

> The main problem of modernism in art in Africa in general (I say in general
> because there are exceptions . . .) seems to be that it suffers from a dependency
> syndrome, with the result that the artist is in a constant struggle to catch up with
> what is happening in the West. There are of course modern artworks that look
> profoundly African, but this look is deceptive. Often, it is no more than a gloss
> over what has originated from the West.[103]

But I would argue against this position. Rather, like Olu Oguibe, I think it is
more important to focus on how art and artists that might *always* have been
seen as marginal to European modernism have made significant contributions
to creating new and dynamic cultures that address and contest this marginalization locally and across postcolonial communities. Oguibe tells us:

> Shouting against Eurocentrism is a been-there, done-that. What is required now
> is that we read within the frames of a larger historical moment that modernism
> ever was, namely the struggles of colonized peoples to contest their predicament
> and forge their modernity, as well as subsequent complications and reconfigura-
> tions of that predicament and their meaning and implications in the postcolonial
> milieu.[104]

In writing their modernity, Moroccan artists articulated a space for their work
within and against dominant discourses emerging around them. In a 1981 interview, Abdellatif Laâbi insisted that even in its failures, the work of the cultural
actors of the 1960s and 1970s succeeded in inspiring future generations of
artists and writers.[105] Today Moroccan artist collectives and projects that seem
to move more easily, but not yet freely, beyond confining experiences of alienation and integration, between home and exile, between memories of the past
and the future, and exhibit their work to heterogeneous publics at home and
in the larger art world, do so in large part due to the work of the first discursive museum. The lack of a physical building and the absence of an audience

haunts artists but does not mean that tactical architectures of art and frameworks of understanding cannot be built.

In her work on patrimony in Jordan, Irene Maffi cites Jocelyne Dakhlia's work on memory and text in North Africa, stating: "In the North African Muslim tradition the notion of heritage is passed down less by built patrimony than by textual transmission."[106] The written or oral text rather than the physical place becomes a site of memory and transmission, and what becomes an object of memory is rigorously constructed and remembered. In her book *Impasse of Angels*, Stefania Pandolfo has shown and performed this dynamic of memory and discourse in a Moroccan context, creating a textual space of memory through the polyphonic collection of enunciative voices. Her book has become a "dialogical space of a locution," a space that does not map out subjects of knowledge but rather performs their construction and dissolution.[107] In their discursive museum Moroccan artists created patrimony through textual constructions and dissolutions. In so doing they articulated art, performed memory, and transmitted patrimony more effectively and more substantively than other, physical, museums in Morocco.

Five

Taking Art to the Streets:
The Ephemeral Outdoor Museum
as Contact Zone

Every summer, cultural festivals take place all over Morocco. From June through August 2006, more than fifteen festivals of art, music, and cinema were staged in beachside towns and large urban areas. With displays and performances that mix elements of folklore, technology, the "traditional," and the "modern," the streets of Moroccan towns and cities become an animated scene for the articulation of Moroccan contemporary culture. So animated, heterogeneous, and pluralistic has this festival scene become that the semiofficial newspaper for the Islamist PJD (Justice and Development) party has called these street festivals "vectors of decadence," and, ironically, certain Moroccan artists have requested legal protection from the state not to be marginalized. This stance of both Islamists and marginalized artists on restricting the nature of festivals was critiqued in the cover story of the January 5, 2007, edition of the Moroccan magazine *Telquel*, in which the editors listed ninety things in Moroccan society that they are "sick of" *(y en a marre)*. Included was a surprising entry on "des rabat-joie pendant la saison des festivals" (the wet rags of the festival season):

> Antifestivals have found a newspaper to support their cause: Attajdid, the semi-official daily newspaper of the PJD that, once the summer has come, never misses the opportunity to judge these artistic manifestations "vectors of decadence" for Morocco. This point of view denies the millions of happy festivalgoers the occa-sional musical free oasis in the grand cultural desert of Morocco. Likewise, we

are sick of the attitude of Moroccan artist unions who reproach the "foreign invasion" in festivals (understand this as the invasion of groups that are more modern than they are). Currently, in December this conglomeration of "has been"
artists even concocted a legal project to "protect the marginalized Moroccan artist
in artistic manifestations." Yes, but who will protect us from them?[1]

As the article asks, why deny millions of Moroccans the pleasure of cultural
experience vis-à-vis the vast desert of existing elite cultural institutions?

As we know, this metaphor of the desert to describe the situation of the arts
in Morocco is not a new one. Most recently, in a comment on the lack of art
infrastructures, virtual artist Hassan Darsi filled a gallery space with sand, plexi-
glassed the entrance so that visitors could see him, and spent several days in
this space with two artists and a cat.[2] Perceiving Moroccan state museums as part
of a lifeless, arid cultural environment in contrast to the life-giving, fertile nature
of the festival works well in parallel with Barbara Kirshenblatt-Gimblett's
metaphor of the museum as a "form of internment—a tomb with a view," in
contrast to the multisensory "environmental performance of culture" in festivals.[3] As she writes, "Though museum exhibitions can also be considered a form
of environmental theater—visitors moving through the space experience the
mise-en-scène visually and kinesthetically—they tend to proceed discursively.
Arts festivals are generally less didactic and less textual," and "they require selec-
tive disattention, or highly disciplined attention, in an environment of sensory
riot."[4] Indeed, whether listening to young *gnawa*-fusion bands, observing painters at work, or witnessing someone pulling a bus with his teeth in a faith-
inspired test of strength, the experiences that the festival offers both Moroccans
and foreign tourists are overwhelming in their richness and diversity.[5]

One of my favorite sensory moments at a festival occurred in Rabat in the
summer of 2005. Standing under a tree in the late afternoon on the corner of
Avenue Mohammed V and Al Forat across from the central roundabout of the
old ville-nouvelle, which faces the train station, a curious mix of people (old,
young, Moroccan, African, and we) listened to a band. The musicians had
arranged themselves in a circle under the tree, and the audience stood around
them enjoying the smell of a particularly fragrant plant as the evening brought
in cooler air. We listened quietly to their music, which was inspired by a mixture of elements: *gnawa,* mellow Bob Marley, rock, and the classical strains of
an Arab orchestra. Every now and then we could hear cars going by and the
drums of a folkloric *gnawa* group that was moving up and down Mohammed
V nearer the medina, but the scene by the tree was one of idyllic calm as people lingered in the oasis to take in the sounds of the group and escape the city
traffic for a moment.

Although Moroccan art festivals could be seen as fairs and spectacles that have little to do with museums, they have long functioned as an antagonistic model for the Moroccan museum and demonstrated how a museum institution could interact with its public and what multilayered spaces of experience it could create. Moroccan cultural festivals are not merely undisciplined carnivalesque events that stand in opposition to the museum as it might have been perceived in late nineteenth-century European cities.[6] Rather the arts festivals work within a general history of museum transformation in the United States and Europe over the past four decades—from the modernist formalized aesthetic experiences of the 1960s to the populist transformation of museum space into "antimuseums" in the 1970s to the growth of the museum as part of a culture and entertainment industry in the 1980s and 1990s—as a new way of staging and experiencing culture. Rather than being object-centered visual displays, today's museums have the potential to engage all the senses and, most important, initiate multiple conversations among traditionally unequal groups. In other words, to borrow from James Clifford's reading of Mary Louise Pratt, museums can function as "contact zones" that function less as centers or destinations and more as "zones traversed by things and people."[7] Art festivals, of course, are destinations, but they are not restricted in the same way as a closed building that is meant to withstand time. Rather they draw on the palimpsest nature of the street to engage with multiple histories and experiences of the environment. They are ephemeral by nature, and, as Erin Manning tells us: "An engagement with the ephemeral represents all that is anathema to rationalist discourses that attempt to confine knowledge within prescribed disciplines and systems of understanding."[8]

Festivals can make claims about the identity of heterogeneous Moroccan communities by going beyond reductive and exclusionary architectures of the nation in their acceptance of plural and pluralistic staging of culture.[9] They also, and perhaps more important, encourage people to reflect on more intimate and immediate relationships, such as those among the spectator, art, and the city itself. The wall-less nature of these spaces of cultural representation and the freedom with which people can move in and out of various performances invite a transformation in the identity of art institutions from that of a hierarchical architecture of knowledge to that of a more democratic and dynamic form of cultural exchange and process. In writing of the future of the museum, Tony Bennett argues that it is time for the museum to give way to "new forms of expertise that, in facilitating a less hierarchical exchange of perspectives, may allow a renovation of the museum's earlier conception as a conversable civic space that . . . functions across the relations between different cultures. This it must do if it is to be of any value at all."[10] In a country in which material museums are seen as a failure, the visible but ephemeral outdoor museum is an important site to be explored for its staging of art and Moroccan culture as a potentially conversable civic space.

Although public transcripts of the imaginary museum of the 1960s and 1970s limited the extent of dialogue between the Moroccan public and modern art, there were many conversations to be had about visual art and its vision of Moroccan modernity. In his novel *La querelle des images* (The quarrel of images), Abdelfattah Kilito presents a Morocco that is in constant negotiation if not contestation with visual images that have come to Morocco from the West. Kilito writes, "The image is, to a certain point the subject or hero of this book."[11] But in the midst of this struggle of images and words is another subject, another hero, a Moroccan subject whose world is being redefined in the struggle over representation. Kilito's examination of the play between the world of images and the Moroccan subject asks us to rethink Susan Sontag's formulation that "a society becomes modern when one of its chief activities is producing images."[12]

How do Moroccan spectators of the image challenge its claim to modernity? How are local memories erased or replaced by global images that do not correspond to a local reality? In the chapter of his novel titled "Ciné-days," Kilito describes a 1960s cinema that was a site of imagination and contestation between a working-class Moroccan audience and the cowboy-Western movies it watched. In its acceptance and rejection of the narratives and cultural values the Western staged, the cinema audience performed negotiations of local agency, practices of modernity, and the dissemination of global socioeconomic possibility. If the cinema as described by Abdelfattah Kilito is one space of discursive polyphony, by its wall-less nature the outdoor museum has the potential to go even further as a site of negotiation and contestation.

Art festivals are one form of what I call the ephemeral outdoor museum. Flexible in its identity, the ephemeral outdoor museum can do many things judged impossible in the confines of a physical museum. A mobile site and temporary site, it has the promise of serendipitous interaction with heterogeneous publics and dislodges the idea that culture is an object to be located in a central static and symbolic temple. Gustavo Buntinx writes of the need to break from a neocolonial logic that asserts that there is one museum location and one model of museology.[13] Likewise, in his work on South African national parks, David Bunn asks:

> What might it mean to go outside the museum? In the first and most important sense, this would imply the recognition that museum space is never singular. Instead, it should be understood as one element of a series of real or imaginary

articulated zones, and it is this very articulation that makes possible what Tony Bennett calls . . . "the development of new forms of civic self-fashioning."[14]

This "civic self-fashioning" is not just about becoming a better citizen of the abstract nation but rather is a fundamental rethinking of the relationship between arts, museum practice, and the local environment of the city. City streets, squares, and parks become places of exchange and transformation in art. This museum model underlines the idea that both art and the museum are social processes in which "a power-charged set of exchanges, of push and pull" occurs; for the museum these exchanges occur in the collection itself among the visitor, the curator, and the history of relations that define the objects and their subjects.[15] Museums have the potential to turn their collections outward and transform the environment around them.

This chapter is not just proscriptive, however. Rather it asks the question How have Moroccan artists engaged with the potential, promise, and problems of the outdoor museum when existing exhibit spaces and nonexistent museums failed them? In describing various attempts by Moroccan artists to bring art to the streets over the past forty years, I hope to show how ephemeral outdoor museums have functioned in different contexts such as the Djemaa Al-Fna in Marrakesh and the town of Asilah and to what extent they were able to reach the audiences they sought. In displaying modern art in public squares and spaces, cultural modernists of the 1960s and 1970s struggled with and against various European and Moroccan museum models of the time in order to interact with a new and diverse public. But, ironically, much as in the disciplining process that occurred in the public transcripts, their concern for maintaining cultural hegemony replicated many of the hierarchical power structures of the traditional museum that they wished to avoid. More seriously, many of their well-intentioned efforts remained at the level of rhetoric, with limited positive effects for local inhabitants of the spaces they sought to create. Their attempts to bring art to the streets should not be read as anxiety-ridden failures, however. In many ways they presaged the art festivals of the present and showed progressive artists and curators of the twenty-first century that the street should be the fundamental space for their work.

La Source du Lion art collective is a compelling illustration of the powers of contemporary art to transform urban environments into dynamic and vibrant spaces of social exchange. In describing the collective's project to transform a colonial-era Casablanca park and the Family Portrait Series it conducted in the Maârif, I aim to illustrate how this group of artists uses museological practices of collecting, preserving, and displaying art and educating the public in order to create public space in Casablanca for the type of artistic exchange that earlier generations of artists desired. Likewise, the tactical curation of Abdellah Karroum in his work with L'appartement 22 seeks to redefine public space and public discourse by redrawing its boundaries. Finally, the Aït Iktel project to build a conceptual community museum brings museological practices "to the street" in a rural context, defining along the way the role of the museum in a diasporic community. These efforts to think outside the physical museum while using its tactics point the way forward in thinking of the future of public spaces for art and culture in Morocco.

Taking Art to the Streets

In 1967 the *L'opinion* commentator "Ben" scolded both the state and Morocco's privileged classes for creating a public space devoid of art. In his column "Read This," Ben challenged his readers:

> Make the tour of all the public establishments (ministries, prefectures, provincial offices, theaters, post offices, banks, cinemas and airports) and show me with your finger one authentic painting by a Moroccan artist. Don't forget to pass by those villas that resemble palaces and whose construction cost 50 to 100 million francs. The state and its privileged servants, can't they purchase some paintings, decorate their rooms and show what our national artists produce?[16]

Why was the public sphere so devoid of Moroccan contemporary art? Why were new public spaces such as airports, post offices, and government buildings, which were supposed to project images of a new and technologically modern Morocco, so utterly vacant of both "traditional" and "modern" Moroccan artwork? The painter Hamid Alaoui also proclaimed the need to fight the ugliness of this official aesthetic: "A visual education should equally occur at the level of the masses through the maintenance and decoration of public squares, of the street, by national artists. . . . It is necessary to fight against a repressive imagination and to denounce it where it is found: that is to say fight the ugliness that has become invasive."[17] According to Alaoui, art should be used to brighten an otherwise depressing economic, social, and political landscape further dulled by the installation of a faceless bureaucratic culture. Art should fill public space and bring a message of progress, beauty, and the potential of transformation to the general public.

While newspapers and cultural journals served as spaces of public interaction in the imaginary museum, the public that participated in these art worlds was quite limited. So artists associated with the Casablanca School of painting did perhaps the most radical thing possible during this period: they took their imaginary museum from the page to the street and created temporary outdoor museums of modern art that appeared to unsuspecting publics and reached larger and more diverse audiences. However, on the level of display, Moroccan outdoor museums of the late 1960s and early 1970s struggled with modernist exhibit dynamics from European and American models of the museum—models that themselves were being challenged and rethought in Paris and New York. During this period, European and American museums that alienated the audience by distancing them from art both physically and socially were losing their authority to museums "of architectural diversity and multiple use, of expanded subjectivities and aesthetic traditions, of anti-élitist education and popular entertainment . . . of hybrid intensity and interaction with the street."[18] The outdoor museums in Marrakesh and Casablanca predate the 1977 Pompidou Center as the epitome of a "museum without walls, or at least without fixed and impenetrable walls," and in some respects, their failure to fulfill their mission is their avant-garde attempt to literally knock down walls without completely rethinking the museum itself.[19] However, the act of merely moving art outside and not changing the ways it was displayed was not enough to bring about the type of exchange that artists desired. In certain ways, the intervention of outdoor museums into the *space* of the city was not radical enough. Likewise, the rehabilitation of Asilah into a town of the arts for more diverse publics ironically excluded local residents from its conception and thus created an aesthetic space at the price of a sustainable community. By reading the politics of space in the historical outdoor museums that follow, I hope to show that well-intentioned rhetoric did not always translate into desired results.

The first initiative to take artwork out among the public occurred in 1969 when six painters from the Beaux-Arts School of Casablanca decided to take their paintings to the Djemaa Al-Fna in Marrakesh.[20] The choice of the site was a provocative one. Djemaa Al-Fna is one of the largest open squares in Morocco, fabled for its lively and heterogeneous public, including both Moroccan and African traders from across the Sahara. It is a true contact zone of historical periods and cultures, and men and women meet there to sell both mystical and secular products and to exchange news and tell stories. To this day, it is home to lively oral traditions, with small crowds gathering as storytellers tell their stories. In an article that covered the exhibit, *Lamalif* described the scene: "Marrakesh . . . . Housewives with their bags, old salesmen propped up on their canes, young people, strollers from all ages, approach and look at the paintings on the wall."[21] This was the general public that the painters wanted to engage. They approached and tried to woo their new audience.

Lamalif recorded some of the conversations from the event. The journal presented the following three exchanges in their coverage of the exhibition, and the choices were not without significance: in each, the painters are portrayed as facilitating educators that valorize public interpretation of their art. In the first dialogue, the painter encouraged the viewer *not* to think about art as a set of elements that need to be understood in a specific frame of knowledge or through extensive education, that art can only be understood by those who know its rules:

> What do you think of it?
> I don't understand very well.
> There is nothing to understand. Simply ask yourself if it says anything to you.[22]

In seeming defiance of Bourdieu's conclusions (published that same year) that "considered as symbolic goods, works of art only exist for those who have the means of appropriating them, that is, of deciphering them," the painter here attempted to extract art from the set of criteria that give it value, out of the social sphere that gives it value, and put it in the hands of a new public with new and subjective criteria.[23] European institutions and the Moroccan bourgeoisie would not be the only ones to define how to understand a work: the everyday Moroccan should also hold that power.

In the second exchange we see yet another attempt to open the world of aesthetic judgment to the viewer and legitimize his or her vision:

> What does this mean?
> Whatever you want; it is for you to find a definition to give.
> Is that why you haven't put names on your paintings?
> Yes.
> Then I am free to give the interpretation that I want.
> Yes, you are free.[24]

The artist called his viewer "free" to decide on the meaning of his work. The repetition of the word "free" stands out when we remember that this period was one in which people were very careful about what they said in public for fear of imprisonment.[25]

The empowerment of the unschooled public in the first two exchanges was followed by an empowerment of the artists in the third:

> I find that this one has something strange about it, there is no equilibrium. But it is you who must be presenting reality because the world we live in is totally inverted.[26]

Here a member of the Moroccan public at large legitimized the vision of the artist. Although the viewer did not understand the work, he or she claimed that the imagined world of the artist must be reality, because Moroccan life seemed so unreal. This recognition and legitimization are quite powerful considering that deficient and inexistent art institutions forced many artists to create imaginary institutions and publics in order to maintain meaningful environments for their work.

The narrative that framed these exchanges in *Lamalif* provided another commentary on the public interactions and applauded the initiative of the painters:

> People stopped and reflected. They were forced to redirect their surprise by surpassing it. It must be said that the thing was surprising: for the first time in Morocco, painters have dared to go down into the streets and to expose themselves, naked, in front of a public that was not prepared, but that reacted beyond their expectations and hopes, and without a doubt with more spontaneity than a so-called initiated public.[27]

That painters had stripped themselves of the protection of a Western and bourgeois culture industry and dared to go down among the uneducated and untrained masses to search for legitimacy and authenticity is precisely the image that these painters wished to embrace. Moroccan painters looked for a true public for their work that would inspire them to push their understanding of reality. Movements in Europe and the United States during the 1960s had shown to what extent art could be revolutionary and affect change outside the museum. In describing the civil rights movement, Lerone Bennett Jr. wrote, "The important point emerging from this is that the Movement was a double revolution, a revolution in the streets and a revolution in symbols, images, and ideas. The two revolutions unfolded at the same time and were complementary facets of the same reality: the historical explosion of a people in the sudden labor of self-discovery, self-determination, and self-legitimization."[28] Social revolution in the streets brought revolution to visual art and vice versa.[29] The Casablanca artists were hoping for a double revolution, on the level of images and symbols and on the level of the street.

But if we reexamine the dialogue between painters and spectators as reported by the cultural journal, we must ask whether and how anything had really changed regarding the public's idea of art. First of all, we never hear the ends of the conversations. What does the public say after they have been given the liberty to say anything they want? Although *Lamalif* reported that the public reacted beyond the painters' expectations, the journal did not report any public interpretation or substantive critique of the works; intellectual interactions between painter and public remained silent. The voices of the painters and reporters framed the exchanges, but the journal ultimately censored the public. The public transcript as a hegemonic discourse remained in place, with the voices of the dominant group, the cultural elite, narrating.

If we look at photographs of the event, we can see that perhaps taking art to the streets was more a rhetorical representation than a reality, for the grammar of elite museum space remained in place and the heterogeneous pluralistic nature of the Djemaa Al-Fna was erased from images of the event. First of all, the paintings were out of the audience's reach, and the exhibit space itself was cordoned off with metal dividers that evoked protest barricades more than gallery walls. Were the painters afraid that the public would storm their art in an uncontrolled "sensory riot," to recall Barbara Kirshenblatt-Gimblett's expression? Not only were the paintings out of reach; they were so far out of reach that it would have been difficult for the public to see the texture of the paint on the canvas. The physical distancing of the untrained public from the works of art points to the structures of social distancing at work in the space itself. The public might not have been contained in a controlled environment such as the Western museum or gallery, where the physical institution controlled behavior through a directed display path and a socially enforced set of understood rules (Do not touch the art, Do not drink or eat in front of the art, Maintain a quiet whisper for your conversations so as not to disturb the deep musings of fellow visitors). However, the construction of the exhibit took certain elements

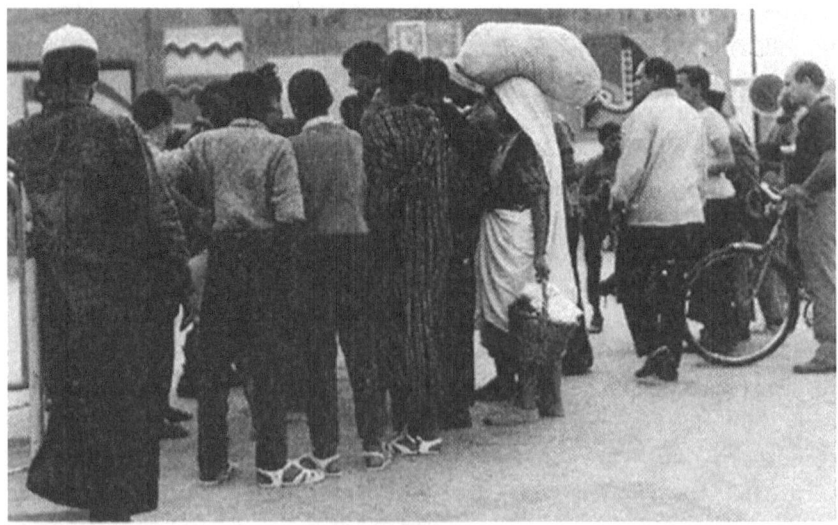

Spectators at the Djemaa Al-Fna Exhibit in 1969. Photograph by Mohamed Melehi.

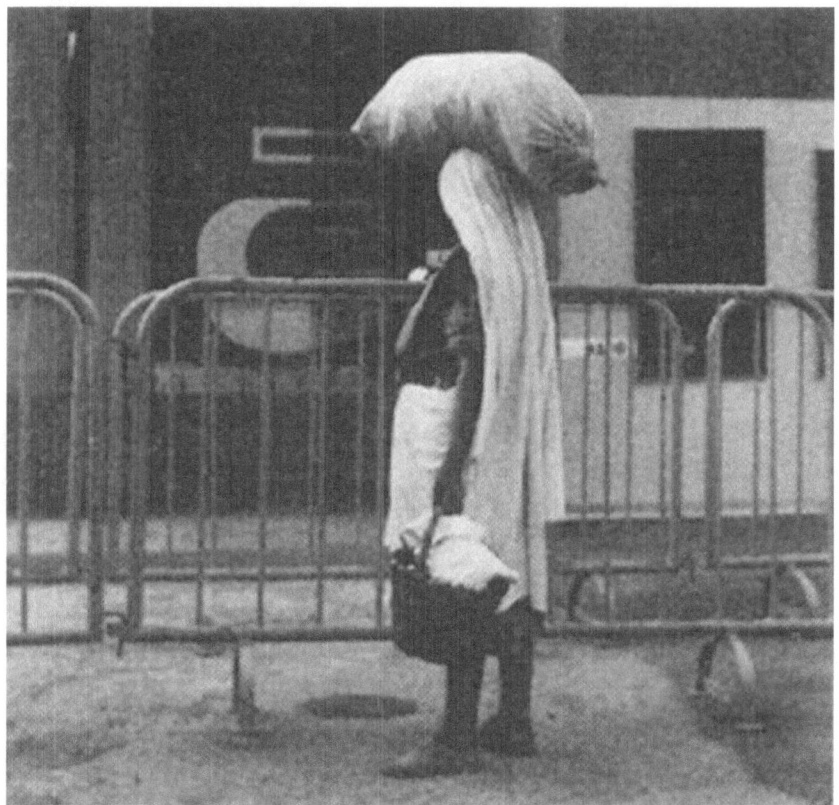

A spectator at the Djemaa Al-Fna Exhibit in 1969. Photograph by Mohamed Melehi.

from this type of disciplinary museum space and projected them into the public square. Although the painters persuaded their audience that the public had the liberty of interpretation and vision celebrating their new perspective on art, an educational process reinforced the old categories of elitist culture. The painters were not the only ones who were receiving an education; rather the public at large was being given a lesson in social manners and taste. They were being taught how to act in front of a painting, how to behave, and how to access culture, based on class models from the nineteenth-century museum.

Let us take a moment to look more closely at the images from the outdoor exhibit. The art public is primarily male and young, and in one image a lone male in a suit, not a djellaba, strains to see the art due to two sets of barricades that separate him from the canvases. Next to him is his bicycle, a symbol of circulation and movement that allows him to pass through different and

competing spaces. In another image, a photograph taken by the artist Mohamed Melehi, we see a mix of men, young and old, primarily wearing Western-
style clothing. Among them stands a woman with a sack of onions on her head.
In this photograph Melehi underlined the visual correspondence between her
form and that of the art. The wave that cuts through the top half of his painting is echoed in the line that traces the contact made between her head and
the sack she is carrying. (Throughout his work from the 1960s to the 1990s,
Melehi was visually occupied by the wave as a symbol of dynamic movement
in Moroccan culture.) Melehi was very conscious of her presence, and as an
artist used her figure to show and underscore how organic and vibrant his own
work—the creation of signs and abstraction of Moroccan culture—truly was.
The woman, perhaps the most subordinate member of the audience—possi-
bly a servant, probably illiterate—was reified as the most essential symbol of
Moroccan organic culture—woman, mother, nurturer, caregiver, food-bearer.
She was then framed in successive shots as engaged with the art, echoing its
core. She might not understand it, Melehi appeared to say, but she was its
source and inspiration. In yet another photograph, the framing of the image
cuts her from the rest of the crowd to concentrate solely on her relationship
to the art. Although she is clearly outside in a space that is accepting of her
presence, the woman is separated from the art by two sets of physical barriers
as well as unseen but present gender and class barriers. The gentle arc of the
woman's head covering as it slides behind her arm is echoed in the art that she
is purportedly staring at, and again, a visual relationship between the two was
emphasized by the photographer. Perhaps most important for me, this image
begs the questions What is she thinking? What is she seeing? How does this
experience of looking at aesthetic modernity relate to her socioeconomic reality? Are the two joined by anything more than their aesthetic forms?

By 1971 a new, more militant rhetoric had developed in the discourse of
progressive painters in Morocco; they stated a new purpose: "envahir le quo-
tidien"—to invade daily life. The same group of painters who had exhibited
in the Djemaa Al-Fna took their work to two sites in Casablanca. First there
was an exhibit in the fall of 1969 in "November 16 Square" in Casablanca, and
then in April and May 1971 the painters started a campaign to exhibit in various
high schools in the Casablanca area.[30] In answer to the question "Why exhibit
to high school students?" an article in *Integral* covering the events replied:

> Because they [the students] constitute a true public with a just way of seeing pre-
> cisely because it is new. We do not need to correct their perception. It remains
> present and encourages a level of communication beyond astonishment. Through
> their presence on the walls of the high school Mohamed V, these painters begin

the process of demystifying an art that does not concern us, the same art that drags behind it the decadent values of a colonial and archaic aesthetic.[31]

The article reveals a level of disappointment about prior public expositions in Marrakesh and Casablanca, intimating that the level of communication that occurred between the public at large and the painters had not moved much beyond an attitude of astonishment on the part of the public. A certain correction of perception, a certain correction of bad taste, had to take place with the public at large; this public failed to understand and communicate with the work. The words of the painter quoted in the *Lamalif* coverage of the Djemaa Al-Fna exhibit—"There is nothing to understand. Ask yourself what it speaks to you"—now ring false. With the students, however, because they were already partly educated, a correction of perception would not have to occur. As Janet Wolff wrote in *Aesthetics and the Sociology of Art,* "The evaluations of works which form the artistic tradition are performed by people who are themselves institutionally and structurally located, with the consequent ideological and partial perspective which this gives them."[32] With one foot in the institutional door, it was implied that the students could understand and evaluate art. Through schooling they had already acquired a certain amount of cultural capital and could better appreciate works of art. The spectator in the street was simply too naïve.

Another article in the same issue of *Integral* provided even further insight into the high school expositions. Titled "Echoes of the Exhibit in High Schools," the article quoted excerpts of students' reactions to the exhibits. The responses were taken from a questionnaire handed out at the end of the exhibit that had been created to "permit this young and attentive public to express its impressions, to record its reactions and to propose suggestions as to the future of this initiative and also to inform the exhibiting artists as to the manner in which their work was received, enabling them to see what sort of communication was established with the public."[33] I would now like to quote and examine at length the reported responses to show not only the range of reaction recorded but also which responses were deemed sufficiently important to be printed by *Integral.*

The first recorded response of the group was the following: "This exhibition allowed us to establish contact with Moroccan painters who are working for a truly national culture. This artistic presence in our school has permitted us to "correct" our perception and our conception of art in general."[34] This first articulation is striking in that it directly contradicts the statement that a young public does not need to be corrected in their perception. Obviously the student who responded felt differently. Although the painters may have been trying to demystify the arts, to a large extent the students had already been programmed to see this art as foreign to their world, something that they had to learn to read correctly and as instructed. The idea that art was important to their development and future in society was already internalized. Perhaps they did not realize the aesthetic value of this highly researched art, but they recognized that an elite art form possessed a social value, indeed a national value, that the public must acquire the means to understand.

The next set of responses addressed the necessity of education and the problem of access to art:

> I am in my last year in high school and I still don't know how to look at a painting. The fact that these painters came to a high school (because they know that hotel lobbies and galleries are not accessible to high school students) is a very important thing. I had only seen painting at the cinema or on the Moroccan news.

> I am twenty years old, and I admit that I had never been in front of a painting. Maybe because I cannot enter into the lobby of large hotels . . . .

> I greatly appreciate the initiative of these painters in the way they have wanted to establish contacts with high school students and speak to them of the art that is being done in Morocco. Until now, I had never seen such an exhibit in a school setting. It was really popular.

> I think it would be very good for this type of exhibit to continue and for this type of exhibit to continue to surpass the rigid and austere framework of galleries.

> They should leave these places in favor of schools, parks, train stations and public squares. In this way art would be popular. I know this is difficult, but I do not think that it would be impossible.[35]

These students stated that they had never seen a work of painting, not because of taste or a lack of desire to do so but rather due to the inaccessibility of art. One student familiar with Moroccan painting due to televised and cinematic coverage claimed that he or she was unable to see a canvas firsthand because lobbies and galleries did not allow young people to enter. The problem was not one of the students' taste; rather, it was the students who were considered distasteful. In an article written in 1997, Edmond El Maleh criticized the continued gallery practice of turning away "dis-tasteful" viewers: "When an adolescent risked entry into a gallery in Casablanca for example, one had one's eye on him just in case he had introduced himself into the gallery in order to swipe something, like maybe an ashtray."[36] Both El Maleh's confirmation of students' complaints and their comments point to an abstract barrier to art more powerful than the physical door of a gallery. These comments point directly to age and class. Art and painting, in the minds of these public school students, belonged to the adult bourgeois elite, and they had no reason to think otherwise.

For two of the students, the association of space, class, and the arts was also linked to physical geography:

> I would like to ask one question: Why do the artists exhibit only in towns? Why don't they go to the countryside?

> Leave the town and go to the markets . . . .[37]

These two comments dared the artists to come through on their populist promises. If artists wanted to popularize visual art, should they not leave Casablanca and Rabat and go where the majority of the uninitiated population resided? These comments reveal the extent to which painting was seen as an urban art and was geographically limited to urban areas. The division between urban and rural culture has always been pronounced in Moroccan society: cities function as sites of learning and culture; rural areas produce agricultural goods and rebels.[38] Artists who claimed modernity wanted to present their art in a modern context. This, in turn, once again excluded subordinated groups in rural and "nonmodern" areas.

The previously examined comments mark the turning point in the recorded responses. No longer humble or laudatory, the remaining responses offer critiques that are at times quite biting. In the following comments, the students displayed a frustration with their own levels of education.

> I am not putting this initiative that I totally approve of in question. But I must admit that I understood nothing of this art.

> I wanted explanations. I was disappointed. I am not educated to appreciate this painting.[39]

These two responses show the frustrated reactions of spectators in front of highly valued art without the perceived tools to understand it and point to the entire problem of cultural capital in postcolonial Morocco. The public was told by artists and the art market what to admire and invest in for its modernity but not how to read or access it. Although artists tried to educate their new public, as the Djemaa Al-Fna exchanges showed, education often functioned on a purely behavioral level in that through art, spectators were taught how to behave. The artists never appeared to discuss their work in the philosophical, ideological, or emotional context in which it had been created. The public at large was never given the terms of engagement.

The last two comments present the end of a spectrum of frustration:

> In my opinion, it is very ugly, abominable. The work executed by these people, who according to me don't merit the name of "artists," is negative. It is simply a waste of time. Art should say something, should recount something that has happened, should critique . . . .

> I know that you consider us ignorant in art. But know that I, as a simple student in the sixth year, can make paintings more beautiful than yours and that will elicit much more of the intelligence of youth today.[40]

The first of these statements is striking in its declaration that the artists represented in the exhibit did not merit the title of artist. What definition of artist was the student working with? One can read that the student was concerned with narrative, with beauty, and with the ability to communicate these concepts through art. Obviously the choice of international abstraction did not speak to his or her aesthetic. But, further, it did not directly speak to him or her at all. The last response shows the mutual frustration of the public at large and elite representatives of the fine arts. This student claimed that he was more in touch with the youth of his time than were the artists and that he could make art that would communicate with the public more successfully than did the work of the artists present—all of this despite his ignorance!

Perhaps because the spirit of the freedom of speech was so missing from Morocco in the 1960s and 1970s, *Integral* did not censor the negative comments from its report. The introduction to the article stated that "the idea of invading daily life, of integrating artistic production into its fabric, does not only preoccupy the artists, it finds itself demanded with lively enthusiasm by the public."[41] The aggressive rhetoric of a welcomed and "demanded" "invasion" of public life once again points to James Scott's concept of a hegemonic public transcript. In his view, subordinate groups are represented by the transcript as "willing, even enthusiastic, partners in that subordination."[42] For the artists and the cultural journal alike, showing the extent and polyphony of art discourse that existed in the public sphere granted a greater legitimacy to their discourse and actions. Although the majority of the comments reproduced were positive in nature, the few negative statements were reported in order to encourage artists to think about problems in their ideological and aesthetic choices and also to testify to the success of artists in finding a passionate and spontaneous public. In a 1973 interview, one of the painters stated: "The importance of the event lies in the fact that each painter that participated had the possibility to speak of his work in front of an extremely varied public, to create a new dialogue."[43] But had there been a dialogue in the true sense of the word? The cultural journals and the artists themselves remained in the position of cultural agents framing, responding to, and correcting student and public reactions. While these cultural actors claimed to participate in a public transcript on Moroccan culture, they were in a position of power to transmit and also manipulate the transcript. That the public was more exposed to contemporary art through their efforts is not to be dismissed, but the extent to which they were engaged is questionable due to the class-based, social-discipline museological models in place.

In 1978 a group of eleven painters led by Mohammed Benaïssa and Mohamed Melehi took their work to the streets in the small coastal town of Asilah and founded an annual art *moussem,* an Arabic term more regularly used for religious festivals than for those of the arts. Benaïssa and Melehi were both inhabitants of the town, and Benaïssa, in the first step of a political career that would eventually turn him into Morocco's minister of foreign affairs, was its mayor. According to Benaïssa and Melehi, they chose to use the term *moussem* and hold the festival in July and August in order to tie it to "existing remains of its [the town's] historical sacred past."[44] The group conducted restoration work on a section of the city ramparts, the Al-Kamra Tower and the Raissouni Palace (the 1909 home of the famous pirate Ahmed al-Raissouni), which was turned into a "Palace of Culture" with art studios and a hall. But the work that was done in preparation for the festival was not just about the restoration of the past. Rather the spirit of the project focused on the establishment of a site for exchange on modern art for heterogeneous publics. In writing about the project, Benaïssa and Melehi argued:

> There is no common ground where the Arab Muslim intellectual—artist, writer or poet of the Third World—can meet his counterparts from the "the other world." This limits their communication through dialogue and an exchange of experiences that should be open, intimate and direct. There needs to be a common ground . . . for much needed communication within a human framework that includes students, teachers, workers, farmers, craftsmen, civil servants, and housewives.[45]

The Asilah festival was designed to provide an international venue for the arts and to transform life in a city that was, in the words of Benaïssa, "a disgrace, lots of garbage, the sewage was a total disaster, the walls had collapsed, no electricity."[46] And thus, in true modernist fashion, modernity (through art) would cure the town of its insalubrities and reconfigure its social relations.

It is arguable whether the residents of Asilah were particularly happy when the artists came to paint the exterior walls of their homes with abstract geometric murals under the slogan "Culture and Art for Development." However, as

Benaïssa exclaimed in 2004, their work had the intended effect of restoring buildings, attracting attention for tourism, and improving the quality of life in the city:

> We now have a generation of kids who were 8, 9 years old when the festival started, and who are now in their thirties. A generation who has opened its eyes and has been influenced by art, as a medium to enjoy life, and also to mobilize the resources of imagination and creativity—without imagination, without creativity, without a clear vision, no matter what means you have, you don't bring about sustainable, viable development. With art you cannot end poverty, but you can bring about the end of misery.[47]

Asilah was a success in the eyes of its modernizing cultural agents and also according to those artists from abroad who participated in the festival. The African-American artist and filmmaker Camille Billops states that the inaugural festival was a moment of great excitement and exchange in the international art world. She had come to Asilah to participate in Robert Blackburn's printmaking workshop, conceived "as an open, democratic space where printmaking was the common language."[48] Artists from around the world worked together in shared visual languages, and during the workshop, even the crown prince Sidi Mohamed, now king of Morocco, was found among the onlookers.[49] One cannot, and should not, deny the festival its success as a site in which art transformed the city and created a new place of exchange. In fact, for its work in rehabilitation, the festival organizers, under the name the Al-Mouhit Cultural Association, won the 1989 Aga Khan Prize, and that summer more than 150,000 people filled the streets of Asilah.[50] It was and continues to be one of the most important art festivals in Morocco.

However, despite the international recognition the festival has received, informal conversations I have had with Moroccan artists, writers, and curators over the past eight years reveal a deep disillusionment with the festival. Some see it as merely a step in Mohammed Benaïssa's political career; others question its relevance for local artists, seeing it as purely a tourist event, a beautiful scene that provides a backdrop to a spectacle for foreign visitors. Thus, perhaps it is not too surprising that in French contemporary art curator Bernard Collet's literary text *Paradis Beach: Récit d'Asilah* (Paradise Beach: An account of Asilah), he makes no mention of the festival. Rather than describing the murals that continue to grace the walls of the town, he focuses on young Moroccans who feel trapped in a cycle of unemployment, who befriend the tourists and prostitute themselves to escape a seemingly static universe. For the festival has not been the perfect picture of community-building and interaction. Eunice Lin questions the nature of local participation in the restoration process and the subsequent development plans, writing that the majority of the town's population was not involved in the decision-making process and participated only on the level of providing labor and supplies.[51] In her critique of the project, she writes that Benaïssa and Melehi wanted to transform the city into a shared space between artists and residents. But

> the reality, however, is that the influx of large numbers of the cultural elite for two months every summer seems to have had the result of alienating the residents who feel they could not understand or participate in these cultural happenings. Also, there have been complaints that the artistic and architectural elements that were installed in the town to beautify it or that were part of the festival are not respective of the local residents' wishes or even of their traditions. They feel that the work represents only the ideas of particular artists, either those visiting, those influenced by Melehi, or Melehi himself and his ever-present "wave" motif.[52]

Lin also notes that although local incomes increase sharply during the summer months, as a result of choosing culture and tourism as its principal sources of revenue, the town suffers from lack of steady employment and a high rate of teenagers who succumb to drug abuse.

Lin's most serious critique as an architectural historian, however, ironically reflects the complaints of artists against the state that I outlined in chapter 1: the renovation of the town provided a veneer of beauty without deeper restoration efforts:

> The unstated emphasis of the project seems to be one of aesthetics—creating the picturesque by beautifying the appearance and maintaining the character of the town vs. the historic preservation of the valuable heritage of the town. There is little published material describing any of the structures or materials involved in the rehabilitation and no statements hinting at strict regulations or studies of the historic fabric of the city. If it is this picturesque quality that improves as the rehabilitation continues, then its appeal as a tourist attraction increases since the town acts as a "stage set" for the *Musim*.[53]

Although gallery barricades were taken down and art literally entered into the fabric of the city, Asilah as an outdoor museum failed to engage in some of the more important work of a museum: the detailed cataloguing and preservation of its collection. Did Benaïssa and Melehi's worthy project create only a veneer of beauty and the rhetoric of artist–resident exchange? Why were local voices still not taken into account?

Intellectuals and artists often expressed their frustration with populist projects by condemning the lack of national supporting structures and institutions that could "educate" and "elevate" the masses. However, in reducing individual responses to the voice of the monolithic masses and in silencing discordant voices, artists and intellectuals struggled to see the myriad possibilities that existed outside their state-centered vision of Moroccan culture and aesthetic modernity. One can have no doubt that the Moroccan public at large, as untrained and unaccustomed to modern art as it was, did react to the art, and that on some level, subtle, unconscious, or momentary as it might have been, the artwork changed their way of seeing. In Melehi's second photograph in this chapter, the woman carrying a bundle on her head stares intently at the canvases in the Djemaa Al-Fna. How did she interpret these signs of modernity, these technologies of cultural modernity, through her own reality? How did art speak to or reflect her world: her life, her neighborhood, and her city? In Asilah, how could art change the way that people lead their lives in a deeper fashion than by just mural-painting the surface?

Returning to the "Source": Art and the Local Environment

Although the cultural modernist elite of the 1960s, 1970s, and 1980s could not fully respond to an uninitiated audience, at the turn of the twenty-first century, urban artists and a former museum director returned to the streets and unexpected viewers in order to interact with an abandoned public and involve them more directly in the world of art and cultural memory. Today, using museological processes such as collection, preservation, display, and education and developing multisensory interactions that target sight, smell, hearing, and touch, these actors create new contact zones. Their art and community projects function to underline the idea of a museum as a process that builds ideas, collections, and communities from multilayered memory and histories rather than as an institution that didactically instructs and socially conditions. Three examples of these community projects that rely on the participation of local residents to define a relationship between immediate spaces, their histories, and the future are the Casablanca art collective La Source du Lion's L'Hermitage Park and Family Portrait projects, Abdellah Karroum's work with the space L'appartement 22, and the Aït Iktel community museum.

The art collective La Source du Lion (The Lion's Spring) was started in Casablanca in 1995 by artists Hassan Darsi, Mohamed Fariji, and Rachid L'Moudenne. The name of the group refers to the ubiquitous lion as a national symbol of Morocco, a symbol that persists despite or perhaps due to the fact that in Morocco lions have been extinct for a very long time. La Source du Lion may refer to a mythological level of national representation, but in many ways the collective is about discovering the nation from the ground up, focusing primarily on smaller units such as the city, neighborhoods, parks, and families. Furthermore, the name is not only symbolic. Rather, the collective has conducted museal projects on the lion in all its manifestations: pictorial representations, video projections, moving installations, written accounts of encounters with lions at the 'Ain Sebaa Zoo, and the restoration of the lion statues in Hermitage Park.

The mission statement of the group performs its commitment to the city of Casablanca and its inhabitants. Rather than presenting a manifesto, the collective asks a series of questions, inviting the beginning of a dialogue rather than stating a unidirectional mission:

> How can we combine long-awaited artistic desires with the needs generated by the city itself, its anarchic and galloping expansion, its inexorable quest for urbanity often paid for at the cost of its humanity? How can an artistic project be conceived on the scale of a city like Casablanca and its inhabitants in a context where art has little effect on reality? How can art generate new experiences, experiment with new processes in order to activate new desires in a social project? How can we reconsider the nature of art itself and its possible confluences with the human and the urban? These questions bring us today to confront a more global context through the city, Casablanca, but also through a "modernity" that is applied as the only method of global development.[54]

These questions go to the heart of the problem: in an out-of-control megacity that has purportedly lost its humanity, how can art have a meaningful role in engaging both the city and the capitalist drives of modernity that have defined and dominated its development?

Mohamed Zafzaf has described Casablanca as a spiritual wasteland that has abandoned its humanity. In his 1999 short story "Une nuit à Casablanca" (A night in Casablanca), cars zigzag and collide on the slippery streets of the city at night. It is raining, and intoxicated men and women circle the peripheries of the city searching to prolong the evening high. As fog rolls in from the Atlantic, they lose sight of their destinations and the city streets become the site of accidents and their accidentals: chance encounters, injuries, broken bodies, and death. During the day, its arteries open to social and economic mobility; at night, the avenues serve as vehicles of destitution for marginalized peoples seeking to escape reality. Human interaction and intimacy take the form of shared whisky, rolled joints, robberies, and car crashes; no true or meaningful communication is possible. And thus for Zafzaf, the city at night is where the drive for modernity takes a wrong turn, where history veers off track.

One need only look at the extensive shantytowns that are scattered throughout Casablanca to see how the city fabric has failed many of its inhabitants and how urban planning builds upon and renders concrete the unequal development that has accompanied Morocco's modernization process. In homage to its namesake, one of the newer Casablanca neighborhoods, Haj Californie, is resplendent with large gated villas, watered gardens, and manicured lawns. This utopist image of "Western" industrialized society contrasts starkly with the proliferation of neighboring shantytowns, tented communities, or empty lots with small trash piles that seem to be eternally burning. For the "citizens" in these communities, there is often no running water and sparse electricity. As the city builds upward and outward, these are the people left behind.

The way in which Casablanca is constantly morphing is not new; in fact, one can say that the city has always resisted a fixed and homogenous spatial identity. As Susan Ossman remarks in her book on the city, Casablanca is a "chantier" (construction-site) city: a work in progress without memory.[55] In the commercial city center of high-rise offices and glass-paneled corporations, even the street names defy the politics of memory. After Morocco achieved independence, streets named after French political, historical, and literary figures were renamed after Moroccans in an attempt to reconfigure Casablanca as a Moroccan city and not the essentially colonial one it had once been, for Casablanca had been but a small town before the French Protectorate. Although the signs have changed, the street names still bear their colonial markers and are referred to by residents as "Rue Lieutenant Mahroud, Ex-Chevalier Bayard," and the like. Like precolonial Arab and Amazigh memory, new and imaginative English-language signifiers in Casablanca's lexicon of identity, such as Haj Californie, seemingly stand apart from a colonial past but are profoundly linked to global capitalist expansion and do not exist independently of past narratives of colonial modernization. Casablanca is a palimpsest in the true meaning of the word: it is a cityscape that continues to be written into and upon the many layers of its history. While such writing aims at the erasure of certain pasts, stubborn traces remain and are carried in its text.

It is this complex palimpsest of memory that La Source du Lion wishes to engage, and it started the process through a long-term project to restore and preserve the many layers of history in L'Hermitage Park in Casablanca, otherwise known as Larmitaj in Moroccan Arabic. This park, once a botanical garden during the French Protectorate, was in a state of utter abandonment and neglect when the group decided to focus their artistic activities on it in 2002. Faced with mountains of trash and homeless populations exiled from the modern city, the collective desired to intervene into the site artistically and attract the public's attention to this lost space of urban beauty and human potential. The first step in the project was to construct a model of the site to be displayed with a detailed inventory of the contents of the park, which revealed the following objects, among others: plastic bags (various colors but predominantly black), plaster, glass, various cartons, plastic and aluminum containers (from coffee, yogurt, and drinks), beer cans, glass from bottles, paper, animal waste, car parts, radios, various metals, marble, cigarette butts, and human feces. In July 2002 the group exhibited an architectural plan for the space; a collection of photographs documenting the refuse; a report on the condition of the trees, plants, and gardens; and all the technical studies pertaining to the project at the Villa des Arts in Casablanca (formerly one of the most progressive and interesting galleries in Casablanca). The group wrote an open invitation to the city to participate in their project. In September workshops began to construct an architectural model of the space with the participation of artists and nonartists alike. In April 2003, the Villa des Arts hosted another exhibit for the project and an international meeting for artists called the Passerelle Artistique in order to discuss shared concerns about city environments. Two weeks later, refuse from half of the park was removed in about two thousand truck runs. In October 2003 the group started an open dialogue about the park's future with the mayor of the city and restored a small building in the park to be used as an art activity and environmental awareness space for children. The following summer, international artists returned to the park and worked on the project together.

Work continued until 2005, when the Mohamed VI Foundation for the Environment offered to complete the restoration project. At first, artist and community projects were integrated into the final landscaping; however, in 2008

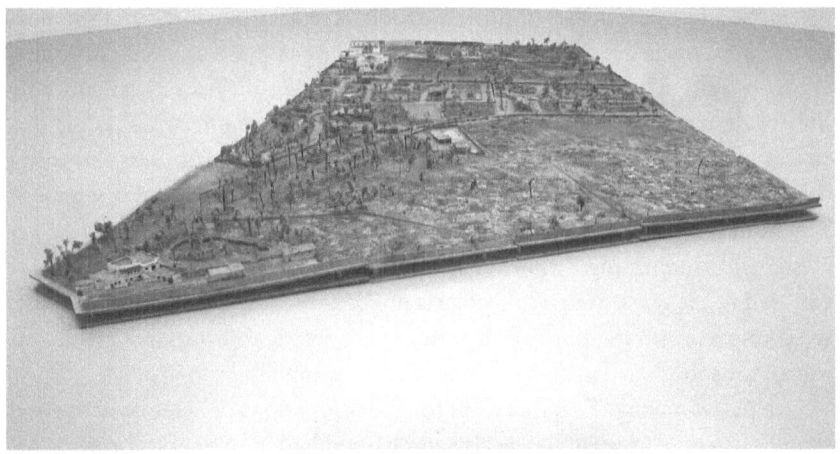

La Source du Lion, *Projet de la Maquette,* 2002–2003. 17 square meters; mixed materials on wood. Scale 1/100. Courtesy of Hassan Darsi.

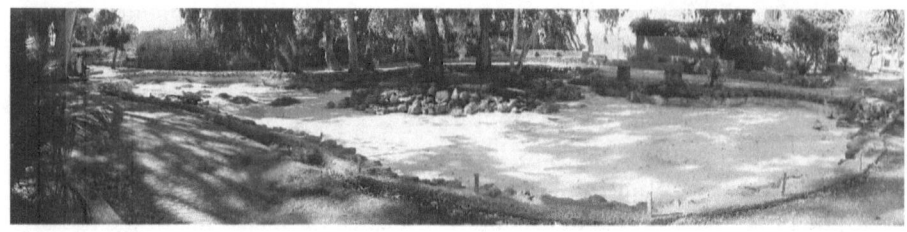

La Source du Lion, *Restauration sommaire* (Summary restoration). Lime and water. From *Passerelle artistique VI,* July 2007. Courtesy of Hassan Darsi.

the final plans by Atelier Vert, the agency contracted by the state, revealed a completely different park that was much less imaginative and removed many of the human-scale projects designed by the collective in collaboration with neighborhood groups. Among the many differences, restored merry-go-rounds and children's playgrounds are slated for removal, two colonial villas are to be torn down, and the original artist ateliers for children are to be dismantled. Not only is the botanical colonial history of the park to be buried, but so is the more recent memory of those residents of adjoining neighborhoods who were involved in the planning and imagination of the space, perhaps the most important part of the project for Hassan Darsi and La Source du Lion.

In creating and co-curating memory, the project was a success. The garden became the site of storytelling circles (Conte de l'Hermitage) and art workshops and was a pleasant place for city dwellers to go. When asked about the interaction between artists and the public, Darsi says that although the relationship between the two was still essentially one of producer and consumer, their project has pushed the public to redefine what they see as art and who they understand artists to be: "I think that first and foremost the public discovers [us as] citizens that take on initiatives in their city. At each encounter there is a debate between people. When they approach the nature of the actions and learn from artists who they are and what they do then the exchange becomes truly interesting. I think that the dialogue goes really well."[56] What we can read in the work of this collective is not only the intense desire of its artists for communication with the public but a recuperation of the city's past by its inhabitants, both artists as citizens and citizens interested in art.

In his own work, Darsi searches for new formations of heterogeneous and plural existence throughout the city and has worked to reinhabit former colonial geographies in the city, not with distant history and nostalgic stories but from the ground up by exploring how people who live there today contribute to the city's palimpsest of memory. What is striking about the art collective is that although it is interested in the memory of the city, it is entirely without nostalgia.[57] Rather than focusing on the lost past of the city, the group works on the present and the future of neighborhoods and their residents. In 2002 Darsi set up his studio in the Casablanca neighborhood of the Maârif and invited families to go there and pose for their portraits. His aim was to engage with his neighbors but also to recover the cosmopolitanism of the neighborhood by exploring the diversity of its current inhabitants.

Built in the 1920s, the Maârif was home to a multinational and heterogeneous group of southern European workers and in this sense was one of the most cosmopolitan neighborhoods in colonial Casablanca. Cohen and Eleb describe the neighborhood during the colonial period:

> There was a strong sense of belonging, and residents even felt that they were more Maarifian than Casablancan. . . . It functioned as a tightly knit, multicultural society (mostly of Mediterranean origins) and was based on a system of mutual cooperation, even though some hierarchical order between classes and nationalities did continue to exist.[58]

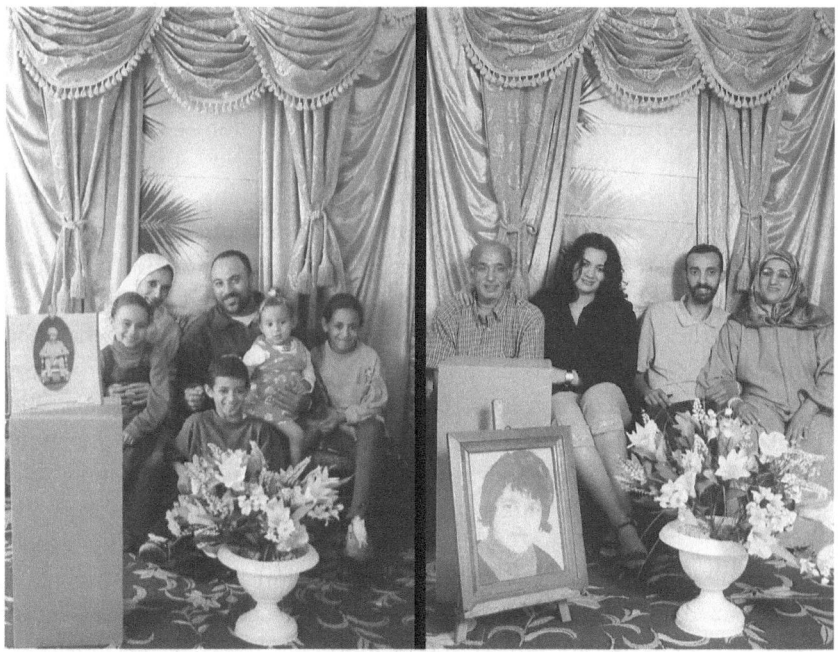

Portraits de famille, Série II, Visages casablancais. Portraits numbered 1/21 and 2/21. Digital prints, 30 cm/47 cm. July 2002. Courtesy of Hassan Darsi.

Today the Maârif is primarily a commercial neighborhood with expensive designer boutiques, cafés, and restaurants that attract upwardly mobile young people. However, behind the veneer of its central avenues, it is still a "quartier populaire," home to a working-class population, with snack bars and ambulatory fruit-sellers. Its public faces are both extremely polished and run-down: boutiques shine while apartments look gray with pollution, wealthy Moroccans mingle with pickpockets, and a police presence is distinctly felt. Darsi's project sought to document a new postcolonial cosmopolitanism in the neighborhood through the idea of the family portrait.

As artist Florence Renault describes this idea, "Families, of diverse nationalities, living in Casablanca came to pose in front of the camera—under the gaze of the artist—and brought with them a personal object chosen in a consensual fashion" (lasourcedulion.org). Families posed with this object on a kitschy interior set with heavy velvet fabrics and a poster of a sunset that references interior decorating practices in many Moroccan homes. The project not only documented various families in Casablanca but also challenged the very definition of what produces a family, how various constellations of people form in the city and what they value. The series of resulting photographs created a new map of the neighborhood on a purely human scale; the images speak of a new type of cosmopolitan family in the city with photographs of extended families, nuclear units, ethnically diverse couples, and unmarried people. Renault concludes, "If the artist involves himself, during the time of the meeting and the taking of the photograph, in the intimacy of the family, it is to give to both those who look and those who are looking, the scale of their city in the most beautiful dimension, a human dimension."

While Darsi's "Family Portrait Series" worked to chronicle life in the unseen and intimate interior of city life, the project also revealed another form of participatory curatorial practice. Participants would bring objects that they wanted to display and catalogue. Sometimes these were other family portraits that would be placed on a pedestal, creating an intertextual palimpsest within the portrait. Other times the object would be a cherished guitar, a Qur'an, or something else that was intensely personal. The curatorial practice was a consensual process within the family that chose to display it and also between the family and the photographer and artist. Such a process was able to invite heterogeneous groups to participate in the creation of memory and meaning.

La Source du Lion performs the potential of art to exhibit, to catalogue, to engage, and to transform space and memory. The project is not caught up in the national politics of memory that have turned medinas into preservation safaris and refuse to consider anything that postdates the colonial period as patrimony, as though the modern nation has produced no culture of worth. Rather, rejecting nostalgia for both the precolonial and the postindependence periods, the artist group focuses on the now. They collect memory from city sites and the people who live in them to deepen the signification and relevance of the city and, most important, to claim memory as a process that is multi-voiced and participatory. Hassan Darsi puts it best when he says, "I am here to raise questions. . . . There is no model."[59] Indeed, rather than leaning on models of the past, Darsi's group seeks to raise questions for the future.

Today Casablanca is multicultural and polyglot. Recent waves of migration to the city both from within Morocco and from beyond its borders have produced a new form of cosmopolitanism. Zakya Daoud tells us: "In this rural and ruralized city, migrants from all of Morocco join each other in a chaotic melting pot where they bring their heritage and where they invent a new way of life, unique in Morocco."[60] Likewise, Ali Bensaâd writes of transcontinental migratory movements that though desired invisible by the state, produce visible and tangible changes throughout Morocco.[61] La Source du Lion functions as a collective outdoor museum that does not seek to monumentalize a static version of Moroccan culture but that through its small-scale interventions has the power to respond to what is happening and engage in complex social transformations.

I have dwelled on the work of this collective because their artwork is a performance of the potential of the outdoor museum to exhibit, to catalogue, to engage, and to transform space and memory. While capturing the energy and heterogeneous nature of interactions in Moroccan art festivals, they strive to engage memory and art through longer-lasting museological interventions into the city space. In writing of the void of modern art museums in Peru, Gustavo Buntinx describes the work of alternate "museums" in performing contemporary art in the face of nonexistent state architectures. Much like La Source du Lion, collectives across Latin America resort to what he terms "tactical museologies": "Their innovative praxis defines a radical institutionality almost heroically gained by deliberately forsaking the established demands for the long-term, the firmly located, and the well-endowed, opting instead for the small-scale, the mobile, the nimble, even the whimsical and the opportunistic."[62] In a 2007 interview, Darsi responded to the global obsession with the large and monumental museum by joking that his next project would be to put up a billboard announcing plans for the construction of an amazing new museum in Casablanca that would never be built.[63] Although the public and the state might be drawn to monumental institutions, tactical museology is the most exciting, relevant, and promising development for contemporary art and its publics in Morocco.

Through tactical curatorial practice, Abdellah Karroum has also created a dynamic art space that engages the cityscape, blurs the boundaries between public and private space, and creates new space for discourse. Located across from the parliament building on the main avenue in Rabat, Avenue Mohamed V, the space is called L'appartement 22 after the number of the apartment. At first glance, the idea of an art space in an apartment might reflect the continued dynamic of shrinking public spaces for art in Morocco: from marketplaces and museums to banks, to caves, and now to a small apartment. But for Karroum the space is "a project site," "a site of diffusion," and "a space of encounter and discourse."[64] This space has existed since 2002 in multiple physical, virtual, and sonic incarnations beyond the physical boundaries of an enclosed private apartment. By diffusing its activities and exhibits throughout Morocco (and the world) through traveling art projects, a Web site that serves as a site of documentation and research, and a Web radio station that broadcasts interviews with artists in Moroccan Arabic, French, and English, L'appartement 22 works to redefine the idea of public space and public discourse. It practices an "activism beyond frontiers,"[65] whether those frontiers are national, international, social, or political. As Karroum likes to say, his apartment is "my permanent seat in front of the parliament."[66]

One of the first projects that Karroum curated at L'appartement 22 was the JF–JH (Individualités) (Young Woman–Young Man [Individualities]) exhibition, in which artists Younès Rahmoun and Safaa Erruas lived together in the apartment from October 10 to November 27, 2002, and created artworks in the presence of one another. For the opening, Karroum used a live feed to project the street into the stairway and corridors of the apartment building. Not only was this a visual link between the activity of the street as something fundamentally related to the art action within the apartment, but it also spoke to a radical reconfiguration of social space. As Karroum explained, "The live video projection of images from the street into the site of exhibition shows that the artist is not disconnected from his society. The artist looks at and listens to the world. There is in this collective proposition a will to re-tie the work to the rest of the city, in a co-presence."[67] The act of two unrelated and unmarried people of the opposite sex living alone in a small apartment for a month went against moral conventions in Morocco. As Karroum explained to me, "The point was to ask how one can construct something together and to show that two people of the opposite sex alone in an apartment create more than just 'immoral' acts of crime, but rather works of art."[68] Through this exhibit Karroum sought to fundamentally redefine the conventions of public space, blurring their boundaries and creating new spheres of discourse. The pieces of art that Rahmoun and Erruas created spoke to the idea of intimacy, danger, violence, and resistance, with respective installations that took the shape of a child and that consisted of razor blades attached to the wall of the room. In many respects, from the idea of the exhibit to the individual pieces that were displayed, "JF–JH" succeeded in creating multiple detours from conventional societal discourse on sexual taboos to deeper reflections and discussions of intimacy and individuality within Moroccan society.

Another project that Karroum led in order to engage life on the street and invite the public to enter into spaces of reflection was the outdoor weaving and display of a carpet that replicated the exact dimensions of the apartment itself. Through the symbolic exteriorization of the space and the transposition of its architecture onto the street he sought to transfer discourse created within "a space of exile" into a public sphere in which the everyday city could leave its imprint. Bringing the private out onto the street and displaying the space was a means to enlarge its engagement with the city. For Karroum the concept of exhibition fundamentally exists as an expedition, a movement outward, a movement toward encounter and discovery:

> The expedition mode is first of all an alternative strategy of an overture; it claims the possibility of existence of the "margin" as an active zone for encounters and the life of artwork. The movement from exhibition to expedition is in my mind the path to take to arrive at the function of art, at a possible autonomy, in societies of the Maghreb as well as elsewhere. . . . The expedition mode as an art practice inscribes the concept of "bricolage" as an alternative to its dependence vis-à-vis crushing local and international conventions.[69]

The expedition is a fundamentally nomadic practice that resists the static and monumental edifices of the traditional museum for active strategies of expanding public contact with art, its ideas, and its overtures to discussion. This nomadism is a concept I will discuss further in the conclusion.

It is the small-scale, nimble, and mobile that has been most successful in another art-in-the-streets project, though in this case "the street" is more metaphorical than urban. In the 1990s the deeply disappointed former director of museums in Morocco, Ali Amahan, moved away from the static and monolithic nature of the national museum to create a more meaningful structure: the community museum at Aït Iktel. Recall that Amahan, still employed by the Ministry of Culture as a senior researcher, is the one who proclaimed: "I am not interested in national museums of the Third World. Memory that is useless is useless to preserve."[70] In this new project, which won the 2001 Aga

Khan Prize in Architecture, Amahan invited the local community to create a public but nonofficial space where cultural memory can be housed (in the form of exhibits and performance), where cultural memory and skills can be passed down (workshops), and where culture can grow through education (classes that teach reading and writing, computer rooms, etc.).[71] As he notes:

> The museum enables people to see the potential of the community as an essential asset for development, through its institutional heritage (systems for social organisation, mobilisation, solidarity, etc.) and ancestral knowledge, in such domains as governance of "public" community affairs, and technology. As an example, the Association has brought the solidarity between the community and its diaspora (emigrants) into play, which can provide both the intellectual and material requirements for implementing and running projects.[72]

For Amahan and the Aït Iktel project, bypassing the nation in favor of local and diasporic communities has brought forth the change and positive development that state modernization once promised. For a government official to abandon state architectures is significant. He has clearly signaled his dissatisfaction with the national museums as carriers of meaning in the lives of many Moroccans, especially those beyond the city limits of urban centers, but even those within them. It is as though Amahan acted on the comment of the Casablanca student who urged the cultural elite to take their projects to the country.

At Aït Iktel, the local community of a small Amazigh village and its diaspora relatives, located primarily in France and Belgium but also in the larger Moroccan cities, have come together to preserve their history in a meaningful way and to plan for the future through development. Diaspora funding does the work to preserve a cultural memory made distant and significant through expatriation. But what is most interesting is that instead of funding museums to keep memories of "traditional" or reified culture intact, the museum actually uses its infrastructure as a place to imagine a new present and future in a concrete way, not just symbolically. The museum itself is a community center where computer training is offered in the same building as cultural projects such as the promotion of local music and the distribution of microcredits for women carpet weavers. Through art and technology in *their* museum, the community members of Aït Iktel have created an alternate model of modernity that recognizes the role of art and development in their community and is tailored to their needs and wishes. Unlike in Asilah, this community museum is for and of the community. And unlike in the living museum that is the Fez medina, there are plenty of spaces to imagine the future.

Fatima Mernissi puts it best in her spirited introduction to her book on NGOs in the rural High Atlas mountains: "The test is simple: If you are among those who repeat that everything is going badly in Morocco and that nothing is happening, you are obsolete! You are no longer a Moroccan, you are a dinosaur!" To be a Moroccan, Mernissi argues that one must be "plugged into the Morocco that is moving, that is a civil society that is in the process of blossoming." In her description of communities that have organized in the mountains and desert regions of the Moroccan south, Mernissi praises the ingenuity and creativity of villages that have significantly improved their lives. She rebaptizes villages whose names begin with the marker of family descent *aït* (which literally means "people of")—for example, changing Aït Iktel into Aït-Débrouille, which means People-of-Getting-It-Done—and goes as far as to write, "To find the trust in oneself, is to find the power to dream differently, to invent a new identity for oneself. And these peasants give an example of solidarity and participatory modernity that large cities like Casablanca and Rabat can barely imagine." Mernissi argues for participatory forms of memory and recollection. In a short section on the importance of creating rural museums that she had written before Amahan helped to organize the community museum, Mernissi insists, "The rural child is more at risk than the city child because there are no rural museums where ancestral objects are available to admire and inspire."[73] The model of the museum as repository that she proposes has been far surpassed by a community center that not only exhibits cultural wealth from the past but also functions as a meeting place for discussing visions of the future.

In chronicling the work of artists and cultural actors to bring art and the museum outside to the street, it was not my intention to critique the failures of postindependence groups and sing the praises of today's collectives but rather to show the historical evolution of the ephemeral outdoor museum. That artists can come closer to meaningful interactions with diverse audiences and effect change in local communities in Morocco today is largely due to the experience gained from the work of those who preceded them. It is also due to a refocusing of their projects from large and monolithic starting points such as the "nation" and its "people" to smaller and more engagable spaces such as the city, the village, the neighborhood, and the park. When asked about the grim future of the Arab world, poet Abdellatif Laâbi wrote: "Defeats, like victories, in the process of struggle constitute a valuable patrimony of the experience of people and authentic movements of liberation."[74] Painter Fouad Bellamine echoes this definition of patrimony, stating in 2004: "We have created a relationship with the tactile, and with painting itself. And with this support, even if we imported it, there has been a writing and discourse that has forged itself over five decades and there have emerged strong personalities who have become part of Moroccan patrimony."[75] The ongoing struggle, the ongoing process, to create meaningful art, communities, and institutions is in itself an important part of Moroccan patrimony.

Conclusion

Rethinking the Museum in Morocco

In *Le Maroc en mouvement: Créations contemporaines* (2001), Brahim Alaoui and Nicole de Pontcharra of the Institut du Monde Arabe speak of Moroccan artists, both literary and visual, as "the face of modern Morocco, that of the freedom of thought." They declare that "the time has come for artistic creation to be recognized as primordial in the projects of a modern society."[1] This type of statement is not new. One might argue that the Moroccan state and various individuals, collectives, and corporations *have* recognized and promoted visual art as the face of their modernity since the country gained independence. The problem has always been deemed by artists a lack of deeper commitment to public infrastructures that would promote visual art, freedom of expression, and public access to the arts in Morocco across classes. Perhaps this is just the universal complaint of progressive artists who lament the use of their work to enrich a small and elite population; after all, art markets and art appreciation have always had an elite identity. But in a postcolonial context, the combination of the perceived emptiness of symbolic gestures toward modernity from the state and the difficult negotiations of the international art market have pushed artists to a more intense level of frustration. In 2003 the Egyptian writer Sonaallah Ibrahim rejected his country's top literary prize in protest against government policy, and in January 2004 the Moroccan writer Ahmed Bouzfour turned down the Moroccan national prize for literature, claiming that no one in Morocco reads his work and that the state uses the prize as a symbolic institution to broadcast its modernity to the rest of the world while doing little to lower illiteracy rates, develop publishing infrastructures, or promote freedom of expression. In a statement given to the BBC, Bouzfour said that he hoped to receive a prize one day from "a government that wants and is able to eradicate illiteracy, to send all the country's children to school and ensure that they don't end up in the streets."[2]

Bouzfour's 1999 short story "La valise rouge" (The red suitcase) is the story of unrecognized, unvalued art itself—in short, the story of Moroccan literature in relationship to its environment. A man appears in a city carrying a heavy suitcase that he guards very carefully. Throughout the course of two days, he tries to visit an insurance broker who is never there. He mills about the neighborhood with the onerous suitcase constantly at his side. At the end of the story he is robbed and stabbed by someone he recognizes but never identifies. The thief opens the suitcase to find only a sheet of paper and, dissatisfied, he promptly throws it into a trashcan. The last lines of the story tell about Kawthar, a secretary from the insurance company leaving the building to buy milk, finding the paper in the trashcan, and reading her own story as it is happening: "She skipped directly to the bottom of the page to read the final words: . . . *And she rushed off . . . toward the closest shop . . . to buy some milk.* Kawthar looked at the two dirhams that she held in her left hand, dropped the piece of paper, emptied the trashcan and rushed off toward the closest shop to buy some milk."[3] Bouzfour's story is symptomatic of the frustration artists feel in the face of a perceived public and value system that recognize neither their work nor the importance of the arts in the life and history of the country. Exemplifying this condition, the story was published for the first time in French translation in a booklet published by the Institut du Monde Arabe as a free gift to those who attended the Fifth Euro-Arab Book Salon. Pointing to both the Moroccan state's absence and the powerful but phantasmagoric legitimization of an exclusionary Western culture industry, the insurance agent who can certify and protect value is never there. The work of literature or art as a portable space that holds the heavy story of the country is carelessly discarded into the trash after it is revealed to be monetarily insignificant by the local population—the suitcase is not filled with gold, so the state and the public have no use for it. It offers no immediate rewards.

The work of Moroccan visual artist Mohammed Bouafir echoes Bouzfour's critique and sense of frustration with the place of art in Moroccan society. Bouafir combines textiles and canvas in provocative critiques of Moroccan society, and in one untitled work displayed in a special exhibit in the Oudaya Museum in 2000 we can read his approach to the idea of Moroccan art as worthless trash. In this piece a clear trashbag containing an abstract canvas is hung on the wall. At first the piece intimates that modern art in a Moroccan context is ultimately disposable; it is consumed by those who have use for it, only then to litter the Moroccan landscape, incapable of becoming an organic part of it. Yet despite its status as trash, Bouafir argues that art can and should have value in its local environment. A black upward-pointing triangle on the canvas creates vertical movement in the piece and suggests the gesture of pulling something up from the ground. As in Bouzfour's story, for Bouafir, Moroccan contemporary arts and literature need to be pulled out of the trash and be given value and a *place* of value in Moroccan society.

Frustration with the state and its symbolic institutions has increased across the postcolonial African and Middle Eastern world. Katya Garcia-Anton writes, "Indeed artists find it exceedingly difficult to exhibit their work through the lack of infrastructure and interest of the public and government. In its present social, political and economic quagmire how should Africa proceed?"[4] Many African and Middle Eastern artists have found the answer to this question outside the confines of nation-state, both literally and symbolically. If the state cannot support their work through recognition of its value, and in fact fails to secure both freedom of expression and patrimony, the natural step has been to move toward another identity and another art that reflects a state of being and creation located in alternate communities. Many Moroccan artists have chosen to practice in Europe or the United States and participate in an international community of artists that situates itself in global points of unbelonging, in exile, or in migration. However, this move away from the state does not necessarily imply a move away from or beyond the nation. As I have shown in the case of the ephemeral outdoor museum, alternative art communities have formed in Moroccan cities and villages and in a diaspora that regularly returns to invest and build a future in Morocco. These communities interrogate the usefulness and even the relevance of the official categories of art, nation, and modernity produced by the state and conceive of more inclusive and engaging models of creation and preservation of memory in Morocco.

It is important to underline that the nation is not abandoned but rather is redefined from another constellation of points that valorize process over monument, interrogation over edification. L'appartement 22 founder Abdellah Karroum's curatorial practice derives from a deep engagement with the symbols and grammar of national and global identity politics. As he writes,

> As soon as one starts to reflect in terms of nations or continents, misunderstandings surge up on the subject of identity paradigms. I choose not to bypass them, but rather to introduce myself into their symbols and representations, from

which arises the necessity to interrogate contemporary art, its issues and its net-works. . . . Art is not tied to a single territory. It operates in permanent round trips between convictions, beliefs, ideologies, ecologies, languages and taboos, in order to propose a world that is convivial, or simply, livable.[5]

In my conclusion to this book on multiple museums in Morocco, I would like to discuss three contemporaneous museological models that exist in tension with one another in early twenty-first-century Morocco. The first is the long-awaited construction of the National Contemporary Art Museum, the second a curatorial practice that conceives of exhibitions as nomadic expeditions, and the third a portable literary museum that emerges from exile. The coexistence of these three models at the beginning of the twenty-first century reveals how multiple actors, firmly invested in art museums as important collective spaces for art, memory, and communal interaction, critically challenge each other, revealing the fictions inherent in monolithic discourses on art, modernity, and the nation.

The National Contemporary Art Museum

It appears that Moroccan artists will finally get their National Museum of Contemporary Art, though the exact date is still uncertain. Workers broke ground for construction of the building in January 2006, but by summer of 2009 the museum was still but a skeleton of a building rising from the corner of Avenue Allal Ben Abdallah and Avenue Moulay El Hassan in Rabat, and the construction work to date has been minimal if any. Despite the slow progress, the future museum has attracted the attention of the public. A medical laboratory across the street from the construction site has already named itself the medical laboratory of the museum district, and one Casablanca blogger conveyed her excitement about and anticipation of the museum in the following entry:

> I was pleasantly surprised today to see that work is effectively taking place on the construction site of the National Museum of Contemporary Art in Rabat. Yaaaaaay, our first museum of this kind, our very own Pompidou center, our national Guggenheim! I dare not start to fantasize on the long days spent in the hallways of what could become the best Rabat attraction, but in any case, the presentation is appetizing. A permanent collection (it would make me rejoice to see some giraffe sculptures by that talented Ouzzani and those other "moujates" [waves] of that dear Melehi brightening the hallways. . . . Do you hear me Mr. Achaâri?), temporary collections, auditorium, public multi-media library (truly public?!), a workshop area and the true "must-have" . . . an art bookshop. . . . Yum, yum, delicious![6]

The writer is ready to consume the space and the commodities the museum promises to deliver, and the models she refers to for comparison in her comment, the Guggenheim and the Pompidou, are quite revealing. The Guggenheim has replicated itself through corporate models and starchitecture, but, most important, has succeeded in producing *desire* for itself: a museum with momentous spaces and international recognition and power. It seems as though everyone wants their local Guggenheim, and this Moroccan blogger is no exception. Her second model, the Pompidou, that bastion of populism and accessibility, points to a different desire and ultimately a concern: for the Moroccan National Museum of Contemporary Art to be truly accessible and public—to create a truly public multimedia library unlike the invisible library of the Rabat Villa des Arts with it empty ateliers and inaccessible technology.

On paper, the Ministry of Culture promises a museum that will "promote, sensitize and initiate a wide public to contemporary works of art." The future museum will group together trends and developments in painting and will ensure the conservation of these works for the future. It will "actively participate in the cultural life of the country by favoring exchanges between the public and artists, likewise it will offer an opening on the world of international art and its movements in choosing its exhibits, all the while preserving its cultural identity."[7] A three-level building of 6,813 square meters, the museum will contain a parking structure in the basement, conservation labs, a reception area, a lecture room, offices, security posts, a bookstore, an auditorium, an educational center, a multimedia library, and a café in addition to 1,500 square meters for a permanent collection and 780 square meters for temporary exhibits. In short, the museum building has all the necessary infrastructures to fulfill its mission, and its outer skin reflects a neo-Moorish style that blends into the capital's architectural style.

However, the success of this museum counts on something else less tangible than the building and its amenities. Although it might be possible to erect a *building*, constructing a *museum* is another type of venture. Chilean critic Justo Pastor Mellado describes such a tension in his work on Latin American museums: "It frequently occurs that the *building* of a museum is confused with *constructing* a museum."[8] Thus we should ask how well this museum will work, what pieces will actually fill its collection, and how it will engage and intervene in Moroccan patrimony. What practices will it instigate? And how will it draw on a public community of artists and intellectuals eager to help in its construction?

Although various Moroccan curators and artists have been contacted by the Ministry of Culture to collaborate on the acquisition of works and the development of exhibits and programs, these conversations have had few follow-ups and have resulted in feelings of exclusion for those who are invested in curating the contemporary in Morocco. Likewise more substantial conversations on widespread arts education have not taken place with artists and educators. Already a certain resignation has settled into the Moroccan art community that value, quality, and innovation will be sacrificed for political alliances and friendships within the ministry.

In 2004 Abdellah Karroum organized a three-day conference on art and its institutions that brought together Moroccan and French museum professionals, artists, journalists, and academics. In the first roundtable of the conference, the new National Museum of Contemporary Art took center stage as artists and curators voiced their concerns and their sense of exclusion from the process of conceptually building the museum. Painter Fouad Bellamine noted the superficiality of his meeting with museum officials: "The other day the director of the museum invited me to lunch in order to ask me which painters should be included in the collection. The next day, she will lunch with another person and then another, and each will have their own responses. This is an absurd question. What is the very notion of this museum in our time?" The question that Bellamine posed after he dismissed the museum's overtures underlines a feeling that the long-awaited structure has ironically already become outdated, that the repository museum model will not succeed, and that the state will have added yet one more empty museum to its inventory. Dounia Benqacem, museum director of the Miloud Foundation (a private museum in the rural south founded by painter Miloud Labied), echoed this sentiment, wondering if the museum will be just a cemetery for modernist painting: "What kind of museums are we going to have in relation to others? Dead museums? Cemeteries for artworks? We do not want this." Is the ministry merely building a beautiful edifice? Who will visit the museum if there is barely any arts education in the country? Artist Maria Karim engaged this concern, exclaiming: "There is no arts education, so for whom are we constructing a museum?! Personally, I believe that it doesn't serve anyone to say 'Yes, we too in Morocco, we have a museum.' I don't think that there is a political will that sees much further than this type of statement."

However, as the discussion continued, disillusionment with the museum turned into making the most of the structure and recognizing its importance and the political will that has led to its construction. Art critic and journalist Aziz Daki made the most passionate retort to those who voiced concern over the lack of a public for the museum:

> I would like to react regarding the inutility of a museum faced with a public that
> would not come. This is a convincing argument because if we were to go now
> to the Villa des Arts, it is most probable that we wouldn't even find a cat. When

a structure as important as a museum is essential, should we ask ourselves questions about the public or not? . . . We must have [a museum.] And through its quality, we must work to attract a public through methods of communication, through media promotion, awareness raising, and political will. First there must be a structure because this is not a luxury but a necessity.[9]

Likewise Dounia Benqacem stressed the necessity of a state institution that can survive beyond the idiosyncrasies of private institutions and the often forced departure of their founding personalities:

It is certain that private initiatives, while praiseworthy, cannot replace the involvement of the state in a cultural project that translates a political vision. As we can see today in Morocco, the few spaces of exhibition that count and whose creation was contingent on the needs and desires of individuals, of personalities, have disappeared, or their missions have been hijacked with the disappearance of these same individuals.[10]

Benqacem was specifically referring to the problematic and forced departures of Sylvia Belhassan from the Villa des Arts in Casablanca and Sakina Rharib from the Omar Ben Jelloun Foundation in Marrakesh. At the Villa des Arts in Casablanca, Frei Belhassan, who made significant progress in bringing contemporary art to a more heterogeneous Casablanca public, resigned in 2004 after a struggle with the corporate directors over curatorial authority and pressures to change the nature of the gallery to include more conservative works.[11] Since her departure the institution has been unable or unwilling to find a permanent replacement, and it is run by corporate managers who do not have training in art collection. When speaking of the struggle of talented young artists, Belhassan declared that in Morocco "there's simply no place for them."[12] After all her public work in Casablanca, Belhassan has withdrawn to her home in the countryside outside of Rabat and is now focused on private consulting.

Meanwhile, in Marrakesh the director of the Musée de Marrakesh–Omar Benjelloun Foundation, Sakina Rharib, was fired in early 2004, supposedly for her valorization of contemporary art over traditional arts. Petitions against her dismissal circulated electronically in the Moroccan art world and beyond. One such petition, headed "A Museum in Peril," collected 656 signatures and many messages of support for Rharib, including posts such as the following:

We are with you. We are with the Museum of Marrakesh, an institution that permitted Moroccan art and culture to show itself and find its adoring public.

Coherent and interesting exhibits with an important focus on contemporary art— a space of prestige and culture in the medina.

Dearest Sakina, you managed to conquer the fatalism that wanted to turn the old medina of Marrakesh into a cultural desert.[13]

Sylvia Belhassan also posted a comment exclaiming that she would sign the petition a thousand times: "We need the Museum of Marrakesh and Sakina Rharib, this incorruptible space in the Moroccan cultural landscape. Art should open our spirit, not close it."[14] In a separate interview, writer and artist Mahi Binebine exclaimed that the firing of Rharib had resulted in the fall of "a haven of peace and culture."[15]

Whereas private institutions risk closing or changing direction on the whims of the corporations or personalities who run them and have no responsibility to the public, in theory a state-run museum answers to the government and the interests of the general public it represents. While it can whither away in practice through inattention or lack of state funding, once a state institution is founded, it is much more difficult to close or make disappear. And as Benqacem concluded, "Small private initiatives on the level of art development are not sufficient to satisfy the need and desire of the public."[16]

Nomadic Museums: The Museum as Project, the Exhibition as Proposition

Although Benqacem argued that the state is still an important and necessary actor for the artists, large, edifying structures are not necessarily the best way to reach a public far removed from art and far removed from the attention of the state. To return to critic Justo Pastor Mellado, he wrote, "It is very probable for museums to be built without being constructed, without being edified or even edifying, in the educational sense."[17] As I have argued, ephemeral museums and their tactical museologies stage interventions into local environments, resisting edification and producing new ways to engage history, memory, and the present. Nomadic museums do very much the same thing; however, rather than investigating one space, these conceptual museums are defined as a process in motion that changes and responds to new contexts and that needs movement to dislocate stratified concepts, disorient vision and creation, and disrupt the fixed and the permanent.

Abdellah Karroum's nomadic curatorial practice developed in 2000 through the initiation of a series of expedition projects. Karroum created portable art actions that took the progressive definition of the museum as a site of discovery, an encounter with art, and an invitation to enter discourse to various places that, in the words of Karroum, were "territories that were far removed from the official contexts of contemporary arts."[18] That same year, in a 2000 keynote address on museums in the twenty-first century, Barbara Kirshenblatt-Gimblett asked: "What if exhibitions were regarded as an interface or agent or catalyst? An exhibition, if indeed the project produces an exhibition, could then be anything, but not an end in itself."[19] Articulating their visions thousands of miles apart, both curator and theorist sought to liberate the exhibition from the physical museum and turn it into a process, an agent, a project that celebrates its unfixed nature. This liberating view of the museum exhibit as a project, as an exhibit in progress, speaks to the heart of what the expedition projects seek to accomplish. Karroum's curatorial practice is to curate contemporary issues, not just objects, and through movement, nomadic exhibits invite a reorientation of vision on the part of the artist and the spectator, producing conversations with and within diverse environments.[20]

By the summer of 2008, Karroum had curated four expeditions within Morocco with French and Moroccan artists, one expedition in Cameroon, and one expedition in France. For the first expedition, Karroum, Younès Rahmoun, and Jean-Paul Thibeau traveled to an Amazigh village in the Rif in June and July of 2000. They rented two rooms in a local family's house and used the flat area over a water tank for their art projects and discussions. As Karroum explains, the point was not to go into remote areas and display objects of art. Nor was the purpose to educate villagers about art and turn them into public spectators. Rather the aim of the displacement was to invite artists and local people to participate with one another in discussions about life, to see the artists as fellow creators in the world and hear how they talk about the process of creating. For the artists it was an opportunity to meet new people, learn about their ways of seeing and comprehending the world, and create new ideas together.[21] The second expedition took place in 2001 in various marketplaces in the Atlas Mountains and the north of Morocco, and it included Karroum, FBWN (Joachim Desarménian), and Pascal Sémur. The three men set up a little white tent in each community market and held open discussions between themselves and various marketgoers. The main theoretical questions that fueled the artists' discussions were "What are new media in art? Is oral contact a new medium?" and "What are differences between real and virtual contact?"[22] But as Karroum says, "One of the most important objectives was to explore the gaps between expected exchanges and the real discussions that took place."[23] Expedition 3 took performance artist and dancer Christine Quoiraud to Merzouga, the Atlas, and the Rif, while Expedition 4 was an open call to artists to meet on a mountaintop near Aix-en-Provence to discuss projects and works in progress. Expedition 5 invited Hassan Darsi to take his family portrait studio to the market in Had Oulad Fraj. Darsi directed family portraits on two successive Sundays in September 2004 and then displayed the photographs in the marketplace in October.

In all of Karroum's curatorial expeditions, the object takes a backseat to

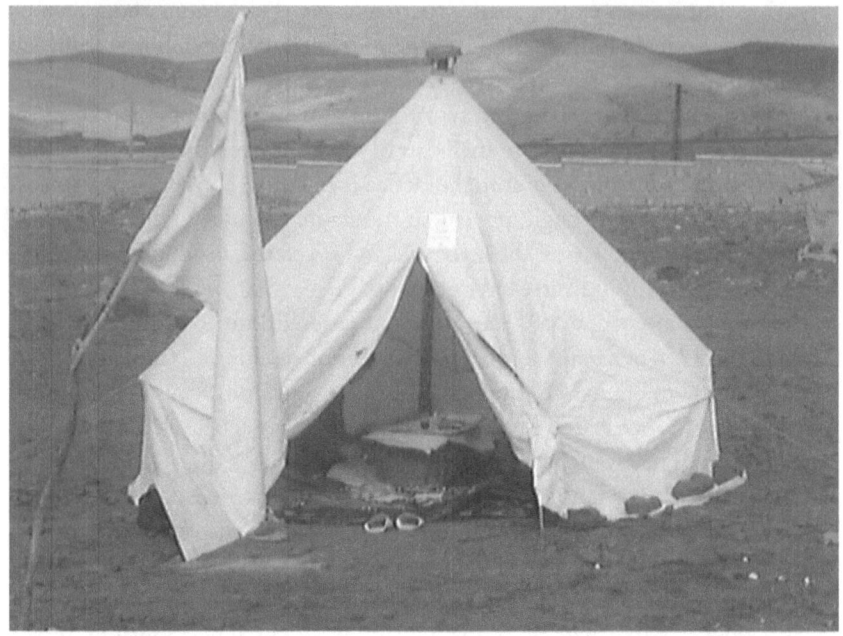

Le bout du monde (The end of the earth), Expedition 2, Azrou Marketplace. Curated by Abdellah Karroum, with artists FBWN and Pascal Sémur, 2001. Photograph by Abdellah Karroum.

discourse and interaction. As he notes: "I would say that in Morocco, many practices of art abandon the use of materials or canvas. These practices do not really leave any traces, or objects."[24] Karroum's idea of nomadic curation of discourse rather than objects can be traced to at least two conceptual starting points: the nomadic communities of the Imazighen in Morocco and the theoretical language of Deleuze and Guattari. From the Imazighen Karroum has drawn on the idea that freedom of movement (*imazighen* means "the free people") is more important than fixed private property. The movement of ideas and art is more important than creating property with art or for art. From Deleuze and Guattari his nomadic practice draws on the idea of the rhizome and the horizontal spread of roots across space. According to Deleuze and Guattari, the nomad is not defined by movement but rather as one who "distributes himself in a smooth space; he occupies, inhabits, holds that space," and "it is in this sense that nomads have no points, paths or land, even though they do by all appearances."[25] It is precisely this ability to distribute oneself across space in a deterritorialized existence that "reterritorializes on deterritorialization itself," that defines the nomadic threat to the state's need to control its bodies and the circulation of capital. In the case of curation, deterritorialized discourse defines the threat to state-controlled categories of art, national identity, and patrimony.

Karroum is certainly not the only artist-curator to practice this type of theoretical and physical nomadism. Palestinian-Lebanese-British artist Mona Hatoum explains, "I think better when I am on the move. . . . The nomadic existence suits me fine, because I do not expect myself to identify completely with one place. They are all provisional bases from which to operate."[26] Using the language of military maneuvers—"bases" and "operations"—Hatoum describes her art as constant war without the idea of a territorial "return." Two Moroccan visual artists, Abdelaziz Taleb and Abdellatif Benfaidoul, also focus on complete deterritorialization through their work in and on video. As the mission statement of their art collective proclaims, Videokaravaan is a "nomadic program" that includes, among other things, a database of video artists and filmmakers from the Middle East and North African region. Videokaravaan travels "through various countries using presentations and discussions to expand the current aesthetics of video and media practices, diversify the Western perspective of art from the Arab world, and to acquaint the West with Arab artists."[27]

Unlike the national museum, which preserves reified identity categories, the model of a nomadic caravan enables the artists to cross borders and escape otherwise imprisoning architectures, and the idea of constant movement between the Arab world and the West complicates a dynamic that had art and its exhibits flowing unidirectionally out of Morocco. Videokaravaan's exhibitions are clearly not an end in themselves but rather the beginning of new conversations outside the constricting spaces of older forms of museums. Most important and radical, perhaps, the proclaimed nomadism of the project unravels the notion of the state and its role in the arts. The Videokaravaan project is inherently stateless, primarily defined as traveling *through* countries rather than originating from or returning to them. Likewise, in a recent project titled OVNI 2005: Resistances, Videokaravaan waged a war against "single thought and its aggressive economics, a hegemony inherited directly from colonialism and ethnocentrism that seemed to be things of the past, but has taken on new strength with the expansionism of the USA and the empire of transnational corporations."[28] Using another form of nomadic identity, OVNI, which is French for UFO, the group has created an "Observatory Archive" of independent documentaries and agit-prop. Not only has Videokaravaan proclaimed itself stateless; by adopting the UFO as its symbol it declares itself "alien" to a planet of nation-states and transnational corporations protected under the aegis of the United States. Resisting location, true to its name, the project plays with the status and threat of the "unidentifiable" vis-à-vis the hegemony of the United States.

The use of video projection as opposed to canvas enables a different type of circulation of images that decenters and dislocates, however momentarily, the museum and gallery space for the more interiorized spaces of spectatorship. Different rules of seeing apply. In a piece created for a February 2005 exhibit in Oman titled The Circle 3, Moroccan video artist Abdulfatah Alzeen projects a work by Chaïbia on a small black television screen. Chaïbia's image loses its depth but appears to gain motion, and the viewer is forced to question this displacement of her work from the white cube of gallery space to the black box placed squarely on a desk that appears to be part of a suite of office furniture. Is the artist commenting on the commercialization of Chaïbia's work and its circulation in the West, its "easy" consumption? Or is he rather drawing on the possibility of bringing the work of a marginalized woman into the most pervasive medium of Arab spectatorship, television? While the physical work is situated in a museum or gallery far from the view of the Arab world, Alzeen allows the image to travel virtually, theoretically reaching a new audience whether in Oman or elsewhere in the Middle East. Alzeen's use of a television monitor rather than projecting his images on a wall evokes the primacy of mass media in the world today and plays with the concept of broadcast television and domesticity. This play ultimately brings art into a space that is more widespread and meaningful than a museum in a Middle Eastern context: the living room, a space where families—men, women, and children—sit, eat, talk, and work. At the same time Alzeen plays with the video monitor's limitations and thus incites a certain nostalgia for the painting itself. As Liz Kotz observes in her article "Video Projection: The Space between Screens":

> Monitors are awkward, badly designed, and a constant reminder of the medium's link to broadcast television, domestic furniture, and all the degraded industrial uses of video technology. Mounted on the ubiquitous gray utility cart in institutional settings, monitors disrupt the gallery and museum space. . . . Who among us would not prefer the luminous image freed from its ungainly support?[29]

Indeed who among us would not prefer to see Chaïbia's work freed from the black box that frames it. And yet the mediation of the black box reminds the viewer that art framed in a white cube is just as distant and removed from a Middle Eastern public at large. The black box has the potential to deterritorialize the image in a conscious manner that reveals the politics of the act.

In many respects, the nomadic work of Abdellah Karroum, the Videokaravaan collective, and other artists succeeds theoretically where Hussein Tallal and André Elbaz's articulations of their universality as artists do not because they do not accept the category of universal as it has been historically produced in the West. Nor do these artists accept the global in its retracing of late capitalist politics. And yet, beyond questions of theory, the reality of the art market resists complete deterritorialization, especially where funding is concerned. When Videokaravaan traveled to Agadir, Morocco, in April 2004, the project was funded entirely by European institutions: the European Cultural Foundation, the Prince Claus Fund, the Hubert Bals Fund, the Rijsakademie Van Beeldende Kunst, and the Institut Français of Agadir.[30] Although the material circumstances for the production of their work cannot sever themselves from state foundations, the collective can accept assistance from multiple national sources.

The Portable Literary Museum

Although the nomadic museum and its disorienting networks produce new conversations and practices of art and memory, they are limited to those who have the freedom to move. In their postnational concerns, artists and curators who define themselves as nomadic participate in a certain network of privileged movement. What happens when one cannot move, when one is stuck at borders, and when one lives in exile?[31] The conversation quickly returns to territory, to the object and how portable memory can serve as the site of collection.

Poet Abdellatif Laâbi has created a museum in exile that can be picked up and carried. Although national museums spin celebratory narratives about the continuity of Moroccan culture using the aesthetics of art as a screen from social injustice and nomadic curators abandon objects for discourse, Laâbi's literary museum houses a national memory on the failure of the state and its promises of modernity and through verse creates a haven for discarded objects. Exhibiting neglected art objects and celebrating various underrecognized but important artists from Morocco, Laâbi's collection of poems titled *Petit musée portatif* (Small portable museum) addresses themes of abandonment, undervalued memory, imprisonment, betrayal, and disappointment, as well as home, love, and family.

Ever since André Malraux introduced the idea of the imaginary museum, writers have created and curated dream museums in literary and photographic forms. Combining text with images of objects, these literary museums remind us of the museum as a utopic space for carrying memory and imagining personalized narratives of culture and history. For Laâbi, the personal literary museum is even more significant because both the nation and its institutions of culture have failed him profoundly over the course of his life. In 1966 Laâbi founded the cultural journal *Souffles* and in so doing gave a space and voice to imaginary art museums, cultural transformation in light of decolonization, and political dissent. However, the journal ultimately cost him his freedom when he was arrested for subversive activities against the state and the full run of *Souffles* and its Arabic edition, *Anfas,* were used as proof against him. Incarcerated from 1972 to 1980, Laâbi led an extremely difficult life in prison, but his ideals and desire to write did not abate. Shortly after his release, in 1985, he left Morocco with his family to live in France. In 2002 his museum book appeared as a physical realization of the discursive museum of the 1960s produced by *Souffles.* Less optimistic than those spaces of the 1960s and tinged with a certain melancholy, his personal museum is accessible to visitors only through the intimacy of reading.

The book itself is a beautifully printed collection of thirty-one poems and thirty-two images: eighteen gouache illustrations by Abdallah Sadouk, photographs by Laydi Maroufi, and reproductions of paintings. The poems vacillate thematically between meditations on art objects such as mirrors, stools, and tables and portraits and homages to artwork and artists from Laâbi's intellectual circle of the 1960s, becoming what writer Françoise Ascal has termed "a constellation of object-companions without which exile would be even more cruel." In the preface to the collection, Ascal describes these objects-in-orbit as "anchored in lands defined by perfumes, flavors, lights, more than by administrative limitations. . . . Among the objects chosen, very few make reference to childhood or to heritage, in the strictest sense of the word. They are essentially part of adulthood and its liberty."[32] The poems, as objects in a portable museum, function to carry the memory of Laâbi's absent friends and a nostalgic image of Morocco to give him places of hope and inspiration while in exile from the nation-state that prevented him from living in his homeland.

By devoting time to thinking and writing the poem-objects, Laâbi performed the function of a curator, separating works from their daily functions in order to examine them closely for their aesthetics, history, and cultural significance. In his hands they do not function as symbols of the nation or Moroccan culture or as stepping-stones toward an avant-garde metadiscourse on art but rather appear as traces of his personal memory and a desire for community. Although the order of the poems was imposed by the structure of a book with page numbers, Laâbi did not create a unidirectional narrative walk through his collection. The reader can open the book to any page at any time. And thus this personal museum does what the National Museum of Contemporary Art will be unable to achieve: it combines contemporary art, photography, artisanal production, and works of art from varying periods of history and geographical locations into a structure that allows these multiple temporalities to coexist without teleological judgment or narrative.

The table of contents, as one potential walk through the museum or unstructured inventory of memory, illustrates this dynamic. The first poem refers to an artist and the last to a studded chest. Here are the titles in order:

> Laura Rosano, Inkwell, Kacimi, Stir-ups, Gharbaoui, Chinaman, Portrait of the mother, Embroidered pillow, Rain sticks, The father, Shelf I, Round table, Circumcision chair, Saladi, Syrian tables, Farzat, Shelf II, Mahdaoui, Moucharabieh screens, Miloudi, Chebaâ, Hexagonal table, Tunisian mirror, Square table, Bazaine, Carpet from Zemmour, The garden of delights, Red chest, Qur'anic diploma, Indian head, Studded chest.[33]

A compilation of poems about people, objects, and ideas from Morocco and beyond its borders, the eclectic collection has the ability to assemble itself without the constraints of a national museum to subsume all history into the nation or of an encyclopedic museum whose aim is to collect everything possible and reorganize the world. As a portable museum, the collection acquires further depth of meaning and association when it can be viewed from multiple locations. What connections are made when one reader can enter the museum from a library in Rabat and another can view the collection from a bookstore in Paris or at home in New York? Although the territorial identity and history of the objects is made clear in their titles, the museum itself is outside of territory and thus allows for and in fact encourages a multiplicity of meanings.

Let us now turn to the collection and more closely examine a few of its objects: a painting by the artist Mohammed Chebaâ, an inkwell, and a table. The poem "Chebaâ" is a focused meditation on one of Chebaâ's paintings. The opening lines describe the forms that dominate the canvas, but through this study of form the poem functions to evoke both a personal history of imprisonment and an art-historical and postcolonial struggle against containment and categorization.

Chebaâ	Chebaâ
Dans les trois carrés	In the three squares
le rond	a circle
et la demi-lune	and a half-moon
d'étranges voyageurs	of strange travelers
prenant la mésure	measuring
de leur liberté	their freedom

Ils hésitent	They hesitate
entre le dedans et le dehors	between the inside and the outside
tels d'anciens prisonniers	like former prisoners
rêvant de la cellule bien rangée	dreaming of the well-kept cell
de la fenêtre étroite	of the narrow window
d'où ils admiraient	from which they admired
un bout du ciel	a piece of the sky
le plus fabuleux de leur vie[34]	the most incredible of their life

On the one hand, Laâbi links Chebaâ the person and Chebaâ the canvas to the history of Morocco's postindependence period: the metaphorical prison of colonialism and the excitement of possibility during that time of intellectual dynamism. He describes Moroccan intellectuals as former prisoners of a colonial system that restricted their view. This imprisonment, he argues, encouraged them to fight against reductive visions of Moroccan culture and to see more clearly and intensely what future lay ahead. The poem reflects upon the safety of narrow categories and well-ordered narratives such as those of home and nation, but ultimately rejects them as imposed prisons as well. And thus, simultaneously, the poem is a personal reflection on the postcolonial injustice that Laâbi experienced as a prisoner of the nation-state he participated in re-imagining—the nation-state that betrayed him and tried to force a narrow window on the "most incredible" piece of sky that he could see.

In another poem, titled "Inkwell," Laâbi focuses on a small artisanal object in order to comment on the process of writing and the location of culture. As in "Chebaâ," Laâbi starts this poem with a description of an art object in order to meditate on a deeper history of cultural production. He links the ceramic inkwell, a font of creativity, to the richness of both Fez and Andalusia, referencing a historical empire that extends beyond both the city and the nation-state. In this Laâbi identifies his cultural heritage as a writer as more universal than just Moroccan or Fassian (Fez was the city of his birth); this heritage goes beyond current administrative borders. The inkwell is described as a citadel, a place that serves to defend and protect one from forces that might destroy civilization. Although ink no longer fills its cavity, the ink's replacement with metallic birds that signify pens shows that the inkwell continues to nourish the creative act in the present. The writing utensils represented as birds link writing back to the sky of the previous poem and symbolize both the freedom and the ability of the arts to look to the future.

In another poem on an artisanal object, "Round table," Laâbi focuses on a table that might or might not be considered art in order to initiate reflection on state neglect and community undervaluation of Moroccan arts in all their forms.

Table ronde	Round table
A force de manger dessus	Due to eating on it
on oublie sa fêlure	we forget its cracks
ses gravures cunéiformes	its cuneiform etchings
ses senteurs d'huile vierge	its odor of virgin oil
de Meknès	from Meknes
On la nettoie	We clean it
sans la moindre caresse[35]	without the smallest caress

Laâbi restores the table lovingly through the act of writing, noting its utilitarian function while at the same time exploring the artisanship that went into making it. This table, like Moroccan arts in general, is not to be just consumed and thrown out. The poem reflects the loss of exile, where something once ordinary reappears with greater value. His condemnation of the table's neglect is not only a reference to the personal neglect of an object but also makes a larger argument about state neglect of the arts when read in context with other poems in the collection.

Combining people, contemporary art, artisanal objects, and sculptures from around the world, Laâbi wishes his museum to be a site in which the variety of human experience and its cultural forms exist without hierarchical judgments or arguments based on nation, race, or civilization. Because it does not seem possible for this collection to exist at any physical site, either in Morocco or elsewhere, the museum remains portable and unfixed in nature, belonging to Laâbi and his readers.

In her review of Mai Ghoussoub and Souheil Sleiman's 1997 exhibit Displaces, art critic Shaheen Merali asks: "Does the notion of belonging have any place on a fluctuating nomadic globe. . . . We find ourselves eventually floundering in the zone that intercedes between exile/homelessness/displacement/unbelonging."[36] Although Merali looks on space and belonging with a certain nostalgia—"We find ourselves eventually floundering"—her question is relevant for an art world that celebrates constant movement while too often neglecting to recognize the impossibility of movement for many artists and the need to hold onto objects and the memory they can carry.

Open Conclusions for the Museum

Tunisian writer Abdelaziz Belkhodja places the museum at the center of his imagined North Africa of the future. In his novel *2103, le retour de l'éléphant* (2103, the return of the elephant), Belkhodja starts with the premise that by the beginning of the twenty-second century, due to its dependency on oil and its xenophobia couched in antiterrorist discourse, the industrialized West has fallen. In contrast, the North African Republic of Carthage has assumed the heights of utopic civilization due to its abilities to reverse processes of pollution and desertification through the creation of glass tiles that produce energy. The Republic of Carthage resembles a Garden of Eden that stretches across the Mediterranean region, including even former Andalusia. In an ironic echo of current European Union discourse, Belkhodja writes: "The Andalusians begged us so much that we finally accepted their candidacy to our Union. They cost us a lot, it's true, but Andalusia and us, it's an old love story! And in love, one doesn't count."[37] The novel's story centers around a young American industrial spy named John who tries to find the secret formula of the tile but ultimately falls in love with this open and free society. The descriptions of Carthage that Belkhodja pens focus on North Africa's long, rich history, and at every turn he places monuments and museums.

The museum as a space of memory is of utmost importance to Belkhodja in his depiction of a victorious, powerful North Africa. In his description of the Museum of History, Belkhodja imagines the ideal museum as a technologically advanced encyclopedic museum:

> John glides down the Avenue of the Philenes Brothers on the moving sidewalk and arrives at the top of the Corniche. There he discovers an imposing monument. On the porch, he reads: Museum of History. He enters. On his left, a first pavilion displays "The Punic Period," then a second: "The Roman Period," then "Byzantine Occupation" and successively "The Arab Conquest" "Oriental Dynasties" "Berber Dynasties" "Turkish Conquest" "French Protectorate." What's this? laughs John. That's weird! The French Protectorate? That's a good one! He continues reading: "Contemporary History" with sections for "Independence" "Second Republic" "Third Republic" "Republic of Carthage."[38]

Belkhodja constructs a space in which history is framed from a non-Western point of view and the Western colonial presence is but one short period in a long, rich, and ultimately victorious history. The French Protectorate becomes a joke in Belkhodja's imperial rooms of memory, and the Western tourist is finally presented with a powerful representation of North African history and culture.

In this futuristic museum virtual experience mixes with the display of preserved artifacts, but the effect of the museum is one that any encyclopedic institution desires: all who enter are inspired to read, to learn, to discover their humanity. As John's experience attests:

> Never in his life did he desire as much to read, to learn, to discover. Essentially, this visit taught him that ultimately, all is simple, that History is not a succession of events without many ties between them, but rather a path that is traced for the elevation of the human spirit. Sometimes the spirit falls into decadence and sometimes, aspiring elevation, it finishes by reaching a superior level.[39]

With underlying nods to Hegel, Belkhodja uses the museum to articulate a theory of universal history based on the elevation of the spirit, but what interests me most in his text is the centrality of the museum in the utopic civilization that he proposes. The belief in the importance and the potential of the museum in North Africa has not disappeared but rather remains as a central architecture in his neo-Enlightenment universe.

Moroccan artists, curators, intellectuals, and politicians all believe in museums and their fundamental role in an open and progressive society. Although a singular imagined Western modernity and a singular imagined universal art museum may have evaded or been neglected in Morocco, museums in Morocco exist in multiple materials and discursive forms that question this lack and attempt to move beyond it. In so doing, museums in all their incarnations become theaters in which memory, history, development, citizenship, identity, patrimony, environment, relationships to the world, and questions of taste can be staged, debated, presented, and displayed. Artists have not abandoned the potential of a museum; rather they have become its curators. And rather than producing poorer imitations of grandiose and outdated national architectures imported from the West, these curators have developed a proliferation of museological projects that meaningfully engage both local and global communities. Outdoor and ephemeral, literary and portable, or essentially nomadic and radical, these museums are not merely urban edifices or monuments but rather critical scapes of engagement.

When called on by the state to participate in the creation of the National Museum of Contemporary Art, artists and curators do not refuse. They do not refuse because they want the better state institutions that discourses of modernity have promised. Yet they also recognize that the state can never be the be-all and end-all and that their projects are of the utmost importance. Countermuseums do not serve as substitutes for the missing institution that has haunted the cultural elite for the past fifty years, but they do fundamentally redefine what a museum should do. In operating from the margins they maintain a critical involvement with state discourses and continue to reveal the fictions housed in both real and symbolic sites of discourse, revealing that out of degeneration or stagnation can rise innovation and hope. Through art and its visible, invisible, stationary, ephemeral, and mobile museums, Moroccans have not only found ways to address lack but have also forged meaningful new communities and relationships to memory that can perhaps transform not only museums but also history and move it forward in another direction.

Notes

Introduction

1. Kilito, "The Flower-Bed," 37.
2. Pandolfo, "The Thin Line of Modernity," 124.
3. Moroccan National Tourist Board, *Morocco: Museums*, 3.
4. Ibid., 4.
5. Ibid., 6, 12, 18.
6. Ibid., 1.
7. Ali Amahan, interview by the author, Ministry of Culture, Rabat, May 19, 2000.
8. Rharib, "Le mot musée," 51.
9. Touzani, "Les musées marocains," 48.
10. Szwaja and Ybarra-Frausto, "Foreword," xiv.
11. Among these studies I have found Wendy Shaw, Irene Maffi, and Heghnar Wautenpaugh's recent works on the Middle Eastern museum the most interesting and inspiring. Shaw, *Possessors and Possessed;* Maffi, *Pratiques du patrimoine et politiques;* Wautenpaugh, "Museums and the Construction of National History." For studies of African museums, see Gaugue, *Les états africains et leurs musées.*
12. Fehr, "A Museum and Its Memory," 59, emphasis mine.
13. Kratz and Karp, "Introduction," 4.
14. Mitchell, "The Stage of Modernity," 17.
15. Preziosi, *Brain of the Earth's Body,* 3, 40.
16. Bennett, "Difference and the Logic of Culture," 56.
17. Cooper, *Colonialism in Question,* 115.
18. Rabinow, *French Modern,* 9.
19. Ferguson, *Global Shadows,* 32–33.
20. Majid, "A Moroccan Star Is Born."

21. Ferguson, *Global Shadows,* 189.

22. Laroui, cited by Pandolfo in "The Thin Line of Modernity," 124.

23. For excellent projects of this type, see Chakrabarty, *Provincializing Europe,* and many of the essays in Mitchell, *Questions of Modernity.*

24. De Boeck and Plissart, *Kinshasa,* 57.

25. Ibid., 34.

26. "La rançon d'une societé à deux vitesses: violence et répression." Diouri, *A qui appartient le Maroc?* 37.

27. This evocative phrase is taken from Pierre Bourdieu: "Like the so-called naïve painter who, operating outside the field and its specific traditions, remains external to the history of art, the 'naïve' spectator cannot attain a specific grasp of works of art which only have meaning—or value—in relation to a specific history of artistic tradition." Bourdieu, *Distinction,* 4.

28. These concepts are developed further in the body of the book, but their phrasing comes from Clifford, *Routes,* 8, and Bennett, "Pedagogic Objects, Clean Eyes, and Popular Instruction," 370–371.

29. Muhairi, cited by Hassan Fattah in "Celebrity Architects Reveal a Daring Cultural Xanadu for the Arab World," *New York Times,* February 1, 2007.

30. http://www.lord.ca.

31. Mikdadi, "Arab Art Institutions and Their Audiences," 56.

32. adonis, "Le manifeste du 5 juin 1967," 3.

33. See the work of Hamid Irbouh, Stacy Holden, and Muriel Girard for scholarship that retrieves voices about art and restoration from the colonial archives. Amina Touzani's thorough and insightful analysis of the Moroccan Ministry of Culture from Independence to the beginning of the twenty-first century is based on her work in various ministerial archives in Morocco in French and Arabic. On the conditions of these archives, Touzani writes, "The Ministry of Cultural Affairs in Morocco is a department without memory because up to this day, it has not been able to organize its archives. In effect, there doesn't exist the smallest administrative cell to proceed to the collection, analysis and diffusion of the archives or at least their preservation. The question that haunts us is the following: Is there really something to preserve?" ("Les musées marocains," 16–17).

34. Becker, *Amazigh Arts in Morocco;* El Maleh, "Ahmed Cherkaoui ou la passion de la signe"; Khatibi, *L'art contemporain arab;* Ossman, Susan, *Picturing Casablanca.*

1. Degeneration and Decay in the National Museum

1. Touzani, *La culture et la politique culturelle au Maroc,* 227.

2. It is not my aim here to examine Benjamin's theory of redemptive recuperation through decay and to analyze its full relevance for a theory on the decay of museums. Rather I am borrowing fundamental concepts such as decay as critical practice from his work in the Arcades Project and *Trauerspiel* as starting points for thinking about museum decay in a Moroccan context.

3. Benjamin, "Paris, Capital of the Nineteenth Century," 163.

4. Tranchant de Lunel, *Au pays du paradoxe,* 188. The Protectorate Fine Arts Administration was called by different names throughout the Protectorate period, including alternately Service des Beaux-Arts and Service des Arts Indigènes. This vacillation in names points

to a vacillation in attitude toward the Moroccan arts. Were they fine arts or indigenous arts, a distinction that separated them from European fine arts?

5. Koechlin, "Du passé à l'avenir," 10.

6. Ricard, *Maroc: Les guides bleu,* 255.

7. Ibid., 194.

8. Girard, "Invention de la tradition et authenticité sous le Protectorat au Maroc."

9. This comparison came from Lyautey's critique of the French plunder and destruction of Algerian culture, which he had witnessed while stationed there. By the early twentieth century the situation in Algeria was lamentable. The Roman camp at Lambèse had been pillaged by French soldiers, the amphitheater destroyed. Monuments in Constantine and the thirteenth-century oratory in Tlemcen had been demolished in order to make room for parking lots for tanks, and a thirteenth-century *madrasa* had been torn down to put up a city hall. Stone slabs with historical and religious inscriptions had even been used in the construction of pavements (Ricard, *Pour comprendre l'art musulman dans l'Afrique du nord,* 305–6). In Morocco, in addition to French urban planners, architects, and modernists, Lyautey appointed administrators who had witnessed the destruction in Algeria to be conservators of culture, and articles and pamphlets published during the early years of the Protectorate for the most part began with a statement acknowledging the errors committed in Algeria: "If the Algerian experience was acquired at the price of weighty errors, it has a least served to educate" (Ibid., 308). This rhetoric is significant because it disassociates the Protectorate in Morocco from the governments of other North African colonies as a more "modern" and successful administration while insisting that Moroccan culture was older and purer than that of Tunisia or Algeria. The rhetoric of the superiority of preserved culture in Morocco extended to the realm of artisanal production and was articulated on all levels. For example, Alfred Bel, one of Lyautey's cultural attachés, believed that Moroccan craftsmen were more agile, more active, and in general more intelligent than Algerian workers (Bel, *Les industries de la céramique à Fes,* 11). The past was a site to preserve for the future, and by claiming that Moroccan culture was distinctly distanced from both Europe and the other North African colonies, the administration could clearly articulate and orchestrate the parameters of Western modernity. For a nuanced and well-documented treatment of French policy toward art and architecture in Algeria, see the work of Nabila Oulebsir (e.g., *Les usages du patrimoine*).

10. Fleury, cited by Girard in "Invention de la tradition et authenticité sous le Protectorat au Maroc" (M. Fleury, directeur PI de l'instruction publique, des Beaux-Arts et Antiquités à M. Pérignon, chef du cabinet civil du résident général, le 18/8/1924, n°3498 SGP, Dossier 475 AP 174, "Arts indigènes et industrie du tapis," Fonds Lyautey, Archives Nationales de France).

11. Tranchant de Lunel, "Le Maroc artistique," 24.

12. Tranchant de Lunel's comments on the ills of modernity echo theories on the decay of modernity as found in the work of Walter Benjamin, in particular the famous essay "Art in the Age of Mechanical Reproduction."

13. See Jukka Gronow's treatment of Bourdieu in *The Sociology of Taste,* 11.

14. Tranchant de Lunel, "Le Maroc artistique," 24–25.

15. Girard, "Invention de la tradition et authenticité sous le Protectorat au Maroc."

16. Ricard, cited by Girard in ibid., note 30, reference incomplete ("Ricard, 1930, p. 19").

17. Irbouh, *Art in the Service of Colonialism,* 60, 15.

18. Holden, "When It Pays to Be Medieval," 313.

19. Ricard, cited by Girard in "Invention de la tradition et authenticité sous le Protectorat au Maroc" (H. R. D'Allemagne, "La résurrection et la conservation des arts indigènes au Maroc," Liasse 710, Fonds Ricard).

20. Ricard, cited by Girard in ibid. ("Enquête sur l'influence du tourisme sur les arts," handwritten note by P. Ricard, no date, Liasse 616, Fonds Ricard).

21. Ricard, *Maroc: Les guides bleu*, 194.

22. Throughout this section I use the term *Berber* because it was current in colonial discourse. In the rest of the book I use the more current and nonperjorative noun *Imazighen* and the adjective *Amazigh* instead of *Berber*.

23. On Berber-Arab relations under the Protectorate, see Burke, "The Image of the Moroccan State in French Ethnological Literature."

24. Champion, *Le Maroc et ses villes d'art*, 85.

25. Laâbi, "Le gâchis," 8.

26. Ricard, *Maroc: Les guides bleu*, 256. "L'homme à l'ânesse," Moulay Mohammed, "Ben Hamara," was a pretender to the Moroccan throne and fought against Moroccan Moulay 'Abd Al 'Aziz, uniting his efforts in 1904 with those of the Algerian marabout rebel Bou 'Amana. He was eventually captured and thrown to the lions.

27. Oulebsir, *Les usages du patrimoine*, 109–11.

28. Armstrong, "A Jumble of Foreignness," 241.

29. Gardiner, *Barbary Holiday*, 33.

30. European tourists could visit the collections outside visiting hours by announcing themselves to the guard. This treatment did not apply to Moroccan visitors.

31. Gardiner, *Barbary Holiday*, 156.

32. For further reading on received ideas of Islam and Islamic history in nineteenth-century Europe, see Said, *Orientalism*, and Burke, "The First Crisis of Orientalism."

33. Armstrong, "A Jumble of Foreignness," 203.

34. Karp, "Culture and Representation," 14.

35. Kirshenblatt-Gimblett, *Destination Culture*, 388.

36. See Bennett, *The Birth of the Museum*.

37. For excellent scholarship on the Louvre as an imperial museum, see Porterfield, *The Allure of Empire*, and McClellan, *Inventing the Louvre*. Likewise for the Musée Social, see Horne, *A Social Laboratory for Modern France*, 80.

38. Direction Générale de l'Instruction Publique des Beaux-Arts et des Antiquités, *Historique 1912–1930*, 150.

39. Rabinow, *French Modern*, 287.

40. Holden, "When It Pays to Be Medieval," 299.

41. Bennett discusses this concept in depth in chapter 7 of his book "Museums and Progress: Narrative, Ideology, Performance," in which he considers "the different ways in which, in their late nineteenth—and early twentieth-century formation, museums, fairs and exhibitions functioned as technologies of progress. . . . Indeed, it was quite common at the time for museums and the like to be referred to as 'machines for progress.'" Bennett, *The Birth of the Museum*, 10.

42. Ibid., 186.

43. Serghini, "The National Role of the Fine Arts and Folklore School of Tetuan," 25–29.

44. Senones, "The Antiquities Museum in Rabat," 43.

45. Gaugue, *Les états africains et leurs musées,* 28.

46. Koffi, "Socio-Historical Factors for Improved Integration of Local Museums," 87.

47. Sekkat, "L'action culturelle au Maroc," 72.

48. The modernization process in Moroccan museums was indicative of a larger global reform and modernization of museums. The decolonization process caused European and American museums as well as postcolonial museums to rethink the way that ethnographic exhibits were constructed and ushered in a period of slow reform in the 1960s and 1970s. For further reading on ethnographic museums and their politics, see Karp and Lavine eds., *Exhibiting Cultures.*

49. Ferguson, *Expectations of Modernity,* 235.

50. Rostow's five stages to modernity include traditional society, the preconditions for take-off, the take-off, the drive to maturity, and high consumption. For a succinct analysis of these terms, see Spybey, *Social Change, Development and Dependency,* 21–22.

51. Shana Cohen's translation of the document as cited by Salmi in *Crise de l'enseignement et reproduction sociale de Maroc,* 85: Cohen, *Searching for a Different Future,* 58.

52. For further reading on this period, see Diouri, *A qui appartient le Maroc?* Vermeren, *Histoire du Maroc depuis l'indépendance;* and Daoud, *Les années Lamalif.* For perhaps less substantiated scholarship but an excellent read, see Perrault, *Notre ami le Roi.*

53. Becker, *Art Worlds,* 165.

54. Duncan, "Art Museums and the Ritual of Citizenship," 88–89.

55. Zoellick, "When Trade Leads to Tolerance," A 13.

56. Diouf, cited by Garcia-Anton in "Dak'Art 98," 88.

57. For an example of recent scholarship that discusses this concept in greater depth, see Kirshenblatt-Gimblett, *Destination Culture,* and Dominguez, "The Marketing of Heritage."

58. In his essay on the politics of late twentieth-century state-run museums in Zimbabwe, Dawson Munjeri describes the extent to which the black majority in Zimbabwe has actually been discouraged from visiting state museums. Munjeri, "Refocusing or Reorientation?"

59. *Morocco Tourism* 53 (Summer 1969): 56.

60. For further reading on how international hotels such as the Hilton were instrumental in disseminating images of modernity and liberal democracy around the world during the 1960s, see Wharton, *Building the Cold War.*

61. *Morocco Tourism* 54 (Autumn 1969): 72.

62. "Mr. Playboy in Morocco," 60.

63. Wang, *Tourism and Modernity,* 46, 49.

64. Kirshenblatt-Gimblett, "From Ethnology to Heritage," 1.

65. Roditi, "Benkemoun," *Morocco Tourism* 51 (Winter 1968): 57.

66. Ministère de l'Education Nationale, Service des Monuments Historiques des Arts et du Folklore, *Jeune peinture marocaine,* 5.

67. Moroccan poet and president of the Moroccan Writers Association, Hassan Najmi, told me that he had never heard of this poet and did not know his true identity. Hassan Najmi, interview by the author, Rabat, June 16, 2000.

68. *Mechouis* is a Moroccan dish of grilled meats.

69. *Pastilla* is another traditional Moroccan food consisting of chicken, almonds, and raisins baked in filo dough and sprinkled with powdered sugar and cinnamon. This dish

is often served at weddings and is considered a food of celebration due to the time, effort, and expense required to prepare it.

70. Fatma, a common Arabic name for a woman, was the name of the Prophet Mohammed's daughter. It was also the name given by the French to North African women in general, and its specific implication was that of courtesan or even prostitute. On French-produced postcards of Moroccan and Algerian women from the early twentieth century, the caption often read "Fatma on the stairs" or "Fatma entertaining at home."

71. The term *Khamas* refers to manual laborers who under the Protectorate worked for European plantations and who after independence became migrant workers.

72. *Kif* can refer both to a flavored tobacco and to Moroccan marijuana.

73. Fantasias are elaborate presentations involving horses and guns that are conducted during great celebrations, primarily in the Marrakesh area. Today these performances are still held on major holy days but are also performed on a smaller scale for tourists.

74. Maraboutism is a movement in Islam specific to Morocco and West Africa. Julia Clancy Smith defines the term as follows: "In the medieval period, it designated religious reformers issuing from frontier redoubts, or *ribats*. In the nineteenth-century lexicon of eastern Algeria and Tunisia, it meant 'men, devoted to God's adoration and linked to Him, who enjoyed a reputation of saintliness which conferred upon them the title of "waliy," friend of God' (Marcel Beaussier, *Dictionnaire pratique arabe-français*, new ed. by Mohamed Ben Cheneb [Algiers: Jules Carbonel, 1931], 378). The French equivalent of this complex term—marabout—was used and misused throughout the colonial period, giving rise to considerable confusion regarding the precise social and religious identity of the marabout." Clancy-Smith, *Rebel and Saint*, 278.

75. "You-yous" are ululations: exclamations of celebration made by women throughout the Arab world. The sounds are produced by emitting a cry while flapping the tongue from side to side.

76. Izhar, "Made in Morocco," 18.

77. "Ce que nous voulons," 6.

78. Daoud, *Les années Lamalif*, 154.

79. El-Malki, "Manifeste de la revue Pro-C," 7.

80. Balzac, *La peau de chagrin*.

81. Al-Fassi, cited by Cohen in *Searching for a Different Future*, 51.

82. Elbaz, "Jeune peintres où sommes-nous?" 4.

83. Bennis, "L'école marocaine doit affronter toutes les competitions internationales," 4.

84. Bellal, "Qui lèvera le rideau?" 4.

85. Bennis, "Cherkaoui révèle," 4.

86. C. E. Y., "Reflections sur l'art et l'artiste," 44.

87. Jay, "Paris fête le Maghreb," 5.

88. "Entretien avec Amine Demnati," 55.

89. Alaoui, *Cherkaoui*, 184–185.

90. Touzani, *La culture et la politique culturelle au Maroc*, 34.

91. Ibid., 15.

92. Ibid., 56.

93. Ibid., 66.

94. "Table ronde 1," 52.

95. In their essay "Museums Are Good to Think," Arjun Appadurai and Carol

Breckenridge argue that the lack of signage in postcolonial museums in India reflects a freedom of discourse and interpretation. I would disagree with regard to the Moroccan context and rather argue that this is a leftover practice from the colonial period.

96. Due to their expense, these lights are turned on and off by a museum attendant as the museum visitor enters and exits rooms. Although this practice might disturb the image of the museum as an "eternal flame"of culture, it promotes conservation of electricity.

97. In particular see chapter 9, "The 'Alawi Blood Descendants," in Combs-Schilling, *Sacred Performances,* and Waterbury, *The Commander of the Faithful.*

98. Sekkat, "L'action culturelle au Maroc," 78.

99. According to the 1921 *Guide bleu,* the Oudaya Complex provided one of the most interesting and charming walks in Rabat. Monmarché, *Maroc: Les guides bleu,* 193.

100. Mariami, "Journée internationale des musées," 8.

101. This separation reflects the dominant opinion of the Moroccan cultural elite in the 1960s and 1970s that naïve art was for the most part an inferior Moroccan art that was exploited by Europe as an example of Third World primitive art. It had no place in an institution of fine arts. This debate will be discussed at length in chapter 4.

102. Jay, "Paris fête le Maghreb," 5.

103. Ali Amahan, interview by the author, Ministry of Culture, Rabat, May 19, 2000.

104. Crane, "Memory, Distortion, and History in the Museum."

105. Amahan, interview by the author.

2. Marketplace Museums

1. For a discussion of the Western art museum as part of a corporate logic of late capitalism and globalization, see Mathur, "Museums and Globalization"; Krauss, "The Cultural Logic of the Late Capitalist Museum"; Twitchell, *Adcult USA;* and van den Bosch, "Museums."

2. Abdellah Belghazi's museum ventures will be discussed at length in the following chapter.

3. Twitchell, *Adcult USA,* 215.

4. Mount, *African Art,* 39.

5. Holden, "When It Pays to Be Medieval."

6. Gaudibert, "Jeunes peintres marocains où sommes-nous?" 4.

7. Slyomovics, *The Performance of Human Rights in Morocco,* 105.

8. Dagher, "Is There an Arab Market for Fine Art?" 4.

9. van den Bosch, "Museums," 84.

10. For a thorough examination of the move from modernization policies to development through the political and economic liberalization in Morocco, see Cohen and Jaidi, *Morocco.*

11. Roberts, "The Museum and the Crisis of Critical Postmodernism," 70.

12. Wafabank merged with the Banque Commerciale du Maroc in 2004, forming the Attijariwafa Bank.

13. Benaïssa, "Dedicace," ii.

14. Ibid.

15. Ardouin, "Culture, Museums, and Development in Africa," 182.

16. Benaïssa, "Dedicace," ii.

17. Cohen and Jaidi, *Morocco,* 11.

18. Ayoun, "L'enjeu culturel."

19. Benaïssa, "Dedicace," iii.

20. Jacobson, *Art and Business,* 10.

21. Ibid.

22. Rockefeller, cited in the foreword to Lee, *Art at Work,* 12.

23. Jacobson, *Art and Business,* 10.

24. Lahbib M'Seffer, interview by the author, Wafabank Casablanca, May 26, 2000.

25. Bennani, "Prologue," in *La peinture marocaine au rendez-vous de l'histoire,* v.

26. El Maleh, "La peinture marocaine: Tradition et modernité," 17.

27. El Maleh, "Preface," 1.

28. M'Seffer, interview by the author.

29. Ibid.

30. Mayer, "Moroccans—Citizens or Subjects?" 65.

31. Youssoufi, cited by Howe in "Morocco's Democratic Experience," 67–68.

32. Ibid., 67.

33. Cohen, *Searching for a Different Future,* 5.

34. Ibid., 8.

35. M'Seffer, interview by the author.

36. Duncan, "Art Museums and the Ritual of Citizenship."

37. For an in-depth analysis of Casablanca as a modern city, see Ossman, *Picturing Casablanca.*

38. Tallal, cited by Daoud in "Le monde fantastique de Tallal," 40.

39. When I was in Morocco in the summer of 2000, many stores and other places still had portraits of Hassan II gracing their walls. The replacement of portraits from Hassan II to Mohammed VI took place at varying speeds in Morocco, reflecting both the availability of photographs of the new king engaged in appropriate tasks and concerns about respecting the former monarch. Even dead, Hassan II still occupies a large visual space in Moroccan life.

40. Meecham and Sheldon, *Modern Art,* 198–199.

41. For further discussion of the function of the white cube in exhibition construction, see O'Doherty, *Inside the White Cube.*

42. Ossman, *Picturing Casablanca,* 11.

43. Bourqia, "The Cultural Legacy of Power in Morocco," 251.

44. Duncan, "Art Museums and the Ritual of Citizenship."

45. M'Seffer, interview by the author.

46. The creation of bourgeois publics for Moroccan art will be discussed in chapter 4.

47. M'Seffer, interview by the author.

48. Ibid.

49. Slyomovics, *The Performance of Human Rights in Morocco,* 110.

50. Ibid., 2.

51. Laroui, *The Crisis of the Arab Intellectual,* 174.

52. El Maleh, "La peinture marocaine," 17.

53. http://www.ona.ma/.

54. Stauffer, "No Room for Contemporary Art."

55. Ibid.

56. Sylvia Frei-Belhassan, interview by the author, Institut Français, Rabat, May 12, 2007.

57. Oumama Draoui, "Villa des Arts de Rabat: Un écrin pour le savoir," *Le journal hebdomadaire* 284 (January 6–12, 2006), http://www.lejournal-hebdo.com/sommaire/culture/villa-des-arts-de-rabat-un-crin-pour-le-savoir.html.

58. When I visited it in 2007, the library was an empty space waiting to be filled with materials and books. The café was not open on the three occasions that I visited, and the ateliers, each named after a famous Moroccan painter, were not in active use.

59. Bennett, *The Birth of the Museum,* 10.

60. Felicia McCarren at Tulane University is conducting interesting work on the Maroc Télécom phone campaigns in order to analyze how the concept of the "téléphone arabe" creates transnational networks and multidirectional transculturation. See McCarren, "*Téléphone arabe.*"

61. http://www.museeiam.ma/presentation.asp.

62. Cohen and Jaidi, *Morocco,* 124.

63. Appadurai, *Modernity at Large,* 21.

3. A Private Cabinet of Curiosity

1. Gombrich, *Ideals and Idols,* 196.

2. Gaye, "La mémoire retrouvée," 2–3.

3. See Susan Crane's article on the Museum of Jurassic Technology, "Curious Cabinets and Imaginary Museums," and Michael Fehr's account of self-reflexive museum display in "A Museum and Its Memory."

4. For further reading on cabinets of curiosity see Impey and MacGregor, *The Origins of Museums;* Pomian, *Collectors and Curiosities;* Findlen, *Possessing Nature;* Dietz and Nutz, "Collections Curieuses"; and Ameri, "The Spatial Dialectics of Authenticity." See also examples of contemporary digital interpretations on the cabinet of curiosity via the following New York Public Library exhibition: http://www.nypl.org/research/chss/events/curiosities.html.

5. Appadurai, *Modernity at Large,* 9.

6. Unless otherwise noted, Belghazi's statements come from an interview I conducted with him in Bouknadel, Morocco, on May 13, 2000.

7. This statement is part of a press packet that the Belghazi Museum has assembled for internal purposes. It is repeated in slightly different forms both in museum pamphlets and in press articles such as Er-Remah, "De soie, d'or et d'argent."

8. Crane, "Curious Cabinets and Imaginary Museums," 65, 68.

9. Sign in a display case on the ground floor of the Belghazi Museum.

10. Ameri, "The Spatial Dialectics of Authenticity," 64.

11. Alaoui, "Le Musée Dar Belghazi."

12. Kirshenblatt-Gimblett, *Destination Culture,* 165.

13. Kreps, *Liberating Culture,* xiii.

14. Ameri, "The Spatial Dialectics of Authenticity," 64.

15. Ibid., 65.

16. Findlen, *Possessing Nature,* 23.

17. Ali Amahan, interview by the author, Ministry of Culture, Rabat, May 19, 2000.

18. Stafford, *Artful Science,* 238.

19. Alaoui, "Le Musée Dar Belghazi."

20. Laabi, "Esthetique de l'objet," 42.

21. Alaoui, "Le Musée Dar Belghazi."
22. *The Arabian Nights,* trans. Richard Burton, 658–659.
23. *Stories from Thousand and One Nights.*
24. Said, *Orientalism,* 40.
25. For an in-depth and compelling analysis of how Orientalist discourse and stereotypes of Arabs and Africans entered into Western popular culture, see Pieterse, *White on Black.*
26. *Stories from Thousand and One Nights.*
27. Ibid. For further reading about the history of the tales of *Thousand and One Nights,* see Irwin, *Arabian Nights: A Companion.*
28. http://www.alibabaonline.fr.
29. Rosello, *Declining the Stereotype,* 15.
30. Chow, *Writing Diaspora,* 36.
31. *The Arabian Nights,* trans. Burton, 680.
32. *Stories from Thousand and One Nights.*
33. Al-Khoury, *Youssef fi baṭn ūmhu,* 20.
34. Ibid., 21.
35. http://www.bcat-tv.org/rotunda/wunderkammer/wunderkammer.asp.
36. http://www.kirchersociety.org.
37. Bennett, "Pedagogic Objects, Clean Eyes, and Popular Instruction," 347.
38. Huyssen writes, "Perhaps it is time to remember the future, rather than simply to worry about the future of memory." Huyssen, *Present Pasts,* 29.
39. Cohen, *Searching for a Different Future,* 143.
40. Budney, "Who's It For?" 88.
41. "Declaration on the Importance and Value of Universal Museums," 248.
42. Mathur, "Museums and Globalization," 703 (emphasis in original).
43. Kapur, *When Was Modernism?* 321.
44. Laroui, *Esquisses historiques,* 176.
45. Touzani, "Les musées marocains."

4. Imaginary Museums and Their Real Phantoms

1. Noever, "On the Subject," 7.
2. Ibid., 8.
3. Cuno, "Against the Discursive Museum"; Belting, "Place of Reflection or Place of Sensation?"
4. Merz and Molderings, "We'll Stick with It."
5. Buntinx, "Communities of Sense/Communities of Sentiment," 219.
6. These debates presaged debates about the "global" that are ongoing in the contemporary art world today.
7. Kirshenblatt-Gimblett, "The Museum—A Refuge for Utopian Thought."
8. Winegar, *Creative Reckonings,* 10.
9. Foucault, *The Archeology of Knowledge,* 25.
10. Maraini, *Écrits sur l'art,* 21–24.
11. Laâbi, "Prologue," 6.
12. Laâbi's use of the term "old humanisms" may be in direct reference to the work of Moroccan poet and philosopher Mohammed Aziz Lahbabi, who explored the idea of a

new humanism. In works such as *De l'être à la personne* Lahbabi examines the idea of "being" and "man" in both Western philosophy and Islamic thought, attempting to articulate a position for the North African subject that is beyond both traditions, firmly located in a new understanding of the term "human."

13. Cohen, *Searching for a Different Future,* 55.

14. Buntinx, "Communities of Sense/Communities of Sentiment," 223 (emphasis in the original).

15. Wa Thiongo, *Decolonising the Mind.*

16. García Canclini, *Hybrid Cultures.*

17. Alonso, *The Burden of Modernity,* 26.

18. Bhabha, "Of Mimicry and Man," 87–88.

19. Flores Khalil, *The Arab Avant-Garde,* xxi.

20. Aziza, *L'image et l'Islam,* 37–38.

21. The only explicit prohibition of the production of images in the Qur'an can be found in the famous "Satanic verses" (Al-ayât al-Shaytaniyyah). In these verses, the anti-Islamic cults of al-Lât, al-Ozza, and Manat are rebuked for their production of anti-Islamic idols (statues and figurines) and a proscription is placed on idolatry (the worship of said idols). In Islamic scholarship, the Satanic verses are considered highly controversial; scholars have different interpretations not only of their meaning but also of their existence. The only other textual prohibition on figurative representation in the body of sacred writings in Islam comes from the hadiths, the codified sayings of the Prophet Mohammed. Drawing on the work of Louis Massignon, Aziza outlines four formal condemnations. The first is a malediction against the adornment of tombs and the creation of images of saints and prophets. The second states that on the day of final judgment, the "makers of images" will be punished when God gives them the impossible task of resuscitating their work, of breathing life into their representations of animate objects. A third condemnation prohibits the use of fabric or cushions with images on them. According to Aziza, this prohibition is quite contentious, for it is thought that such cushions existed in the bedroom of the Prophet himself. And finally there is a condemnation of the cult of the cross. Despite the formal nature of the prohibitions and condemnations contained in the hadiths, one must remember that the hadiths are an interpretation of the Prophet Mohamed's sayings, codified only in the second half of the ninth century, and they have have never been declared an "imperative" source of religious law.

22. Leaman, *Islamic Aesthetics,* 18.

23. Aziza, *L'image et l'Islam,* 46.

24. Recent scholarship on Islamic art has challenged this point. The work of Oleg Grabar has been particularly important in this light, urging scholars and students of Islamic art not to treat this art through a static and unified vision of Islam but rather to treat it as a force of social and political expression. See Grabar, "Geometry and Ideology."

25. Bahnassi, "Al-Wasiti d'après les maqamats d'al Hariri," 37.

26. Al-Aroussi, *Esthétique et art islamique,* 12.

27. Cited by Maraini in "Introduction," 43.

28. Gaudibert, "Jeunes peintres marocains où sommes-nous?" 4.

29. Some scholars, such as Moulim Al-Aroussi and Khalil M'Rabet, have written that there is no critical tradition vis-à-vis the arts in Morocco. According to M'Rabet, "In the field of Muslim fine arts, there doesn't exist any local critical tradition—except for calligraphy

and miniature painting—that couples artwork with historical commentary or aesthetic principles. All critical heritage that would inform us about the development of taste, about the artistic principles of the past, has not been cultivated by artisan-artists of past periods, or by their contemporaries, men of letters. Doesn't this absence of an art critique perpetuate itself even today?" M'Rabet, *Peinture et identité*, 20.

30. El Maleh, "Ahmed Cherkaoui ou la passion de la signe," 44.

31. "Je suis venu chercher asile dans l'impeccable naïveté." Baudelaire, cited by Boutaleb in *La peinture naïve au Maroc*, 7. This quote can be found in Baudelaire, "Extrait des critiques d'art de Baudelaire sur l'exposition universelle de 1855." In searching for the reference for this line, I came across two other sources on naïve painting that use it as an epigraph (both without citations).

32. Belkahia, Chebaâ, and Melehi, "Situation de la peinture naïve au Maroc," 75.

33. My understanding of this term comes from Calo, "African Art and Critical Discourse between World Wars." Calo acknowledges that the term originated from Gaines, Berger, and Lord, *Theater of Refusal.*

34. David O'Brien discusses the tension between masculinity and feminity in abstract expressionism through the work of the Egyptian-French artist Ghada Amer in his introductory essay in O'Brien and Prochaska, *Beyond East and West,* 17.

35. Daoud, "Un peintre qui promet," 45.

36. See Maraini, "Le rôle historique des arts populaires," 6–10, and, more generally, Price, *Primitive Art in Civilized Places,* 60.

37. Daoud, "Un peintre qui promet," 45.

38. Tallal, "The Artist's Voice," 184.

39. Ibid., 185 (emphasis in original).

40. Stouky, "Réflexions sur la dialectique de la modernité et de la tradition," 40.

41. Kapur, *When Was Modernism?* 291; Winegar, *Creative Reckonings,* 2.

42. This is by all means an incomplete and simplifed definition of nationalism in Morocco. For a detailed analysis of the nationalist movement in Morocco, see Abdallah Laroui, *Les origines sociales et culturelles du nationalisme marocain.*

43. Chatterjee, "The Disciplines in Colonial Bengal," 14.

44. Association de Recherche Culturelle, "Programme de recherche et d'action de l'A.R.C.," 3–9, 5.

45. Khatibi, "Culture nationale et culture de classe au Maroc," 20.

46. Daoud, "Le monde fantastique de Tallal," 40.

47. Elbaz, "L'art doit toucher l'universel," 36.

48. Oguibe, *The Culture Game,* xiv.

49. García Canclini argues that one of the four basic "movements" that constitute modernity is the "emancipation" of cultural fields so that art becomes an autonomous sphere. García Canclini, *Hybrid Cultures,* 12–13.

50. Benaïssa, "Photographies," 22.

51. Maraini, *Écrits sur l'Art,* 19.

52. Daoud, "Les pionniers de l'Art," 32.

53. Maraini, *Écrits sur l'Art,* 19.

54. Armbrust, *Mass Culture and Modernism in Egypt,* 194.

55. Ibid., 22.

56. This instance provides an interesting glimpse of the tightness of the artistic and

intellectual group in Morocco at the time. Both Ben Jelloun and Khatibi were intimately acquainted with Melehi as a friend and as a fellow contributor to the cultural journals *Souffles* and *Lamalif.* In 1971 Melehi became the founder and editor of the journal *Integral,* in which the writers' articles appeared. During this time Melehi was also married to art historian Toni Maraini.

57. Ben Jelloun, "Melehi," 4.

58. Ibid.

59. Melehi's work has a striking resemblance to the 1960s "postpainterly" work of painters Max Bill and Josef Albers. The latter was the founder of op art, a movement that was interested in creating optical illusions through overlapping forms. For more on postpainterly abstraction and op art, see chapter 3 of Lucie-Smith, *Movements in Art since 1945.*

60. Khatibi, "Exposition Mohamed Melehi à l'atelier Rabat," 2.

61. In his later work Khatibi has become much more attuned to questions of political and economic dependency in art, writing in 1997, "The exasperated expression that one often hears 'art has no borders; it is international!' does not take into consideration the economic and cultural implications placed into the conquering structures of political will." Khatibi, cited by M'Rabet in "Écrits en amont," 24–25.

62. Stouky, "Reflexions sur la dialectique de la modernité et de la tradition," 38.

63. Becker, *Amazigh Arts in Morocco,* 178.

64. Shabout, *Modern Arab Art,* 30.

65. Stouky, "Réflexions sur la dialectique de la modernité et de la tradition," 38.

66. C. E. Y., "Reflexions sur l'art et l'artiste," 44.

67. In his contribution to the series "Young Moroccan Painters Where Are We?" which André Elbaz started in a newspaper, Pierre Gaudibert wrote: "One of the great reverberations of the influence of colonialism was in the massive introduction in all the Maghreb of a 'pacotille' (shoddy objects) or bazaar orientalism that permitted a mediocre painter to execute commercial visions of conventional visions and scenes. This painting, also termed 'the arab market,' has multiplied and widely disseminated oases, gazelles, prostitutes, palm trees, minarets, etc." Gaudibert, "Jeunes peintres marocains où sommes-nous ?" 4.

68. Laâbi, "Réalités et dilemmes de la culture nationale."

69. Ibid., 30 (boldface in the original).

70. Laroui, *The Crisis of the Arab Intellectual,* xi.

71. Ibid., 156.

72. Ibid., 166.

73. Ibid., 176.

74. Laâbi, *La brûlure des interrogations,* 80.

75. Hammoudi, *Master and Disciple.*

76. See Armbrust, *Mass Culture and Modernism in Egypt,* and Abu-Lughod, "Modern Subjects."

77. Winegar, *Creative Reckonings,* 188–89.

78. Bourdieu, *Distinction,* 4.

79. Scott, *Domination and the Arts of Resistance,* 4.

80. The extent to which the newspapers circulated beyond their intended audiences is not certain. However, because the act of newspaper-reading is such an established and cherished activity in Morocco, requiring only basic reading skills, it is possible that articles on art reached all sectors of society. As Mark Cohen writes of 1960s Morocco: "For the literate,

the most popular reading material is the newspaper. . . . Total daily circulation is approximately 150,000, although dissemination is wider due to the common practice of reading newspapers aloud for the benefit of illiterate relatives and friends and of passing the papers on to others." Cohen and Hahn, *Morocco: Old Land, New Nation,* 201. Likewise, televised and cinematic news coverage of arts in Morocco also served as a method of widely disseminating information, reaching illiterate audiences who owned a television or had access to one. Starting after Morocco achieved independence, the Moroccan Cinematographic Center, a national agency, produced short documentaries about different aspects of Moroccan life and culture. The first film to deal with painting and the contemporary arts appeared in 1964. It was an eighteen-minute piece titled *Moroccan Painting—Naïve to Abstract,* and the center's catalogue described it as "a short piece that makes our young art of painting known by placing it in the context of Moroccan artistic patrimony." This was the only film produced on the art of painting until 1980, when the series took off with titles such as *The Nostalgia of the Naïve* (1980), *Morocco and Its Painters: Mahjoub Ahrdane* (1982), *Morocco and Its Painters: Hassan Slaoui* (1982), *Morocco and Its Painters: Mekki Meghara* (1983), *Morocco and Its Painters: Fatima Hassan* (1984), *Morocco and Its Painters: Miloud* (1984), *Canvas Painting* (1988) and *Cherkaoui the Abstract* (1988). *Catalogue du Centre Cinématographique Marocain.*

81. "Le peintre Kacimi expose à la Maison de la Pensée," *L'opinion,* June 13, 1965, 5.

82. In his dissertation Abdelhak Sekkat wrote that some young Moroccan painters (no specific names were given) enjoyed their relationship with the emerging bourgeoisie and did what they could to profit from the situation. Sekkat, *L'action culturelle au Maroc,* 65.

83. "Admirez ce chef-d'oeuvre!" *L'opinion,* March 11, 1965, 5.

84. "Une visite s'impose pour se rendre compte du travail accompli." "Les élèves des Beaux-Arts exposent leur oeuvres à l'Ecole," *L'opinion* (June 19, 1965): 4 ; "Exposition de peinture dans la salle vitrée du Harti," *L'opinion,* May 20, 1967, 4.

85. Jay, "La palette étincelante de Larbi Belcadi," 5.

86. "Huit Picasso à la plus intéressante exposition de ces dernières années," *L'opinion,* February 11, 1967, 5.

87. "Nos lecteurs en colère!"

88. "Nos lecteurs en colère: Qu'est-ce que l'émission Arts et Lettres?" *L'opinion,* April 10, 1965, 4.

89. Ibid.

90. "Nos lecteurs en colère: Mlle Arts et Lettres répond," *L'opinion,* April 13, 1965, 4.

91. "Nos lecteurs en colère: Un critique," *L'opinion,* April 16, 1965, 4.

92. "Où est le public de la littérature marocaine?" *L'opinion,* March 21, 1967, 5.

93. During the 1960s cultural correspondents for *L'opinion* included Salim Jay, a poet, and Zakya Daoud, the art editor and editor in chief of the cultural journal *Lamalif.*

94. In 1966 Cohen estimated that the combined circulation of *Le petit Marocain* and its sister publication *La vigie* was 80,000, approximately half of the total circulation numbers in Morocco. Cohen and Hahn, *Morocco: Old Land, New Nation,* 202.

95. *Le petit Marocain,* May 19, 1965, 4.

96. Laâbi, "Lisez 'Le petit Marocain,'" 6.

97. "Le peintre De Pass expose à la Galerie 17," *Le petit Marocain* (May 21, 1965): 4; "Exposition des oeuvres de Lucette Salazzi à la Galerie 17," *Le petit Marocain* (May 8, 1965): 4; "Les artistes Independants ont inauguré leur nouveau local," *Le petit Marocain,* May 23, 1965, 4.

98. Settat is a medium-sized city on the coastal plain directly south of Casablanca and is the largest market town of the area. Hence some of the more organic and florid metaphors used to describe the exhibit itself.

99. "Rabi'a al-fan fî Settat," *Al-'Âlam,* May 2–3, 1965, 5.

100. Ibid.

101. Ibid.

102. Appiah, *In My Father's House,* 149.

103. Araeen, "Modernity, Modernism, and Africa's Place in the History of Art," 412.

104. Oguibe, "The True Location of Ernest Mancoba's Modernism," 420.

105. "Questionnaire by Hassouna Mesbahi. *Journal al-Mostaqbal.* Tunis. 1981," in *Pour Abdellatif Laâbi,* ed. Ripault, 228–29.

106. Maffi, *Pratiques du patrimoine et politiques de la mémoire en Jordanie,* 104.

107. Pandolfo, *Impasse of the Angels,* 3.

5. Taking Art to the Streets

1. "Y en a marre!" *Telquel Online* 253–54 (January 5, 2007), http://www.telquel-online .com/.

2. For more information, read the project description for "L'invendu" at Darsi's Web site: www.lasourcedulion.org.

3. Kirshenblatt-Gimblett, *Destination Culture,* 57, 59.

4. Ibid., 59, 57–58.

5. Historically, *gnawa* music is a sacred music brought by ritual musicians and former slaves from sub-Saharan Africa (the Gnawa) to Morocco. The music is performed to induce a trance and heal those who are believed to be possessed. Today, many contemporary *gnawa* groups have entered the world music scene, collaborating with African-American jazz musicians and other recording artists to produce a new genre of *gnawa*-fusion. For work on the Gnawa and their music, see Kapchan, *Traveling Spirit Masters.*

6. For a sophisticated Foucauldian reading of the relationship between fairground and museum in the nineteenth century, see chapter 1 of Bennett, *The Birth of the Museum.*

7. Clifford, *Routes,* 8.

8. Manning, *Ephemeral Territories,* 6.

9. Of course, not all festivals function this way. In her work on national museums and youth festivals in Mali, Mary Jo Arnoldi shows how the Malian state used festivals to disseminate a certain regulated vision of the nation. Arnoldi, "Youth Festivals and Museums."

10. Bennett, "Pedagogic Objects, Clean Eyes, and Popular Instruction," 370–71.

11. "L'image est, jusqu'à un certain point, le sujet ou le héros de ce livre." Kilito, *La querelle des images,* 10.

12. Sontag, *On Photography,* 153.

13. Buntinx, "Communities of Sense/Communities of Sentiment," 238.

14. Bunn, "The Museum Outdoors," 358.

15. Clifford, *Routes,* 192.

16. Ben, "Lisez ceci: De la peinture," 4.

17. "Entretien avec Hamid Alaoui," *Integral* 2 (1972): 12–16.

18. Roberts, "The Museum and the Crisis of Critical Postmodernism," 71.

19. Ibid.

20. The group of painters consisted of Mohamed Ataallah, Farid Belkahia, Mohamed Chebaâ, Mustapha Hafid, Mohamed Hamidi, and Mohamed Melehi.

21. "Il faut revaloriser et encourager l'art," *Lamalif* 30 (May–June 1969): 48.

22. Ibid.

23. Bourdieu and Darbel, *The Love of Art*, 39.

24. "Il faut revaloriser et encourager l'art," 48.

25. See Slyomovics, *The Performance of Human Rights in Morocco;* Perrault, *Notre ami le Roi*; and Diouri, *A qui appartient le Maroc?* for accounts of political censure and oppression in Morocco during the 1960s and 1970s.

26. "Il faut revaloriser et encourager l'art," 48.

27. Ibid.

28. Bennett, "Introduction," 9–10.

29. This symbiotic relationship between the arts and social revolution during the 1960s and early 1970s can be read across genres in art. Further scholarship on the presence of art forms on the street includes Sullivan, *On the Walls and in the Streets,* and Callaghan, "The Perpetual Present."

30. The composition of the group remained the same with the exception of Mustapha Hamidi, who left the group.

31. "Présence plastique dans les lycées," *Integral* 1 (October 1971): 6.

32. Wolff, *Aesthetics and the Sociology of Art,* 105.

33. "Echos de l'exposition dans les lycées," *Integral* 1 (October 1971): 8.

34. Ibid.

35. Ibid.

36. El Maleh, "Itinéraire," 13.

37. "Echos de l'exposition dans les lycées," 8.

38. Historians of Morocco have discussed at great length the social and political divisions between urban and rural areas of Morocco, between the Makhzen and the Bled es-Siba. During the Protectorate period, French colonial ethnographers and historians further aggravated and calcified this division in their scholarship, and likewise colonial administrators created policy based on these distinctions. For further treatment, see Burke, "The Image of the Moroccan State in French Ethnological Literature"; Laroui, *L'histoire du Maghreb;* and Rivet, *Le Maroc de Lyautey à Mohammed V.*

39. "Echos de l'exposition dans les lycées," 8.

40. Ibid.

41. Ibid.

42. Scott, *Domination and the Arts of Resistance,* 4.

43. "Entretien avec Mohamed Hamidi," *Integral* 3–4 (January 1973): 45.

44. Benaïssa and Melehi, cited by Blood in "A Printmaking Workshop in Morocco" (Mohammed Benaïssa and Mohamed Melehi, *Asilah: First Cultural Moussem July/August 1978* [New Zealand: Shoof Publications, 1979]).

45. Benaïssa and Melehi, cited by Hayes in "Asilah: Common Ground," 12.

46. Benaïssa, cited in "Mohammed Benaïssa on the Asilah Festival."

47. Ibid.

48. Blood, "A Printmaking Workshop in Morocco."

49. Ibid.

50. "Rehabilitation of Asilah, Morocco," 28.

51. Lin, "Asilah, Morocco."
52. Ibid.
53. Ibid.
54. http://www.lasourcedulion.org.
55. Ossman, *Picturing Casablanca,* 21.
56. Hassan Darsi, interview by the author, January 12, 2007.
57. See my article on nostalgia in Casablanca: "Nostalgia and the New Cosmopolitan."
58. Cohen and Eleb, *Casablanca,* 228–29.
59. Derain, *Echo Larmitaj,* 178.
60. Daoud, *Casablanca en mouvement,* 22.
61. Bensâad, "The Militarization of Migration Frontiers in the Mediterranean."
62. Buntinx, "Communities of Sense/Communities of Sentiment," 221–22.
63. Hassan Darsi, interview by the author, Casablanca, May 6, 2007.
64. Abdellah Karroum, interview by the author, Williamstown, Mass., May 24, 2008.
65. Karroum, "Allers/Retours."
66. Karroum, interview by the author.
67. Karroum, "La coprésence fondement de la rencontre."
68. Karroum, interview by the author.
69. Karroum, "La coprésence fondement de la rencontre."
70. Ali Amahan, interview by the author, Ministry of Culture, Rabat, May 19, 2000.
71. The jury citation from the Aga Khan Award stated: "This project has received an Award because it exemplifies a new approach to development, environmental conservation and the improvement of living conditions for rural populations. The success of the project was based on mobilizing the experience of emigrant villagers who brought back expertise after living in modern urban contexts, joining hands with those who remained in order to take charge of their own destiny. As a result, old buildings are now cared for and new installations have been added to provide basic services such as a water-supply network, electricity and education facilities. The cooperation between the villagers has enhanced daily life while preserving the traditions of this isolated and poor population. The success of the project makes it an example for the entire region, bringing hope to rural communities throughout the Islamic world and reinforcing their determination to improve their own lives." Aga Khan Award for Architecture, *The Eighth Award Cycle, 1999–2001,* http://www.akdn.org/agency/akaa/eighthcycle/page_02txt.htm.
72. Amahan, "A Model Community Museum in a Village in the High Atlas," 1.
73. Mernissi, *Les Aït-Débrouille,* 3, 3, 4, 96.
74. Laâbi, cited by Ripault in *Pour Abdellatif Laâbi,* 229.
75. "Table ronde 1," 59.

Conclusion

1. de Pontcharra and Alaoui, "Dans le monde, le désir d'être soi," 128.
2. "'Unread Author' Spurns Book Award," *BBC News Online,* January 23 2004, http://news.bbc.co.uk/go/pr/fr/-/1/hi/world/africa/3424965.stm.
3. Bouzfour, "La valise rouge," 31–32.
4. Garcia-Anton, "Dak'Art 98," 91.
5. Karroum, "Allers/Retours."

6. Blog entry, July 4, 2006, http://eyesonit.blogspot.com/2006/07/un-muse-dart -contemporain-chez-nous.html.

7. Ministry of Culture, http://www.minculture.gov.ma/fr/MAC.htm.

8. Pastor Mellado, cited by Buntinx in "Communities of Sense/Communities of Sentiment," 240 (emphasis in original).

9. "Table ronde 1," 58.

10. Ibid., 53.

11. Sylvia Belhassan, interview by the author, Rabat, Morocco, May 10, 2007.

12. Belhassan, cited by Stauffer in "No Room for Contemporary Art."

13. "Liste des signataires: 'Sauvons le Musée de Marrakech,'" *Emarrakech.com*, April 26, 2004, http://www.emarrakech.info/index.php?action=article&id_article=34155.

14. Ibid.

15. "Oui le musée de Marrakech est en danger," interview of Binebine by Tarik Essadi, *Emarrakech.com* (April 20, 2004), http://www.emarrakech.info/index.php?action= article&id_article=33292.

16. "Table ronde 1," 55.

17. Pastor Mellado, cited by Buntinx in "Communities of Sense/Communities of Sentiment," 240.

18. Karroum, "Expédition no. 1."

19. Kirshenblatt-Gimblett, "The Museum as Catalyst."

20. Abdellah Karroum, interview by the author, Williamstown, Mass., May 24, 2008.

21. Ibid.

22. Karroum, "Le passage du souk."

23. Ibid.

24. "Table ronde 1," 48.

25. Deleuze and Guattari, *A Thousand Plateaus*, 381.

26. "Mona Hatoum Interviewed by Jo Glencross," 69.

27. "Videokaravaan: About," *Videokaravaan*, http://www.videokaravaan.org/about.php.

28. "OVNI 2005: Resistances/ 25–30 January 2005," *Videokaravaan News*, http://www .videokaravaan.org/news.php.

29. Kotz, "Video Projection," 101.

30. "Videokaravaan in Agadir, Morocco."

31. See my work on this, "Bodies on the Beach."

32. Ascal, "Avant-dire," 7.

33. "Laura Rosano, Encrier, Kacimi, Etrières, Gharbaoui, Bonhomme chinois, Portrait de la mère, Coussin brodé, Batons de pluie, Le père, Etagère I, Table ronde, Chaise de circoncis, Saladi, Tables syriennes, Farzat, Etagère II, Mahdaoui, Moucharabieh, Miloudi, Chebaâ, Table hexagonale, Miroir tunisien, Table carrée, Bazaine, Tapis zemmour, Le jardin des delices, Coffre rouge, Diplôme coranique, Tête indienne, Coffre clouté."

34. Laâbi, *Petit musée portatif*, 47.

35. Ibid., 29.

36. Merali, "Displaces," 103.

37. Belkhodja, *2103, le retour de l'éléphant*, 43.

38. Ibid., 67.

39. Ibid., 84.

Bibliography

"Abdallah Hariri et Elvire Alerini exposent dans une banque." *Integral* 3–4 (January 1973): 48.

Abouzeid, Leila. *Year of the Elephant.* Trans. Barbara Parmenter. Austin: University of Texas Press, 1989.

Abu-Lughod, Janet. *Rabat: Urban Apartheid in Morocco.* Princeton, N.J.: Princeton University Press, 1980.

Abu-Lughod, Lila. "Modern Subjects: Egyptian Melodrama and Postcolonial Difference." In *Questions of Modernity,* ed. Timothy Mitchell. Minneapolis: University of Minnesota Press, 2000.

adonis. "Le manifeste du 5 juin 1967." *Souffles* (1968): 1–11.

Adyoun, Ahmed. "L'enjeu culturel." *Le temps du Maroc* 168 (January 15–21, 1999). http://www.tempsdumaroc.press.ma/hebdomadaire/1999/1521janv168/cult3.htm.

Aga-Oglu, Mehmet. "Remarks on the Character of Islamic Art." *Art Bulletin* 6 (1956): 178–202.

Alaoui, Brahim, ed. *Cherkaoui: La passion du signe.* Paris: Institut du Monde Arabe, 1996.

Alaoui, Larbi. "Le Musée Dar Belghazi un patrimoine national à preserver." *Al Bayane,* May 23, 1997.

Al-Aroussi, Moulim. *Esthétique et art islamique.* Casablanca: Arrabeta, 1996.

Al-Faraqi, I. R. "Islam and Art." *Studea Islamica* 37 (1973): 81–109.

Alioua, Khalid. "The State and Control of the Urban Milieu." In *The Moroccan State in Historical Perspective: 1850–1985,* ed. Abdelali Doumou, trans. Ayi Kwei Armah. Dakar: Codesria, 1990.

Al-Khoury, Idriss. *Youssef fi buṭn ūmhu.* Rabat: Dar Nashar Al-Mu'arifa, 1994.

Alloula, Malek. *The Colonial Harem.* Trans. Myrna Godzich and Wlad Godzich. Minneapolis: University of Minnesota Press, 1986.

Alonso, Carlos J. *The Burden of Modernity: The Rhetoric of Cultural Discourse in Spanish America*. New York: Oxford University Press, 1998.

Alpers, Svetlana. "The Museum as a Way of Seeing." In *Exhibiting Cultures: The Poetics and Politics of Museum Display*, ed. Ivan Karp and Steven Lavine. Washington, D.C.: Smithsonian Institution Press, 1991.

Altbach, Philip C., and Salah M. Hassan. *The Muse of Modernity: Essays on Culture as Development in Africa*. Trenton, N.J.: Africa World Press, 1996.

Amahan, Ali. "A Model Community Museum in a Village in the High Atlas." *International Museum Day 2001*. http://icom.museum/imd_rep2001_c.html.

Ameri, Amir. "The Spatial Dialectics of Authenticity." *SubStance* 33, no. 2 (2004): 61–89.

Amrière, Francis, ed. *Maroc: Les guides bleu*. Paris: Hachette 1950.

Anderson, Benedict. *Imagined Communities: Reflections on the Origin and Spread of Nationalism*. New York: Verso, 1991.

Appadurai, Arjun. *Modernity at Large: Cultural Dimensions of Globalization*. Minneapolis: University of Minnesota Press, 1996.

Appadurai, Arjun, and Carol Breckenridge. "Museums Are Good to Think: Heritage on View in India." In *Museums and Communities: The Politics of Public Culture*, ed. Ivan Karp, Christine Mullen Kreamer, and Steven D. Lavine. Washington, D.C.: Smithsonian Institution Press, 1992.

Appiah, Kwame Anthony. *In My Father's House: Africa in the Philosophy of Culture*. New York: Oxford University Press, 1992.

The Arabian Nights: Tales from a Thousand and One Nights. Trans. Richard Burton. New York: The Modern Library, 2001.

Araeen, Rasheed. "Modernity, Modernism, and Africa's Place in the History of Art of Our Age." *Third Text* 19, no. 4 (July 2005): 411–417.

Arce, Alberto, and Norman Long, eds. *Anthropology, Development, and Modernities: Exploring Discourses, Counter-Tendencies, and Violence*. London: Routledge, 2000.

Ardouin, Claude Daniel. "Culture, Museums, and Development in Africa." In *The Muse of Modernity: Essays on Culture as Development in Africa*, ed. Philip Altbach and Salah M. Hassan. Trenton, N.J.: Africa World Press, 1996.

Armbrust, Walter. *Mass Culture and Modernism in Egypt*. Cambridge: Cambridge University Press, 1996.

Armstrong, Meg. "'A Jumble of Foreignness': The Sublime Musayums of Nineteenth-Century Fairs and Expositions." *Cultural Critique* 23 (Winter 1992–93): 199–250.

Arnoldi, Mary Jo. "Youth Festivals and Museums: The Cultural Politics of Public Memory in Postcolonial Mali." *Africa Today* 52, no. 4 (2006): 55–76.

"Arts plastiques: Une nouvelle galerie étrenée par une pléaide d'artistes." *Al Bayane*, May 23, 1997.

Ascal, Françoise. "Avant-dire." In *Petit musée portatif*, by Abdellatif Laâbi. Neuilly, France: Editions Al Manar, 2002.

Association de Recherche Culturelle. "Programme de recherche et d'action de l'A.R.C." *Souffles* 12 (1968): 3–9.

Ayoun, Ahmed. "L'enjeu culturel." *Le temps du Maroc* 168 (January 15–21, 1999). http://www.tempsdumaroc.press.ma/hebdomadaire/1999/1521janv168/cult3.htm.

Aziza, Mohamed. *L'image et l'Islam*. Paris: Albin Michel, 1978.

Bahnassi, Afif. "Al-Wasiti d'après les maqamats d'al Hariri." *Integral* 3–4 (January 1973): 37.

Baida, Jamaa. *La presse marocaine d'expression française des origines à 1956.* Casablanca: Faculté des Lettres et des Sciences Humaines de Rabat, 1996.

Balzac, Honoré de. *La peau de chagrin.* Paris: Flammarion, 1996.

Barringer, Tim. "The South Kensington Museum and the Colonial Project." In *Colonialism and the Object: Empire, Material Culture, and the Museum,* ed. Tim Barringer and Tom Flynn. London: Routledge, 1998.

Baudelaire, Charles. "Extrait des critiques d'art de Baudelaire sur l'exposition universelle de 1855." In *Baudelaire critique d'art: Curiosités esthétiques, poèmes, oeuvres diverses, lettres.* Paris: Club des librairies de France, 1956.

Becker, Cynthia. *Amazigh Arts in Morocco: Women Shaping Berber Identity.* Austin: University of Texas Press, 2006.

Becker, Howard S. *Art Worlds.* Berkeley: University of California Press, 1982.

Bel, Alfred. *Les industries de la céramique à Fes.* Alger: Ancienne Maison Bastide-Jourdan, 1918.

Belkahia, Farid, Mohammed Chebaâ, and Mohamed Melehi. "Situation de la peinture naïve au Maroc." *Souffles* 7–8 (1967): 75.

Belkhodja, Abdelaziz. *2103, le retour de l'éléphant.* Marseilles: Transbordeurs, 2005.

Bellal, Mohammed. "Qui lèvera le rideau?" *L'opinion,* August 13, 1965, 4.

Belting, Hans. "Place of Reflection or Place of Sensation?" In *The Discursive Museum,* ed. Peter Noever. Vienna: Hatje Cantz, 2001.

Ben. "Lisez ceci: De la peinture." *L'opinion,* April 10, 1967, 4.

———. "Lisez ceci: Esthétique?" *L'opinion,* March 18, 1965, 4.

Ben Jelloun, Tahar. "Melehi." *Integral* 1 (October 1971): 4.

Benaïssa, Mohammed. "Dedicace." In *La peinture au rendez-vous de l'histoire.* Casablanca: Editions Espace Wafabank, 1988.

———. "Photographies." *Integral* 5–6 (September 1973): 22–29.

Benjamin, Walter. "Art in the Age of Mechanical Reproduction." In *Illuminations,* ed. Hannah Arendt, trans. Harry Zohn. New York: Shocken, 1968.

———. "Paris, Capital of the Nineteenth Century." In *Reflections,* trans. E. Jephcott. New York: Shocken, 1978.

Bennani, Abdelhak. "Prologue." In *La peinture marocaine au rendez-vous de l'histoire.* Casablanca: Editions Espace Wafabank, 1988.

Bennett, Lerone Jr. "Introduction." In *Tradition and Conflict: Images of a Turbulent Decade, 1963–1973,* ed. and curated Mary Schmidt Campbell. New York: Studio Museum in Harlem, 1985.

Bennett, Tony. *The Birth of the Museum: History, Theory, Politics.* London: Routledge, 1995.

———. "Difference and the Logic of Culture." In *Museum Frictions: Public Cultures/ Global Transformations,* ed. Ivan Karp, Corinne Kratz, Lynn Szwaja, and Tomás Ybarra-Frausto. Durham, N.C.: Duke University Press, 2006.

———. "Pedagogic Objects, Clean Eyes, and Popular Instruction: On Sensory Regimes and Museum Didactics." *Configurations* 6, no. 3 (1998): 345–71.

Bennis, Abdellatif. "Cherkaoui révèle: Le Maroc, invité, n'ira pas à la Biennale de Sao Paulo." *L'opinion,* August 14, 1965, 4.

———. "L'école marocaine doit affronter toutes les competitions internationales." *L'opinion,* August 12, 1965, 4.

Bensaâd, Ali. "The Militarization of Migration Frontiers in the Mediterranean." In *The*

Maghreb Connection: Movements of Life Across North Africa, ed. Ursula Biemann and Brian Holmes. Barcelona: Actar, 2006.

Berrada, Mohammed. "Défaite/destin." *Integral* 3–4 (January 1973): 28–29.

Bhabha, Homi, "Of Mimicry and Man." In *The Location of Culture,* by Homi Bhabha. London: Routledge, 1994.

Blood, Katherine. "A Printmaking Workshop in Morocco: Artist Camille Billops on Her Work with Robert Blackburn." *Library of Congress Information Bulletin* (July–August 2003). http://www.loc.gov/loc/lcib/0307-8/morocco.html.

Bosch, Annette van den. "Museums: Constructing a Public Culture in the Global Age." *Third Text* 19, no. 1 (January 2005): 81–89.

Bourdieu, Pierre. *Distinction: A Social Critique of the Judgement of Taste.* Trans. Richard Nice. Cambridge, Mass.: Harvard University Press, 1984.

Bourdieu, Pierre, and Alain Darbel. 1969. *The Love of Art: European Museums and the Public.* Trans. Caroline Beattie and Nick Merriman. Cambridge: Polity Press, 1991.

Bourqia, Rahma. "The Cultural Legacy of Power in Morocco." In *In the Shadow of the Sultan: Culture, Power, and Politics in Morocco.* Cambridge, Mass.: Harvard University Press, 1999.

Boutaleb, Abdeslam. *La peinture naïve au Maroc.* Paris: Editions du Jaguar, 1985.

Bouzfour, Ahmed. "La valise rouge." Trans. Abdellatif Ghouirgate and Jawida Khadda. In *Onze histoires marocaines,* ed. Mohamed Saad Eddine El Yamani. Paris: Institut du Monde Arabe, 1999.

Budney, Jen. "Who's It For ? The 2nd Johannesburg Biennale." *Third Text* 42 (Spring 1998): 88–94.

Bunn, David. "The Museum Outdoors: Heritage, Cattle, and Permeable Borders in the Southwestern Kruger National Park." In *Museum Frictions: Public Cultures/Global Transformations,* ed. Ivan Karp, Corinne Kratz, Lynn Szwaja, and Tomás Ybarra-Frausto. Durham, N.C.: Duke University Press, 2006.

Buntinx, Gustavo. "Communities of Sense/Communities of Sentiment: Globalization and the Museum Void in an Extreme Periphery." In *Museum Frictions: Public Cultures/ Global Transformations,* ed. Ivan Karp, Corinne Kratz, Lynn Szwaja, and Tomás Ybarra-Frausto. Durham, N.C.: Duke University Press, 2006.

Burke, Edmund III. "The First Crisis of Orientalism." In *Connaissances du Maghreb: Sciences sociales et colonisation,* ed. Jean-Claude Vatin. Paris: Centre National de la Recherche Scientifique, 1984.

———. "The Image of the Moroccan State in French Ethnological Literature." In *Arabs and Berbers: From Tribe to Nation in North Africa,* ed. Ernest Gellner and Charles Micaud. Lexington Mass.: Lexington Books, 1972.

Burkhardt, Titus. *Mirror of the Intellect: Essays on Traditional Science and Sacred Art.* New York: State University of New York Press, 1987.

C. E. Y. "Réflexions sur l'art et l'artiste." *Lamalif* 7 (November 1966): 43–44.

Caisse de Depot et de Gestion. *Bouchta El Hayani expose.* Rabat: Galerie d'art CDG, 2000.

Calinescu, Matei. *Five Faces of Modernity: Modernism, Avant-garde, Decadence, Kitsch, Post-modernism.* Durham, N.C.: Duke University Press, 1987.

Callaghan, David. "The Perpetual Present: Life as Art during the 1960s." In *Theatre at the Margins: The Political, the Popular, the Personal, the Profane,* ed. John W. Frick. Tuscaloosa: Southeastern Theatre Conference and the University of Alabama Press, 2000.

Calo, Mary Ann. "African Art and Critical Discourse between World Wars." *American Quarterly* 51 (3): 580–621.

Catalogue du Centre Cinématographique Marocain. Rabat: Centre Cinématographique Marocain, n.d.

"Ce que nous voulons." *Lamalif* 1 (March 1966): 5–7.

Çelik, Zeynep. *Displaying the Orient: Architecture of Islam at Nineteenth-Century World's Fairs*. Berkeley: University of California Press, 1992.

Chakrabarty, Dipesh. *Provincializing Europe: Postcolonial Thought and Historical Difference*. Princeton, N.J.: Princeton University Press, 2000.

Champion, Pierre. *Le Maroc et ses villes d'art*. Paris: Librairie Renouard, 1927.

Chatterjee, Partha. "The Disciplines in Colonial Bengal." In *Texts of Power: Emerging Disciplines in Colonial Bengal*, ed. Partha Chatterjee. Minneapolis: University of Minnesota Press, 1995.

Chebaâ, Mohammed. "Points de vue sur la biennale." *Integral* 9 (December 1974): 29–30.

———. "Situation de la peinture naïve au Maroc." *Souffles* 7–8 (1967): 73–76.

Chow, Rey. *Writing Diaspora: Tactics of Intervention in Contemporary Cultural Studies*. Bloomington: Indiana University Press, 1993.

Clancy-Smith, Julia. *Rebel and Saint: Muslim Notables, Populist Protest, Colonial Encounters*. Berkeley: University of California Press, 1994.

Clifford, James. *Routes: Travel and Translation in the Late Twentieth Century*. Cambridge, Mass.: Harvard University Press, 1997.

Cohen, Jean-Louis, and Monique Eleb. *Casablanca: Colonial Myths and Architectural Ventures*. New York: Monacelli Press, 2002.

Cohen, Mark I., and Lorna Hahn. *Morocco: Old Land, New Nation*. New York: Praeger, 1966.

Cohen, Shana. *Searching for a Different Future: The Rise of a Global Middle Class in Morocco*. Durham, N.C.: Duke University Press, 2004.

Cohen, Shana, and Larabi Jaidi. *Morocco: Globalization and Its Consequences*. London: Routledge, 2006.

Collet, Bernard. *Paradis Beach: Récit d'Asilah*. Casablanca: Editions Aïni Bennaï, 2003.

Comaroff, Jean, and John Comaroff, eds. *Modernity and Its Malcontents: Ritual and Power in Postcolonial Africa*. Chicago: University of Chicago Press, 1993.

Combs-Schilling, M. E. *Sacred Performances: Islam, Sexuality, and Sacrifice*. New York: Columbia University Press, 1989.

Cooper, Frederick. *Colonialism in Question: Theory, Knowledge, History*. Berkeley: University of California Press, 2005.

Crane, Susan. "Curious Cabinets and Imaginary Museums." In *Museums and Memory*, ed. Susan Crane. Stanford, Calif.: Stanford University Press, 2000.

———. "Introduction." In *Museums and Memory*, ed. Susan Crane. Stanford, Calif.: Stanford University Press, 2000.

———. "Memory, Distortion, and History in the Museum." *History and Theory* 36, no. 4 (December 1997): 44–63.

Cuno, James. "Against the Discursive Museum." In *The Discursive Museum*, ed. Peter Noever. Vienna: Hatje Cantz, 2001.

Dagher, Charbel. "Is There an Arab Market for Fine Art?" Trans. Elie Chalala. *Al-Jadid* 5, no. 27 (Spring 1999): 3–4.

Dakhlia, Jocelyne. *L'oubli de la cité: La mémoire collective à l'épreuve du lignage dans le jérid tunisien*. Paris: Editions la découverte, 1990.

Dallmayr, Fred, and G. N. Devy. "Introduction." In *Between Tradition and Modernity: India's Search for Identity*, ed. Fred Dallmayr and G. N. Devy. Thousand Oaks, Calif.: Sage, 1998.

Daoud, Zakya. "Actions, limites, avatars et dangers des centres culturels étrangers." *Lamalif* 50 (September 1971): 6–10.

———. *Casablanca en mouvement*. Paris: Editions Autrement, 2005.

———. "Le monde fantastique de Tallal." *Lamalif* 16 (November 1967): 37–40.

———. *Les années Lamalif: 1958–1988, trente ans de journalisme au Maroc*. Casablanca: Tarik Editions, 2007.

———. "Les pionniers de l'Art." *Lamalif* 5 (July–August 1966): 32.

———. "Manifesto." *Lamalif* 1 (March 1966): 5–7.

———. "Un peintre qui promet: Chaibia." *Lamalif* 2 (April 15, 1966): 45.

De Boeck, Filip, and Marie-Françoise Plissart. *Kinshasa: Récits de la ville invisible*. Trans. Jean-Pierre Jacquemin. Paris: Renaissance du Livre, 2005.

"Declaration on the Importance and Value of Universal Museums: 'Museums Serve Every Nation.'" In *Museum Frictions: Public Cultures/Global Transformations*, ed. Ivan Karp, Corinne Kratz, Lynn Szwaja, and Tomás Ybarra-Frausto. Durham, N.C.: Duke University Press, 2006.

Deleuze, Gilles, and Félix Guattari. *A Thousand Plateaus*. Trans. Brian Massumi. Minneapolis: University of Minnesota Press, 1987.

de Pontcharra, Nicole, and Brahim Alaoui. "Dans le monde, le désir d'etre soi." In *Le Maroc en mouvement: Créations contemporaines*, ed. Maati Kabbal and Nicole de Pontcharra. Paris: Maisonneuve et Larose, Malika Editions, 2001.

Derain, Martine. *Echo Larmitaj: Un chantier à Casablanca*. Casablanca: Le Fennec, 2006.

Dias, Nélia. "The Visibility of Difference: Nineteenth-Century French Anthropological Collections." In *The Politics of Display: Museums, Science, Culture*, ed. Sharon Macdonald. London: Routledge, 1998.

Dietz, Bettina, and Thomas Nutz. "Collections Curieuses: The Aesthetics of Curiosity and Elite Lifestyle in Eighteenth-Century Paris." *Eighteenth-Century Life* 29, no. 3 (2005): 44–75.

Diouri, Moumen. *A qui appartient le Maroc?* Paris: L'Harmattan, 1992.

Direction Générale de l'Instruction Publique des Beaux-Arts et des Antiquités. *Historique 1912–1930*. Rabat: Protectorat de la Republique française au Maroc, 1930.

10 ans d'independence, 1956–1966. Rabat: Ministère de Transports et de Communications, 1966.

Dominguez, Virgina R. "The Marketing of Heritage." *American Ethnologist* 13, no. 3 (1986): 546–55.

Douglas, Allen, and Fedwa Malti-Douglas. *Arabic Comic Strips: Politics of an Emerging Mass Culture*. Bloomington: Indiana University Press, 1994.

Duncan, Carol. "Art Museums and the Ritual of Citizenship." In *Exhibiting Cultures: The Poetics and Politics of Museum Display*, ed. Ivan Karp and Steven Lavine. Washington, D.C.: Smithsonian Institution Press, 1991.

El Maleh, Edmond Amran. "Ahmed Cherkaoui ou la passion de la signe." *Integral* (December 9, 1974): 44.

————. "Itinéraire: Critique de la critique." *Horizons Maghrebins* 33–34 (1997): 10–15.

————. "La peinture marocaine: Tradition et modernité." In *La peinture marocaine au rendez-vous de l'histoire.* Casablanca: Editions Espace Wafabank, 1988.

————. "Preface." In *Première rencontre de la jeune peinture marocaine.* Casablanca: Editions Fondation Wafabank, 1989.

Elbaz, André. "Jeune peintres où sommes-nous?" *L'opinion,* August 4, 1965, 4.

————. "Jeunes peintres marocains où sommes nous?" *L'opinion,* August 5, 1965, 4.

————. "L'ort doit toucher l'universel et ne doit pas devenir un artisanat national." *Lamalif* 12 (May 1967): 36.

El-Malki, Omar. "Manifeste de la revue Pro-C." *Pro-Culture* 1 (September 1973): 7–10.

"Entretien avec Amine Demnati." *Lamalif* 18 (March 1968): 50–55.

"Entretien avec Ismail Shammout." *Integral* 9 (December 1974): 33–36.

Er-Remah, Khalid. "De soie, d'or et d'argent." *La nouvelle tribune,* December 19–21, 1997.

Ettinghausen, Richard. "The Character of Islamic Art." In *The Arab Heritage,* ed. Nabih Amin Faris. New York: Russell and Russell, 1963.

"Exposition de Miloud." *Integral* (1975): 24.

Fabian, Johannes. *Time and the Other: How Anthropology Makes Its Object.* New York: Columbia University Press, 1983.

Fehr, Michael. "A Museum and Its Memory: The Art of Recovering History." In *Museums and Memory,* ed. Susan Crane. Stanford, Calif.: Stanford University Press, 2000.

Ferguson, James. *Expectations of Modernity: Myths and Meanings of Urban Life on the Zambian Copperbelt.* Berkeley: University of California Press, 1999.

————. *Global Shadows: Africa in the Neoliberal World Order.* Durham, N.C.: Duke University Press, 2006.

Findlen, Paula. *Possessing Nature: Museums, Collecting, and Scientific Culture.* Berkeley: University of California Press, 1994.

Flores Khalil, Andrea. *The Arab Avant-Garde: Experiments in North African Art and Literature.* London: Prager, 2003.

Foucault, Michel. *The Archaeology of Knowledge.* Trans. A. M. Sheridan Smith. New York, Pantheon, 1972.

Gaines, Charles, Maurice Berger, and Catherine Lord. *Theater of Refusal: Black Art and Mainstream Criticism.* Irvine: Fine Arts Gallery, University of California, 1993.

Gans, Herbert. *Popular Culture and High Culture: An Analysis and Evaluation of Taste.* New York: Basic Books, 1999.

García Canclini, Néstor. *Hybrid Cultures: Strategies for Entering and Leaving Modernity.* Trans. Christopher Chiappari and Silvia Lopez. Minneapolis: University of Minnesota Press, 1995.

Garcia-Anton, Katya. "Dak'Art 98." *Third Text* 44 (Autumn 1998): 87–92.

Gardiner, Wrey. *Barbary Holiday.* London: Frederick Muller, 1952.

Gaudibert, Pierre. "Jeunes peintres marocains où sommes nous?" *L'opinion,* August 11, 1965, 4.

Gaugue, Anne. *Les états africains et leurs musées: La mise en scène de la nation.* Paris: L'Harmattan, 1997.

Gaye, Amadou. "La mémoire retrouvée." *Al-Maghrib Culture,* May, 5 1996, 2–3.

Girard, Muriel. "Invention de la tradition et authenticité sous le Protectorat au Maroc: L'action du Service des Arts indigènes et de son directeur Prosper Ricard." *Socio-Anthropologie*

19, Les mondes du patrimoine, 2006. Published online October 31, 2007, http://socio
-anthropologie.revues.org/document563.html.

Gombrich, E. H. *Ideals and Idols: Essays on Values in History and Art.* New York: E. P. Dutton, 1979.

Grabar, Oleg. "An Art of the Object." *ArtForum* 14, no. 7 (March 1976): 1–3.

———. "Geometry and Ideology: The Festival of Islam and the Study of Islamic Art." In *A Way Prepared: Essays on Islamic Culture in Honor of Richard Bayly Winder,* ed. Farhad Kazemi and R. D. McChesney. New York: New York University Press, 1988.

Gronow, Jukka. *The Sociology of Taste.* London: Routledge, 1997.

Guha-Thakurta, Tapati. *Monuments, Objects, Histories: Institutions of Art in Colonial and Postcolonial India.* New York: Columbia University Press, 2004.

Guillemet, Paul. "On the Threshold of Modern Morocco." *Morocco 54: Encyclopédie mensuelle d'outre-mer,* special issue (1954): 9–10.

Hajji, Adil. "Malaise dans la culture marocaine: Effervescence créatrice, blocages structurels." *Le monde diplomatique* (Septembre 2000): 24–25. Published online October 28, 2003, http://www.monde-diplomatique.fr/2000/09/hajji/14232.

Hammoud, Salah Dine. "Arabization in Morocco: A Case Study in Language Planning and Language Policy Attitudes." Ph.D. diss., University of Texas, Austin, 1982.

Hammoudi, Abdellah. *Master and Disciple.* Chicago: Chicago University Press, 1997.

Hayes, Danielle B. "Asilah: Common Ground" *Aramco World* 45, no. 1 (January 1994): 12.

Holden, Stacy E. "When It Pays to Be Medieval: Historic Preservation as a Colonial Policy in the Medina of Fez, 1912–1932." *Journal of the Historical Society* 6, no. 2 (June 2006): 297–316.

Horne, Janet R. *A Social Laboratory for Modern France: The Musée Social and the Rise of the Welfare State.* Durham, N.C.: Duke University Press, 2002.

Hourya. "Art et décoration." *Lamalif* 11 (April 1967): 47–48.

Howe, Marvine. "Morocco's Democratic Experience." *World Policy Journal* 17 (Spring 2000): 65–70.

Huyssen, Andreas. *Present Pasts: Urban Palimpsests and the Politics of Memory.* Stanford, Calif.: Stanford University Press, 2003.

"Il faut revaloriser et encourage l'art." *Lamalif* 30 (May–June 1969): 48.

Impey, O. R., and A. G. MacGregor, eds. *The Origins of Museums.* Oxford: Oxford University Press, 1985.

Irbouh, Hamid. *Art in the Service of Colonialism: French Art Education in Morocco, 1912–1956.* New York: Tauris Academic Press, 2005.

Irwin, Robert. *Arabian Nights: A Companion.* London: Allen Lane, 1994.

Izhar. "Made in Morocco." *Lamalif* 12 (May 1967): 18.

Jacobson, Marjory. *Art and Business: New Strategies for Corporate Collecting.* London: Thames and Hudson, 1993.

Jay, Salim. "La palette étincelante de Larbi Belcadi." *L'opinion,* June 8, 1967, 5.

———. "Paris fête le Maghreb." *L'opinion,* March 24, 1967, 5.

Jeune peinture marocaine. Rabat: Ministry of Education, 1960.

Jusdanis, Gregory. *Belated Modernity and Aesthetic Culture.* Minneapolis: University of Minnesota Press, 1991.

Kapchan, Deborah. *Traveling Spirit Masters: Moroccan Gnawa Trance and Music in the Global Marketplace.* Middletown, Conn.: Wesleyan University Press, 2007.

Kapur, Geeta. *When Was Modernism? Essays on Contemporary Cultural Practice in India.* New Delhi: Tulika, 2000.

Karp, Ivan. "Culture and Representation." In *Exhibiting Cultures: The Poetics and Politics of Museum Display,* ed. Ivan Karp and Steven Lavine. Washington, D.C.: Smithsonian Institution Press, 1991.

Karp, Ivan, and Steven Lavine. *Exhibiting Cultures: The Poetics and Politics of Museum Display.* Washington, D.C.: Smithsonian Institution Press, 1991.

Karroum, Abdellah. "Allers/Retours: L'exposition comme déplacement vers les contextes." *L'appartement 22,* May 14, 2007, http://www.appartement22.com/spip.php?article9.

———. "Expédition no. 1." *Le bout du monde,* June 15, 2000, http://lebdm.free.fr/article.php3?id_article=2.

———. "La coprésence fondement de la rencontre." *L'appartement 22,* August 6, 2006, http://www.appartement22.com/spip.php?article16.

———. *L'appartement 22: 2002–2008.* Paris: Editions hor'champs, 2008.

———. "Le passage du souk." *Le bout du monde* (August 15, 2005). http://lebdm.free.fr/article.php3?id_article=3.

———, ed. *Le colloque, l'oeuvre toujours.* Rabat: Editions Hors'champs, 2005.

Khatibi, Abdelkebir. "Exposition Mohamed Melehi à l'atelier Rabat." *Integral* 1 (October 1971): 2.

———. "Culture nationale et culture de classe au Maroc." *Integral* 5–6 (September 1973): 20.

———. *L'art contemporain arabe: Prolégomènes.* Paris: Al Manar, 2001.

Khuri, Richard. *Freedom, Modernity, and Islam: Toward a Creative Synthesis.* Syracuse, N.Y.: Syracuse University Press, 1998.

Kilito, Abdelfattah. "The Flower-Bed." Trans. Susan Slyomovics. *Mediterraneans: Voices from Morocco* 11 (Winter 1999–2000).

———. *La querelle des images.* Casablanca: Editions EDDIF, 1995.

Kirshenblatt-Gimblett, Barbara. *Destination Culture: Tourism, Museums, and Heritage.* Berkeley: University of California Press, 1998.

———. "From Ethnology to Heritage: The Role of the Museum." SIEF Keynote in Marseilles, April 28, 2004. http://www.nyu.edu/classes/bkg/web/SIEF.pdf.

———. "The Museum—A Refuge for Utopian Thought." In German translation in *Die Unruhe der Kultur: Potentiale des Utopischen,* ed. Jörn Rüsen, Michael Fehr, and Annelie Ramsbrock. Weilerswist, Germany: Velbrück, 2004. http://www.nyu.edu/classes/bkg/web/museutopia.pdf.

———. "The Museum as Catalyst." Keynote address, *Museums 2000: Confirmation or Challenge.* Organized by International Council of Museums Sweden, the Swedish Museum Association, and the Swedish Travelling Exhibition/Riksutställningar. Vadstena, September 29, 2000. http://www.nyu.edu/classes/bkg/web/vadstena.pdf.

Koechlin, Raymond. "Du passé à l'avenir." *Les arts* 161 (October 1917): 3–10.

Koffi, Adou. "Socio-Historical Factors for Improved Integration of Local Museums." In *Museums and the Community in West Africa,* ed. Claude Ardouin and Emmanuel Arinze. Washington, D.C.: Smithsonian Institution Press, 1995.

Kotz, Liz. "Video Projection: The Space between Screens." In *Theory in Contemporary Art since 1985,* ed. Zoya Kocur and Simon Leung. Oxford: Blackwell, 2005.

Kratz, Corinne A., and Ivan Karp. "Introduction." In *Museum Frictions: Public Cultures/*

Global Transformations, ed. Ivan Karp, Corinne Kratz, Lynn Szwaja, and Tomás Ybarra-Frausto. Durham, N.C.: Duke University Press, 2006.

Krauss, Rosalind. "The Cultural Logic of the Late Capitalist Museum." *October* (Fall 1990): 3–17.

Kreps, Christina F. *Liberating Culture: Cross-Cultural Perspectives on Museums, Curation, and Heritage Preservation.* London and New York: Routledge, 2003.

Laâbi, Abdellatif. *La brûlure des interrogations: Entretiens réalisés par Jacques Alessandra.* Paris: L'Harmattan, 1985.

———. "Le gâchis." *Souffles* 7–8 (1967): 1–14.

———. "Lisez 'Le petit Marocain.'" *Souffles* 2 (1966): 5–7.

———. *Petit musée portatif.* Paris: Al Manar, 2002.

———. "Prologue." *Souffles* 1 (1966): 6.

———. "Réalités et dilemmes de la culture nationale." *Souffles* 4 (1966): 4–12.

Laabi. C. "Esthétique de l'objet." *Maroc Hebdo,* December 1996–January 3, 1997, 42.

Lahbabi, Mohammed Aziz. *De l'être à la personne.* Paris: Presses Universitaires de France, 1954.

Laroui, Abdallah. *The Crisis of the Arab Intellectual.* Trans. Diarmid Cammell. Berkeley: University of California Press, 1976.

———. *Esquisses historiques.* Casablanca: Centre Culturel Arabe, 1993.

———. *L'histoire du Maghreb.* Paris: Maspero, 1975.

———. *Les origines sociales et culturelles du nationalisme marocain.* Casablanca: Centre Culturel Arabe, 1993.

Leaman, Oliver. *Islamic Aesthetics.* Notre Dame, Indiana: University of Notre Dame Press, 2004.

Lee, Marshall, ed. *Art at Work: The Chase Manhattan Collection.* New York: E. P. Dutton, 1984.

Lichtenberger, André. "Le commerce français à la foire de Fez." *France-Maroc* 12 (1917): 12–13.

Lin, Eunice M. "Asilah, Morocco: Rehabilitation and the Cultural Festival of Asilah." http://web.mit.edu/akpia/www/AKPsite/4.239/asilah/asilah.html.

Lucie-Smith, Edward. *Movements in Art since 1945.* London: Thames and Hudson, 2001.

Maffi, Irene. *Pratiques du patrimoine et politiques de la mémoire en Jordanie.* Lausanne, Switzerland: Editions Payot Lausanne, 2004.

Majid, Anouar. "A Moroccan Star Is Born." *Tingis: A Moroccan-American Magazine of Ideas and Culture,* January 2007. http://www.tingismagazine.com/review.php?reviewid=41.

Manning, Erin. *Ephemeral Territories: Representing Nation, Home, and Identity in Canada.* Minneapolis: University of Minnesota Press, 2003.

Maraini, Toni. *Écrits sur l'art: Choix de textes, Maroc 1967–1989.* Rabat: Al-Kalam, 1990.

———. "Introduction." In *La peinture marocaine au rendez-vous de l'histoire.* Casablanca: Editions Wafabank, 1988.

———. "Le rôle historique des arts populaires." *Integral* 2 (March 1972): 6–10.

———. "Notes sur les arts plastiques." *Integral* 3–4 (January 1973): 38–39.

———. "Situation de la peinture marocaine." *Souffles* 7–8 (1967): 15–19.

Mariami, Karim. "Journée internationale des musées: A quoi servent ces lieux de la mémoire?" *Libération,* May 20, 1997, 8.

Le Maroc: Aperçu historique. Rabat: Ministère de l'Information, 1966.

Martineau, Gilbert, ed. *Maroc: Les guides Nagel.* Paris: Editions Nagel, 1953.

Mathur, Saloni. "Museums and Globalization." *Anthropological Quarterly* 78, no. 3 (2005): 697–708.

Mayer, Ann Elizabeth. "Moroccans—Citizens or Subjects? A People at the Crossroads." *International Law and Politics* 26, no. 63 (1993): 63–105.

McCarren, Felicia. "Téléphone arabe: From child's play to terrorism—the poetics and politics of postcolonial telecommunication." *Journal of Postcolonial Writing* 44, no. 3 (September 2008): 289–305.

McClellan, Andrew. *Inventing the Louvre: Art, Politics, and the Origin of the Modern Museum in 18th Century Paris.* Cambridge: Cambridge University Press, 1994.

Meecham, Pam, and Julie Sheldon. *Modern Art: A Critical Introduction.* London: Routledge, 2000.

Melehi, Mohamed. "Festival al-Wasiti." *Integral* 3–4 (January 1973): 34–36.

———. "L'exposition maghrébine d'Alger." *Integral* 8 (March–April 1974): 14–15.

———. "Situation de la peinture naïve au Maroc." *Souffles* 7–8 (1967): 73–76.

Merali, Shaheen. "Displaces: Topography of Unbelonging." *Third Text* 39 (Summer 1997): 103–5.

Mernissi, Fatima. *Les Aït-Débrouille: ONG rurales du Haut-Atlas.* Rabat: Editions Marsam, 2003.

Merz, Gerhard, and Herbert Molderings. "We'll Stick with It: Any Interference in the Soundlessness, Timelessness, Motionlessness, and Lifelessness of the True Museum Is Disrespectful." In *The Discursive Museum,* ed. Peter Noever. Vienna: Hatje Cantz, 2001.

Mikdadi, Salwa. "Arab Art Institutions and Their Audiences." *MESA Bulletin* 42 no. 1–2 (Summer/Winter 2008): 55–61.

Miller, Susan Gilson, trans. and ed. *Disorienting Encounters: Travels of a Moroccan Scholar in France in 1845–1846.* Berkeley: University of California Press, 1992.

Ministère de l'Education Nationale, Service des Monuments Historiques, des Arts et du Folklore. *Jeune peinture marocaine.* Rabat: Ministry of Education, 1960.

"La misère de l'artisanat." *L'opinion,* May 29, 1967, 1.

Mitchell, Timothy. "The Stage of Modernity." In *Questions of Modernity,* ed. Timothy Mitchell. Minneapolis: University of Minnesota Press, 2000.

———. "The World as Exhibition." *Comparative Studies in Society and History* 31, no. 2 (April 1989): 217–36.

———, ed. *Questions of Modernity.* Minneapolis: University of Minnesota Press, 2000.

"Mohammed Benaïssa on the Asilah Festival," *Contemporary Art from the Islamic World* 7 (June 2004). http://universes-in-universe.de/islam/eng/2004/03/benaissa/index.html.

"Mona Hatoum Interviewed by Jo Glencross." In *Mona Hatoum: Domestic Disturbance,* ed. Laura Stewart Heon. North Adams, Mass.: Massachusetts Museum of Contemporary Art, 2001.

Monmarché, Marcel, ed. *Maroc: Les guides bleu.* Paris: Hachette, 1921.

Moroccan National Tourist Board. *Morocco: Museums.* Rabat: Moroccan Tourist Board and the Moroccan Ministry of Culture, 1994.

Morocco Tourism, 1968–1971.

Mount, Marshall W. *African Art: The Years since 1920.* Bloomington: University of Indiana Press, 1974.

"Mr. Playboy in Morocco." *Morocco Tourism* 58 (Autumn 1970): 58–60.

M'Rabet, Khalil. "Écrits en amont: Pour une tradition moderne." *Horizons Maghrebins* 33/34 (1997): 22–31.

———. *Peinture et identité: L'expérience marocaine.* Paris: L'Harmattan, 1987.

Munjeri, Dawson. "Refocusing or Reorientation? The Exhibit or the Populace: Zimbabwe on the Threshold." In *Exhibiting Cultures: The Poetics and Politics of Museum Display,* ed. Ivan Karp and Steven Lavine. Washington, D.C.: Smithsonian Institution Press, 1991.

"Musées du Maroc: Le degré zero de la muséologie." *Matrice des arts* 1 (October–December 2005): 46.

Nakano, Aki'o. *Report on Moroccan Urban and Rural Life.* Tokyo: Toyko University of Foreign Studies, 1979.

Nochlin, Linda. *The Politics of Vision.* New York: Harper and Row, 1989.

Noever, Peter. "On the Subject." In *The Discursive Museum,* ed. Peter Noever. Vienna: Hatje Cantz, 2001.

O'Brien, David, and David Prochaska. *Beyond East and West: Seven Transnational Artists.* Champaign, Ill.: Krannert Art Museum, 2004.

O'Doherty, Brian. *Inside the White Cube: The Ideology of the Gallery Space.* Berkeley: University of California Press, 1999.

Oguibe, Olu. *The Culture Game.* Minneapolis: University of Minnesota Press, 2004.

———. "The True Location of Ernest Mancoba's Modernism." *Third Text* 19, no. 4 (July 2005): 419–420.

Ossman, Susan. *Picturing Casablanca: Portraits of Power in a Modern City.* Berkeley: University of California Press, 1994.

Oulebsir, Nabila. *Les usages du patrimoine: Monuments, musées et politique coloniale en Algérie (1830–1930).* Paris: Editions de la Maison des Sciences de l'Homme, 2004.

Packard, Vance. *The Status Seekers: An Exploration of Class Behavior in America.* New York: D. McKay, 1959.

Pandolfo, Stefania. *Impasse of the Angels: Scenes from a Moroccan Space of Memory.* Chicago: University of Chicago Press, 1997.

———. "The Thin Line of Modernity." In *Questions of Modernity,* ed. Timothy Mitchell. Minneapolis: University of Minnesota Press, 2000.

"Le peintre Kacimi expose à la Maison de la Penseé," *L'opinion,* June 13, 1965, 5.

Perrault, Gilles. *Notre ami le Roi.* Paris: Folio, 1990.

Pieprzak, Katarzyna. "Bodies on the Beach: Youssef Elalamy and Moroccan Landscapes of the Clandestine." In *Land and Landscape in Francographic Literature: Remapping Uncertain Territories,* ed. Katarzyna Pieprzak and Magali Compan. Newcastle, England: Cambridge Scholars Publishing, 2007.

———. "Nostalgia and the New Cosmopolitan: Literary and Artistic Interventions in the City of Casablanca." *Studies in 20th and 21st Century Literatures* 33, no. 1 (Winter 2009): 100–122.

———. "Ruins, Rumors and Traces of the City of Brass: Moroccan Modernity and Memories of the Arab Global City." *Research in African Literatures* 38, no. 4 (Winter 2007): 187–203.

Pieterse, Jan Nederveen. *White on Black: Images of Africa and Blacks in Western Popular Culture.* New Haven, Conn.: Yale University Press, 1992.

Pomian, Krzysztof. *Collectors and Curiosities.* London: Polity Press, 1990.

Porterfield, Todd. *The Allure of Empire: Art in the Service of French Imperialism, 1798–1836.* Princeton, N.J.: Princeton University Press, 1998.

"Première biennale des arts plastiques à Baghdad: Manifeste de l'Association Marocaine des Arts Plastiques." *Integral* 8 (March–April 1974): 16–19.

Preziosi, Donald. *Brain of the Earth's Body: Art, Museums, and the Phantasms of Modernity.* Minneapolis: University of Minnesota Press, 2003.

Price, Sally. *Primitive Art in Civilized Places.* Chicago: University of Chicago Press, 1989.

Quantin, J. "Les musées commerciaux au Maroc." *France-Maroc* 10 (1917): 48.

43 artistes. Rabat: Association Marocaine des Arts Plastiques, 1998.

"Rabi'a al-fan fi Settat." *Al-'Ālam* (May 2–3, 1965): 5.

Rabinow, Paul. *French Modern: Norms and Forms of the Social Environment.* Cambridge, Mass.: MIT Press, 1989.

"Rehabilitation of Asilah, Morocco." *Mimar: Architecture in Development* 33 (December 1989): 28–29.

Renault, Florence. "Portraits de famille." *La Source du Lion.* http://www.lasourcedulion.org.

Rharib, Sakina. "Le mot musée absent de la loi du Patrimoine." Interview by A. Benhamza. *Matrice des arts* 1 (October–December 2005): 50–51.

Ricard, Prosper. *Arts marocains: Broderie.* Alger: Ancienne Maison Bastide-Jourdan, 1918.

———. *Maroc: Les guides bleu.* Ed. Marcel Monmarché. Paris: Hachette, 1921.

———. *Pour comprendre l'art musulman dans l'Afrique du nord.* Paris: Hachette, 1924.

Ripault, Ghislain, ed. *Pour Abdellatif Laâbi.* Paris: Nouvelles éditions rupture, 1982.

Rivet, Daniel. *Le Maroc de Lyautey à Mohammed V: Le double visage du Protectorat.* Paris: Denoël, 1999.

Roberts, John. "The Museum and the Crisis of Critical Postmodernism." *Third Text* 41 (Winter 1997–1998): 66–73.

Roditi, Edouard. "Benkemoun." *Morocco Tourism* 51 (Winter 1968): 57.

Rosello, Mireille. *Declining the Stereotype: Ethnicity and Representation in French Culture.* Hanover, N.H.: University Press of New England, 1998.

Royaume du Maroc. *10 ans d'Indépendance, 1956–1966.* Rabat: Ministère des Travaux Publics et Communications, 1966.

Saaf, Abdallah. "The State and the Middle Classes in Morocco." In *The Moroccan State in Historical Perspective: 1850–1985,* ed. Abdelali Doumou, trans. Ayi Kwei Armah. Dakar: Codesria, 1990.

Safi, Louay M. *The Challenge of Modernity: The Quest for Authenticity in the Arab World.* Latham, Mass.: University Press of America, 1994.

Said, Edward. *Culture and Imperialism.* New York: Alfred A. Knopf, 1993.

———. *Orientalism.* New York: Vintage, 1979.

Salas, Angela M. "*Talking Dirty to the Gods* and the Infinitude of Language, or Mr. Komun-yakaa's Cabinet of Wonder." *Callaloo* 28, no. 3 (2005): 798–811.

Salmi, Jamil. *Crise de l'enseignement et reproduction sociale de Maroc.* Casablanca: Editions Maghrebines, 1985.

Salvatore, Armando. *Islam and the Political Discourse of Modernity.* Reading, England: Ithaca Press, 1997.

Scott, James. *Domination and the Arts of Resistance: Hidden Transcripts.* New Haven, Conn.: Yale University Press, 1990.

Sekkat, Abdelhak. "L'action culturelle au Maroc." Ph.D. diss., Université Mohammed V, Rabat, Morocco, 1971.

Senones, Marion. "The Antiquities Museum in Rabat." *Morocco Tourism* 49 (Summer 1968): 43–47.

Serghini, Mohamed. "The National Role of the Fine Arts and Folklore School of Tetuan." *Morocco Tourism* 50 (Autumn 1968): 25–29.

Shabout, Nada. *Modern Arab Art: Formation of Arab Aesthetics.* Gainesville: University Press of Florida, 2007.

Shaw, Wendy. *Possessors and Possessed: Museums, Archaeology, and the Visualization of History in the Late Ottoman Empire.* Berkeley: University of California Press, 2003.

Sontag, Susan. *On Photography.* New York: Farrar, Straus and Giroux, 1977.

Slyomovics, Susan. *The Performance of Human Rights in Morocco.* Philadelphia: University of Pennsylvania Press, 2005.

Spybey, Tony. *Social Change, Development, and Democracy: Modernity, Colonialism, and the Development of the West.* Oxford: Polity Press, 1992.

Stafford, Barbara. *Artful Science: Enlightenment Entertainment and the Eclipse of Visual Education.* Cambridge, Mass.: MIT Press, 1994.

Stauffer, Beat. "No Room for Contemporary Art." *Qantara.de: In Dialogue with the Islamic World,* trans. Patrick Lanagan. Published online September 13, 2005. http://www.qantara.de/webcom/show_article.php/_c-310/_nr-217/i.html.

Stories from Thousand and One Nights. Harvard Classics vol. 16. New York: P. F. Collier and Son, 1909–1914. Published May 18, 2001, at Bartleby.com.

Stouky, Abdallah. "Réflexions sur la dialectique de la modernité et de la tradition." *Lamalif* 55 (November 1972): 38–41.

Sullivan, James D. *On the Walls and in the Streets: American Poetry Broadsides from the 1960s.* Urbana: University of Illinois Press, 1997.

Swingewood, Alan. *Cultural Theory and the Problem of Modernity.* New York: St. Martin's Press, 1998.

Szwaja, Lynn, and Tomás Ybarra-Frausto. "Foreword." In *Museum Frictions: Public Cultures/ Global Transformations,* ed. Ivan Karp, Corinne Kratz, Lynn Szwaja, and Tomás Ybarra-Frausto. Durham, N.C.: Duke University Press, 2006.

"Table ronde 1: La collection et ses réactivations." *Le colloque, l'oeuvre toujours.* Rabat: Editions Hors'champs, 2005.

Tallal, Chaïbia. "The Artist's Voice." Trans. Fatima Mernissi. In *Images of Enchantment: Visual and Performing Arts of the Middle East,* ed. Sherifa Zuhur. Cairo: American University in Cairo Press, 1998.

Tliti, Houcine. "Représentation de l'homme et art pictoral arabo-musulman." *Integral* 5–6 (September 1973): 41–45.

Touzani, Amina. *La culture et la politique culturelle au Maroc.* Casablanca: Editions la croisée des chemins, 2003.

———. "Les musées marocains." *Matrice des arts* 1 (October–December 2005): 47–49.

Tranchant de Lunel, Maurice. *Au pays du paradoxe.* Paris: 1924.

———. "Le Maroc artistique." *Les arts* 161 (October 1917): 12–32.

Twitchell, James. *Adcult USA: The Triumph of Advertising in America.* New York: Columbia University Press, 1996.

"'Unread Author' Spurns Book Award." *BBC News Online,* January 23, 2004. http://news .bbc.co.uk/go/pr/fr/-/1/hi/world/africa/3424965.stm.

Vermeren, Pierre. *Histoire du Maroc depuis l'indépendance.* 2nd ed. Paris: La Découverte, 2006.

"Videokaravaan in Agadir, Morocco." *Contemporary Art from the Islamic World* 7 (June 2004). http://universes-in-universe.de/islam/eng/2004/03/videokaravaan.

Wa Thiongo, Ngugi. *Decolonising the Mind: The Politics of Language in African Literature.* London: James Currey, 1986.

———. *Penpoints, Gunpoints, and Dreams: Towards a Critical Theory of the Arts and the State in Africa.* Oxford: Clarendon, 1998.

Wang, Ning. *Tourism and Modernity: A Sociological Analysis.* New York: Pergamon, 2000.

Waterbury, John. *The Commander of the Faithful: The Moroccan Political Elite, A Study in Segmented Politics.* New York: Columbia University Press, 1970.

Wautenpaugh, Heghnar. "Museums and the Construction of National History in Syria and Lebanon." In *The British and French Mandates in Comparative Perspective,* ed. Nadine Méouchy and Peter Sluglett, 185–202. Leiden: E. J. Brill, 2004.

Wharton, Jane. *Building the Cold War: Hilton International Hotels and Modern Architecture.* Chicago: University of Chicago Press, 2001.

Winegar, Jessica. *Creative Reckonings: The Politics of Art and Culture in Contemporary Egypt.* Stanford, Calif.: Stanford University Press, 2006.

Wolff, Janet. *Aesthetics and the Sociology of Art.* London: Allen and Unwin, 1983.

Wright, Gwendolyn. *Politics of Design in French Colonial Urbanism.* Chicago: University of Chicago Press, 1991.

Young, Robert. *White Mythologies: Writing History and the West.* London: Routledge, 1990.

Zafzaf, Mohamed. "Une nuit à Casablanca." Trans. Abdellatif Gourighate and Jawida Khadda. In *Onze histoires marocaines,* ed. Mohamed Saad Eddine El Yamani. Paris: Institut du Monde Arabe, 1999.

Zoellick, Robert. "When Trade Leads to Tolerance," *New York Times,* June 12, 2004, A13.

Index

Katarzyna Pieprzak is associate professor of French and comparative literature at Williams College.

www.ingramcontent.com/pod-product-compliance
Lightning Source LLC
Chambersburg PA
CBHW020858180526
45163CB00007B/2550